The Matter of My Book

Montaigne's *Essais* as the Book of the Self

The Matter
of My Book
Montaigne's *Essais*
as the Book
of the Self

RICHARD L. REGOSIN

University of California Press
BERKELEY   LOS ANGELES   LONDON

University of California Press
Berkeley and Los Angeles, California
University of California Press, Ltd.
London, England

For Nathan Edelman

"Le guain de nostre estude, c'est en estre
devenu meilleur et plus sage" (I, 26)

Contents

Acknowledgments

I owe a special debt to my friends and colleagues David Carroll, James Chiampi and Franco Tonelli whose comments and questions helped me gain a better understanding of the *Essais*. I am particularly grateful to Robert Griffin for his generous and continued support. I would like to thank Rona Kornblum for the painstaking care with which she typed the manuscript and Laurie Scott for her way with titles.

Introduction

In *De la ressemblance des enfans aux peres* (II, 37) Montaigne claims that whatever he may be, he wants to be elsewhere than on paper and that, above all, he is less a maker of books than of anything else. Although we recognize his familiar insistence on concrete, physical existence and his desire to distinguish himself from those "faiseurs de livres" whose writings he decries, the paradox of his own dependence on words and the book is all too apparent. His preoccupation with language (both its use and abuse), with the act of writing, and with books (his own and those of others) underscores the extent to which he *is* on paper, to which he is foremost the maker of a book.

The questions Montaigne raises by this preoccupation turn about the relationship between life and literature and indicate his own desire that existential life both generate his writing and be its ultimate creation. And the writer's concerns have become those of his readers as we have sought to piece together his personal, intellectual character or to examine the formative role of stylistic expression. These approaches to the *Essais* have presupposed the resemblance between life and literature, the mimetic quality of Montaigne's art as self-portrait. Whether attempting to derive the essayist's attitudes on specific topics (religion, education, politics) or to disclose a more comprehensive or unified picture (the evolution of his thought), or through formalistic analyses to study the articulation of that thought, our primary movement has led us from the essays to speculate on the man.

Montaigne himself readily encourages this movement, this imbalance in the life-literature interplay; that is, the essays invite the reader to speculate on the motives of the writer. At the same time, by his concern with the coincidence between words and things, his sense of language as an airy medium and his ambiguous feelings toward books, and by his essential adherence to them, he shifts our attention to the distinctions between literature and life and to the problematic nature of the interplay itself. In one of those paradoxes that inform the *Essais* (both because they express the richness and complexity of man in the world and signal his inability to master things by reducing them) he suggests both his identification with and his separateness from the book.

In the following pages I attempt to explore the space in which the existential man becomes both the subject and the object of the textual presentation. This does not relegate the work to the category of imaginative fiction (for to do so would be another kind of reductionism) but rather allows room to juxtapose the essays' historical dimension to what we might call Montaigne's artistic vision. I assume textual autonomy both in terms of the integrity of the speaker as persona and of the possibility of esthetic structure or wholeness (in the supposition of the inter-relationships and interdependence of the parts). The risks of distortion are serious in this approach, for if the *Essais* are not exclusively historical, neither are they simply imaginative fiction. And yet all literature involves the transformation of reality just as the writing of history posits structures inhering in the ebb and flow of everyday events. The difficulty (and the interest) in dealing with the essays is to give each domain its due: to acknowledge structure and form where it emerges and at the same time to stress ambiguity, paradox, open-endedness, and diversity; to recognize the presence and function of the essayist in the text as both resembling and differing from the historical Montaigne; to appreciate that the *Essais* are both more than and less than their author.

The present study focuses on Montaigne's book and the act of writing, both as he speaks about them through the authorial voice that glosses and qualifies his own activity and as he fashions the text as empirical writer. The essayist draws our attention to the subject as the text itself yields patterns of movement, "unifying" metaphors or structures that reaffirm the fundamental centrality of the act of writing. In the dynamic that operates through the juxtaposition of commentary and text, in the interaction of the essayist's observations on what he is doing and the activity of writing, we glimpse the very heart of the *Essais*. Among its many faces, the *Essais* may above all else be a book concerned with books and the imperative to write. The essayist's representation of the lost utopia of friendship, his metaphor of self-portraiture, his response to the Delphic injunction "know thyself" and the movement that returns him to himself, his image of the consubstantial book can be seen as functions of the act of writing. The book emerges as the locus of the self, the space where Montaigne finds and founds his sense of being. Why and how that comes about is my central concern.

The richness and complexity of Montaigne's *Essais* inevitably render its study partial and tentative. My own effort is no exception. I have purposely taken a limited, even modest perspective in the hope of pursuing a single thread in depth; the interlocking, weblike quality of the essays has led irresistibly to other major strands, thematic, stylistic, metaphoric, which I have examined in the context of writing and the book. I have sought to avoid the distorting influence of my own concern for order to allow the essayist's preoccupations to emerge. Montaigne himself alerts us to the tendency to treat a matter according to ourselves (II, 50). I have attempted to treat this matter according to itself: to capture Montaigne's own multiple perspectives, to appreciate diversity and paradox, to explore and then go beyond the letter of the text to seek out inner meanings. The result involves a continually shifting ground which must not imitate the *Essais* but elucidate them, which must be faithful to their movement, contradiction, ambiguity while attempting (as Montaigne listens to the voices of his *forme sienne*) to give expression and form to those ruling patterns that lie implicit, hidden, in that body consubstantial which is the essayist and his book.

PART I
THE SECULAR
CONVERSION

1
Friendship and Literature

"un desir fantastique de chose
que je ne puis recouvrer" (III, 3, 820)

I

In that process of self-reflection which is the heart of his portrait,
Montaigne considers his writing as he does his other activities.
Self-study demands that his theme turn in on itself, that the
observer be observed: "j'escry de moy et de mes escrits comme de
mes autres actions, . . . mon theme se renverse en soy" (III, 13,
1069).[1] The purpose of the enterprise, the nature of the
procedure, considerations of style and of language all occupy his
attention, making it difficult for the critic to discuss anything
that the essayist has not already treated himself. As a result,
Montaigne has become the most influential commentator on the
Essais. We have been inclined to accept his point of view, to feel
that his intimacy with the work allows privileged insight; the
essayist's insistence on his truthfulness and sincerity has led us to
make his observations and judgments our own.

Nowhere is Montaigne's word taken more readily than in his
assertion of originality, his claim that unlike other writers he is
one and indivisible with his book. From the opening preface "Au
lecteur" ("je suis moy-mesmes la matiere de mon livre" [p. 3])
through the essay on giving the lie ("livre consubstantiel à son
autheur, d'une occupation propre, membre de ma vie" [II, 18,
665]) to *De l'art de conferer* in the Third Book ("j'ose non

seulement parler de moy, mais parler seulement de moy" [III, 8, 942]), the essayist insists on the unity of man and book, the coincidence of life and writings. The metaphor of the self-portrait—evoking the popular vogue of realistic portraiture in sixteenth-century France—seems to confirm the representational, mirror quality of the *Essais*. Without art or artifice, Montaigne maintains, he seeks to depict himself in his simple, natural, and ordinary fashion.

Taking this lead, readers have tended to treat the *Essais* as personal document, as source of both social and intellectual biography, of the writer's life and times and his ideas and attitudes. And the man depicted in the work—his chronology, his actions and opinions—and the historical context in which he resides do seem to correspond to much of what we know of the existential Montaigne and of the contemporary scene. At the same time, there exist a number of discrepancies between the historical and textual Montaigne that suggest a distinction between man and writer and move the *Essais* closer to the domain of art. Recent studies have indicated, for example, that his friendship with La Boétie may have been more literary than real, that Montaigne is more scholarly, more learned as the essayist in the book than in life.[2] "Je parle au papier comme je parle au premier que je rencontre," he says in the opening lines of Book III, but we are discovering that the effect is self-consciously willed and worked out. The conversational tone with its spontaneous, natural ring—the artless medium of the unpretending man—often veils the studied composition, the careful stylistic casting of ideas. The essayist's depreciation of his writing, his reasoning power, and his memory, the military face of this most unmartial jurist suggest that something other than mimetic fidelity alone determines the portrait of the *Essais*.

The biographical or historical reading of the *Essais* remains incomplete, primarily because it chooses to stress as the whole what is only a part. The work is deeply rooted in historical reality as one pole of the interplay between life and literature, history and art, the central relationship that informs the nature and mode of the work. If we are to appreciate this interplay, we must move from our reading of the work as a personal document, not to undermine its historical dimension, but rather to place it in its proper literary light.

Perhaps no other essay raises these questions more strikingly than *De l'amitié* (I, 28). Montaigne's friendship with Etienne de La Boétie is an accepted historical fact, and what we have come to know of their relationship—gleaned from the *Essais,* the *Journal de voyage,* and Montaigne's correspondence—confirms its central role in his emotional life. The compelling expression of their union in the essay ("par ce que c'estoit luy; par ce que c'estoit moy" [188]); the poignant account of La Boétie's death in Montaigne's letter to his father; the avowal, years later in the intimacy of his journal, that he was overcome with grief upon remembering that death have sustained our belief in the intensity and sincerity of the friendship. Some critics have maintained that the *Essais'* point of origin is the death of La Boétie, as Montaigne sought to compensate for the loss of the "divine liaison" by communicating with his readers.[3] Recently, however, the historical accuracy of Montaigne's portrayal has been questioned, and it has been argued that perhaps our reading has been a sentimental one, verified essentially by cross-reference within Montaigne's own writing. The indelible literary stamp on both the letter and the essay suggests that the friendship described may derive more from books than from actual experience. The death of La Boétie—"moulé au patron d'autres siecles que ceux-cy" (194)—bears a marked resemblance to that of Socrates as recounted by Plato; in *De l'amitié,* distinctions among the various types of friendship, and the central notions of the true friend as another self and of the relationship as the union of two souls, echo both Aristotle and Cicero as literary and philosophical antecedents. The humanist may well have been performing a traditional literary exercise, coloring personal experience with erudition and imagination to discourse on ideal friendship.[4]

There are explanations, both historical and literary, which serve to help us understand the structured and sometimes formal ring of *De l'amitié,* the fact that it reads in part as much like a treatise as the celebration of an experience so profound as to dominate Montaigne's entire life. It could be argued that the passage of a period of eleven to thirteen years between La Boétie's death and the composition of the essay sufficiently dulled Montaigne's exposed emotional nerves to allow him a more detached, analytical perspective. From this affective distance, and through the reflective act of writing essays, he might have been able to move from the particular to the universal, raising his own experience to the larger context of that of other men. Or it may be, since Montaigne was clearly aware of the literary antecedents of his theme, that he sought purposely to imitate the ancients. Given the contemporary esteem for Greek and Latin literature and Montaigne's own reverence for the classics, he may have chosen to work in a familiar and respected medium, especially at this rather early stage in his writing. At that time, imitation of this nature did not mean slavish copying but rather the attempt to add something of one's own, to improve upon the original. Current notions of literary creation expressed by *invention* brought together the sense of working with familiar material drawn from model authors and of finding or tracing new conceptual and expressive modes.[5] For Montaigne to reach back to Aristotle and Cicero and to reconceive and recast their primary matter in his personal idiom was not only to honor his sources but to try out that mental faculty which was itself called invention. Within this context, the earliest essays, which are often considered dry and imitative (dry because imitative) compared to the more personal and original work to come, represent Montaigne's first attempts to test his inventive powers, an activity that we can imagine evolving naturally and irresistibly into the later essays of his judgment. In the opening lines of *De l'amitié* Montaigne states that La Boétie's *La servitude volontaire,* which he intended to use as a centerpiece, was written "par maniere d'essay." It may be that La Boétie's early "trial" of his hand at writing finds its counterpart here in Montaigne's work on friendship.

II

The logic and structure of *De l'amitié* appear to belie the familiar terms of disparagement with which Montaigne opens the essay: "Que sont-ce icy aussi, à la verité, que crotesques et corps monstrueux, rappiecez de divers membres, sans certaine figure, n'ayants ordre, suite ny proportion que fortuité" (183). The syllogistic reasoning which begins the discussion of friendship itself introduces the rhetorical cast and literary flavor of the essay: "Il n'est rien à quoy il semble que nature nous aye plus acheminé qu'à la societé. Et dit Aristote que les bon legislateurs ont eu plus de soing de l'amitié que de la justice. Or le dernier point de sa perfection est cetuy-cy [friendship]." The third term of this progression does not conclude but precedes it, an established fact that frames the essay, that is both its point of origin and its termination: "cette amitié que nous avons nourrie, tant que Dieu a voulu, entre nous, si entiere et si parfaite que certainement il ne s'en lit guiere de pareilles, et, entre nos hommes, il ne s'en voit aucune trace en usage" (184). *La servitude volontaire*—as that substantial element which Montaigne places at the genesis of their friendship and as that which tangibly remains of La Boétie afterward—serves in correlative fashion to open and close the work, as the essayist explains first why he intends to publish the treatise and then why he has chosen not to. The main body of the essay falls naturally into two principal sections: the presentation of a series of relations that do not represent perfect friendship (184-188) and a discussion of the functioning of the ideal relationship (188-194).

Montaigne begins by what through the essays comes to be his characteristic movement toward knowledge, putting his subject into relief by determining what it is not. Proceeding systematically through the various relationships that might be considered true friendship, he describes and eliminates each as something else. That which binds father and child can only be respect; friendship demands a level of communication precluded by this unequal status. The natural tie that joins brothers does not guarantee the harmony and kinship required by perfect friendship. The attraction of the sexes is too impetuous and fickle; marriage is rather like a contractual agreement. And the relationship between men, besides being abhorrent to Christian morality, lacks uniformity and constancy. Each of these associations is measured against the standard of true friendship, variously referred to in these pages from which La Boétie is dramatically absent as *l'amitié* (184, 186), *ces vrayes et parfaictes amitiez* (185), *la parfaicte union et convenance qu'icy nous demandons* (187).

When Montaigne comes to ideal friendship, he evokes his relationship with La Boétie and, in what amounts to a single paragraph, describes the genesis of their friendship: that they knew of each other before ever meeting; that from their first encounter they were profoundly bound to each other; that having so little time to be together and no model to imitate, their wills fused in a quintessential bond. In terms of specific detail, Montaigne mentions only that their initial meeting came at a great feast and gathering in the city, that La Boétie later wrote a Latin satire as an apology on the precipitancy of the friendship, and that they were both adults at the time, La Boétie several years older than he. Aside from these meager references, the gist of which had been given in the opening comments on the *Servitude volontaire* (184), Montaigne's discourse remains essentially impersonal, drawing more on classical models and commonplaces than on what might be called personal experience. The stories of Gracchus and Blosius, and of Eudamidas and his friends, that dominate the presentation function as models to describe the fusion and indivisibility of wills. Quotations from Virgil, Terence, Horace, and Catullus structure the portrayal of that half-life which remains after the death of the friend. Although Montaigne speaks in the first person to declare his personal sense of loss, the borrowed verse clearly serves as a source of both inspiration and affirmation. The essayist's personal statement of his plight as survivor echoes the poetic expression of Horace and Catullus, who portray friendship as the union of souls and the death of one friend as the death of both. What the reader glimpses in this juxtaposition and in the metaphoric quality of Montaigne's description ("ce n'est que fumée, ce n'est qu'une nuit obscure et ennuyeuse" [193]) is the lyric dimension of his own presentation.

Lyric is perhaps an appropriate term to characterize a relationship described essentially in the superlative, whose origins were mysterious, whose driving and binding forces were fundamentally inexplicable, which seemed unbound by time and space. The actual friendship transcended temporal duration through that natural inclination to union which preceded their knowledge of each other. Spatial separation was nullified by the fusion of their souls. Montaigne describes elements that exist on a level above what we commonly consider the realm of human activity, closer to what might be than what is, more an Ideal in the Platonic sense. Over and above the reports they had heard of each other, and the tangible, written word of the *Servitude volontaire* that brought them together, he imagines an inexplicable and fatal force as the mediator of their union ("force inexplicable et fatale, mediatrice de cette union" [188]). His descriptive vocabulary lends to it a transcendental quality as he suggests that this "divine liaison" (190) had its origin in "quelque ordonnance du ciel" (188). As something that participates in the mystery of transcendence, its essential nature is impenetrable to human reason; Montaigne's reference to that "force . . . fatale" as "inexplicable" confirms his inability to explain rationally. And it is not *simply* an inexplicable force he is describing, but "ne sçay quelle force inexplicable." The same formula reappears when he attempts to describe the union of two souls: "c'est je ne sçay quelle quinte essence de tout ce meslange" (189).

Montaigne is concerned with something unusual rather than ordinary, something absolute rather than relative. He ascribes qualities of abstract perfection to his friendship with La Boétie so that the ideal is rendered real in their union. From the introductory remarks of the essay, even before the definition and elaboration of the nature of friendship begins, their relationship stands as the archetype, as the touchstone against which all others are to be measured and judged: "cette amitié que nous avons nourrie . . . entre nous, si entiere et si parfaite que certainement il ne s'en lit guiere de pareilles, et, entre nos hommes, il ne s'en voit aucune trace en usage" (184). On seven other occasions the essayist affirms its perfection in terms like "cette parfaicte amitié" (186), "la parfaicte union" (187), "l'union . . . veritablement parfaicte" (190). What the two friends experienced even exceeded the classical models (192).

The uniqueness of this perfect relationship both demands and reflects the singularity of the participants. Intellectually, Montaigne portrays La Boétie as a man spiritually related to antiquity (184-94), as holding a place in the company of the greatest classical minds: "en cette partie des dons de nature, je n'en connois point qui luy soit comparable" (184). His patriotism too sets him apart from all other men: "il ne fut jamais un meilleur citoyen, ny plus affectionné au repos de son païs, ny plus ennemy des remuements et nouvelletez de son temps" (194). A variety of reasons can help to understand this exaggeration. Since Montaigne's serious intellectual communication occurs through literature, with the writers and thinkers from antiquity, it is not at all surprising that he desires La Boétie to be one of them. In the context of his veneration of the past, he establishes a direct and personal link to that golden time. From a political point of view, to distinguish La Boétie from the Protestants who were making seditious use of the *Servitude volontaire,* it made sense to emphasize his loyalty, even to the point of overstatement. But over and above all this, the hyperbolic presentation of La Boétie as incomparable, the use of the absolutes *point* and *jamais* to single him out among all men for all times evoke a figure wholly consistent with the absolute perfection of the friendship.

Montaigne himself, on the other hand, repeatedly denies his own worth, and in so doing raises a possible objection to the notion of perfection. Clearly the type of friendship he envisages, based on ancient models, demanded an intellectual and moral affinity and equality requiring that Montaigne measure up to his counterpart. If we consider the relationship in Aristotelian terms,

Montaigne's true worth is affirmed by La Boétie's recognition. From yet another point of view, a justified love of self was considered an essential precondition for love of others. While Montaigne does not explicitly derive love from virtue, the Ciceronian echoes are unmistakable in the notion of a perfect La Boétie and a perfect friendship.[6] The essayist's modesty takes on the look of a pose in a context in which he and his friend must stand side by side.

Montaigne's additions to the 1588 edition (forming what we have come to know as the C text) appear in some cases to acknowledge and affirm this principle of equality. The longest interpolation elaborates on love between men, which he had originally called "cet'autre licence Grecque" (187) and had dismissed on moral grounds in one brief sentence. Coming back to the text, he develops this relationship in the detail accorded to other types of association, and then rejects it for its intrinsic differences with true friendship. Montaigne may have felt that summarily to dismiss a pagan practice from the Christian viewpoint, while just and even necessary, was essentially alien to the spirit of the essays. Rarely does he judge that classical world he so admires in that way. He may also have considered it unfair to reject so abruptly that love which was so important a source of friendship in ancient Greece. Since on the part of the beloved the relationship required the appreciation of spiritual beauty and since as well the relationship which began as *fureur* might settle down to what Montaigne is willing to call *amitié* (188), he may have sought to avoid the confusion of what might look like or might "become" true friendship with the genuine item itself. But beyond this speculation, in terms of the dynamics of the essay itself, the impact of this addition is striking. What Montaigne gains is the picture of a relationship whose most dramatic element is the *inequality* of the participants, the *disparity* of their ages, of their appearances, of their esthetic and spiritual qualities. It is on these grounds that he ultimately denies it the name of true friendship: "Je revien à ma description, de façon plus equitable et plus equable" (188). By that process of negative definition Montaigne gives a central place to the spiritual nature of the relationship and to the equality of the two friends.

Similar emphasis derives from other additions where Montaigne attempts to achieve a balance between the constituents. The famous definition of love, "par ce que c'estoit luy; par ce que c'estoit moy" (188), which is less an explanation than an affirmation of its ineffable mystery, serves by its very construction to suggest equilibrium and reciprocity. While the phrase may represent Montaigne's desire to express the disinterested nature of true friendship, the way it was constructed supports the notion of balance. The *exemplaire de Bordeaux* reveals that when he originally decided to express the inexpressible he qualified his negative ("si on me presse de dire pourquoy je l'aymois, je sens que cela ne se peut exprimer") by adding "qu'en respondant: Par ce que c'estoit luy." Perhaps struck by the one-sidedness of what he had just described as the binding of two souls, as their mingling and blending, Montaigne evened the construction and the thought by including La Boétie's recognition of him: "par ce que c'estoit moy."

This is precisely the effect he achieves in the next paragraph when he elaborates on aspects of their coming together through the dominant use of the third-person-plural reflexive: "nous nous cherchions," "nous nous embrassions."[7] And at the same time, to the sentence written earlier, "c'est je ne sçay quelle quinte essence de tout ce meslange, qui, ayant saisi toute ma volonté, l'amena se plonger et se perdre dans la sienne," Montaigne adds "qui, ayant saisi toute sa volonté, l'amena se plonger et se perdre en la mienne, d'une faim, d'une concurrence pareille." The addition sustains much more effectively the concept of *meslange* with which he began. But what is most striking is that Montaigne again adds himself as the second term of the equation and insists that La Boétie's movement toward him corresponds to his own toward La Boétie, "with equal hunger, equal rivalry." Further on in the essay, the axiom of equality on which the friendship rests appears forcefully in the Aristotelian concept of the friend as another self.[8]

In almost every case the additions to the 1580 text embellish the notion of commonality and union that Montaigne originally placed at the very center of the essay. This motif, woven through the essay as the essential characteristic of perfect friendship, dominates through its rich and varied vocabulary. Montaigne stresses the oneness of the relationship by the repeated use of *union* (187, 188, 190), by his image of the two souls pulling *uniement ensemble* (189), and by his expression of uniqueness as *la chose la plus une et unie* (191). On three separate occasions this oneness is described as *convenance* (186, 187, 190), which as a noun deriving from the Latin verb *convenire* evokes the state of union as well as the dynamic which brings it about. Montaigne speaks of this coming together as *se mesler* (188) and *confondre* (188), and variously of its mode as *correspondance* (185), *couture* (186), *conference [conferre: rassembler]* (186), *liaison* (190), *confusion* (190) [linked etymologically and semantically to *confondre*]. The notions that the two friends hold everything in common between them ("volontez, pensemens, jugemens, biens, femmes, enfans, honneur et vie" [190]), that they are as a single soul in two bodies (190), that their relationship is indivisible (191) state and restate from differing angles the central theme of oneness. On two occasions Montaigne purposely lends religious overtones by referring to the *saincte couture* (186) and the *divine liaison* (190). The mysterious forces which mediated the bond, and which Montaigne suggestively notes may reveal "quelque ordonnance du ciel" (188), explain in part his insistence on the ineffability of the experience. The idea that total immersion and loss of oneself lead to discovery of oneself, the characterization of the union as "une si ardante affection," where the love as flame is clearly apparent, suggest that Montaigne's experience parallels the mystical union with God. While it has an active, one might even say violent, beginning (*se plonger, se perdre*), it is sustained by reason (189) and assumes over the long run a moderate, even, and gentle warmth. The analogy emerges in muted tones to reinforce what we have called the lyric dimension of the essay.

The expression of what Montaigne calls the most singular and unified of all things reaches its apogee in the image of the friend as another self: "Le secret que j'ay juré ne deceller à nul autre, je le puis, sans parjure, communiquer à celuy qui n'est pas autre: c'est moy. C'est un assez grand miracle de se doubler . . ." (191). From this point, the essay turns downward to lay particular stress on the rarity of the perfect friendship, on the difficulty of meeting a man equal to it, on the impossibility of even finding a good judge of it. The anecdote of the young soldier unwilling to trade his prize horse for a kingdom but ready to exchange it for a friend, "si j'en trouvoy," puts this into relief. As if foreshadowing the picture he paints in the final pages of the essay as he describes his own life since La Boétie's death, Montaigne portrays the soldier as a man who properly values friendship and who is alone.

The body of the essay has moved through what we have called negative definition to put before the reader his unique concept of friendship. It has excluded relationships that cannot be called friendship and eliminated friendships that cannot be called true, as if peeling away outer layers and discarding them—for both what they are and what they are not—to disclose the essential core of wholeness, union. But the paradox of the core is that we arrive at it not to possess it but to lose it. For the essential thrust of the essay is to describe not what Montaigne has but what he does not have, not what is presence but what is absence. The presentation constructed to highlight oneness and totality concludes by confirming partialness and division. Montaigne describes his life since La Boétie's death in terms dramatically opposed to those that characterize their friendship: from the *vol hautain et superbe* (186) he descends to drag wearily along ("je ne fay que trainer languissant" [193]); from *jouyssance* (186), life becomes *ennuyeuse* (193); from the multiple expressions of wholeness (*liaison, confusion, convenance,* etc.), there remains only a fragmented part ("il me semble n'estre plus qu'à demy" [193]). The lyric hyperbole of the perfect friendship finds its counterpoint in the poetic overstatement of its loss:

> My pleasures all lie shattered, with you dead.
> Our soul is buried, mine with yours entwined;
> And since then I have banished from my mind
> My studies, and my spirit's dearest joys.[8]

This sense of incompleteness, of something physically missing, is furthered by the unfulfilled promise of a rich and polished picture to occupy the best spot, the center of our attention. Montaigne opened the essay by disclosing the intended structure of his book: "Il [the painter whose manner he would imitate] choisit le plus bel endroit et milieu de chaque paroy, pour y loger un tableau élabouré de toute sa suffisance; et, le vuide tout au tour, il le remplit de crotesques, qui sont peintures fantasques, n'ayant grace qu'en la varieté et estrangeté" (183). Since in characteristic fashion he claims to be unequal to the task demanded by the center, La Boétie's *Servitude volontaire* will serve as the "tableau riche, poly et formé selon l'art," appropriately framed by the essays, "crotesques et corps monstrueux."[9] And thus the reader proceeds, from these comments on the excellence of this book, which brought them together, through the exposition of friendship to discover at the conclusion that the projected center, like the friend, is missing. The *Servitude volontaire* stands at the origin of friendship and the essay as well, and the anticipation of finding it accompanies the experience of reading. Montaigne indicates at the very end that he changed his mind about including the treatise after it was published by Protestants in a seditious context. This may indeed be so, but it does not explain why Montaigne allows the reader to anticipate its inclusion throughout the essay from beginning to end. Why did he choose not to modify his opening remarks by explaining his change of mind? Through comparative studies of additions to the text, we have become all too aware of Montaigne reading and rereading, adding and deleting, clarifying, elaborating, until satisfied—for the time being—that the text expresses what he intends, not to appreciate his care and sensitivity as a writer. Clearly the impact on the reader of this unrealized expectation derives from the internal disposition of the essay, for the parallel between its culmination in the absence of both the friend and his work is too striking to be gratuitous. And, interestingly, La Boétie's twenty-nine sonnets, which Montaigne had occupy the center temporarily in the editions published during his lifetime, he removes in the manuscript that becomes the *exemplaire de Bordeaux*. Montaigne again left his remarks promising the *Servitude volontaire* standing, just as he left his promise of the sonnets standing. In the following essay, which was to contain the sonnets, he added the enigmatic phrase, "Ces vers se voient ailleurs" (196). It may be, as has been suggested, that someone else published them between 1588 and 1592, although no such edition has ever been found. They too are absence.

III

If we had placed the *Essais* in the context of autobiography or confessional literature we probably would have been more skeptical of the historicity of its claims and assertions. Because of its inherent subjectivity we would have given art its due (as transformation of reality) and looked to the text for the elaboration of a speaker whose integrity was independent of its exterior counterpart. Differences between the historical fact and the self-portrait would have served to establish the independence of the text. But in spite of elements such as first-person narrative, self-disclosure, and the claim of historical accuracy which the *Essais* share with these other genres, we properly set it apart. Its unsystematic and incomplete record of the speaker's life, its locus in the present, and its self-depreciation distinguish it from the chronological, retrospective structure of autobiography and its frequent self-justifying intent. We take the essays essentially at face value with these differences in mind, and sustained by Montaigne's biography—ironically drawn in the main from the essays themselves—we read the work literally. We have devised a number of responses to the nagging question of historical veracity, responses that minimize the importance of discrepancy, which put it aside to preserve the work as "truthful." We are given to saying that the essays essentially concern the life of the mind and thus permit a certain license in the presentation of external detail; or that the psychological universe portrayed is infinitely more complex and therefore necessarily different from the life of the man in the world; or that all art by its very nature involves some degree of transformation of reality. These considerations are in part true and our understanding of the essays has been enhanced by them. Basically, however, they speak around, not to, the question.

Our comments on the essay on friendship may shed light on these observations. If *De l'amitié* is an idealization of a historical friendship, a lyric dramatization of the past written to illuminate the present; if the individuals presented and the relationship described are more literary than real, and the disparities between the life and the writing as striking as the resemblances, perhaps we must consider the meaning of the text not in its relation to that life but as a function of the internal dynamics of the *Essais* themselves. We take the first step in that direction when we see the essay as a literary exercise, as the speaker essaying friendship, for the validation of this reading comes from contextual consider-ations: other essays reveal the semantic force of *essayer*, which is not explicit in *De l'amitié* itself. Or again, when we posit the symbolic value of the idealized La Boétie by relating his past presence and present absence to the larger context of Montaigne's quest for self-knowledge. But in both cases we risk sliding between biographical concern and textual consideration, for the conclusions—in the first case, that Montaigne is in dialogue with his books or, in the second, that he is compensating for the loss of the required "other"—treat the essay essentially as a function of the historical man. Instead of looking outside the work to confirm the integrity of the man depicted inside the essays, it may be more fruitful to consider him in relation to himself as the speaker of the other essays. If he is different from the exterior model, then what he is and why he is may derive from what we might call his textual life. To recognize the independence of the basic speaker of the *Essais* is not to reduce the work to purely imaginative fantasy, nor is it to make the textual Montaigne a fictional character. It is rather to underscore the aesthetic wholeness of the text by seeking to uncover the intrinsic relationships of its composite parts.

If we consider *De l'amitié* from this perspective, a number of aspects surface within the larger context of the *Essais*. The lyrical, ahistorical nature of the friendship suggests that its significance lies beyond the literal, that its import is figurative. Rather than being essentially retrospective, seeking to depict what is past for its own sake, the essay reaches back only to illuminate the present. In *De l'amitié* itself, and in what becomes through the work a characteristic mode of thought, what something is emerges through the depiction of what it is not. Just as Montaigne describes those associations that are not true friendship in order to reveal what true friendship is, so also does he evoke a presence to define absence. By calling up a past envisioned as ideal, the present as real comes into focus as counterpoint.

Whether one's reading of the *Essais* stresses Montaigne engaged in self-portraiture or embarked on the correlative search for self-knowledge, the reality of the moment is negativity. In its simplest terms, the moment is an empty canvas to be filled (the blank pages of the book) or the ignorance of the self yet to be discovered. Montaigne evoked this emptiness or absence in concrete terms in a 1588 addition to *De la vanité*: "Il n'y a personne à qui je vousisse pleinement compromettre de ma peinture: luy seul [La Boétie] jouyssoit de ma vraye image, et l'emporta. C'est pourquoy je me deschiffre moy-mesme, si curieusement."[10] As if the friend, when he disappeared, actually carried off a physical presence, leaving the essayist with the current void. This metaphoric representation allows negativity to be conceptualized, for what is not can only be imagined as the negation of what was. In order for Montaigne to articulate his present sense of fragmentation, of instability, he must conceive of unity, wholeness, stability, the very elements with which he composes the friendship.

If Montaigne had not had La Boétie he would have had to invent him.

By the death of La Boétie and the dissolution of union, the speaker depicts renunciation. The images of smoke and night which describe his existence negate life; his flight from pleasure into *ennui* and languor diminish his vital forces. The texts quoted blur distinctions between the missing friend and the survivor to include Montaigne in death: "Ille dies utramque Duxit ruinam"; "Tecum una tota est nostra sepulta anima" (193-94). The real sacrifice of life is replaced by a symbolic death that will allow Montaigne to reconstitute an existence from point zero. He holds the unique advantage of being both dead and alive to the world at the same time, enjoying the ethical superiority of renunciation, the psychological and aesthetic distance that accompanies withdrawal, and the practical gain of potential return to and interaction with the world. The death of the friend, then, is not only the destruction of unity and plenitude but self-negation as well; not only the friend and the wholeness realized by the two parties in friendship, but the self as well is lost. The moment of total presence becomes the time of complete absence.

IV

The Edenic moment, that mystical fusion in oneness that confers plenitude and confirms integrity dissolves; the metaphorical death as exclusion from the fullness of being leaves a fragmented, alienated soul, errant in the instability of the world of becoming, seeking a means of return. A familiar falling away whose very terms compellingly recall the Adamic fall from grace through original sin and suggest a dialectic reminiscent of Christian conversion.

Augustine provides us with the vocabulary with which to describe the setting for conversion. In Augustinian terms, form was bestowed on shapeless matter at creation, through God's recall of both matter and spirit to Himself. The form impressed on man was the divine image itself, and it conferred participation in being, in that principle of order and unity which is God. When Adam sinned, contact between the image and the divine model was diminished; the image remained permanently rooted in the nature of the intellectual soul, but obscured. Distanced from God through the deformation of his true image, excluded from being, man experienced alienation, multiplicity, disequilibrium.

Christ offers the possibility of a re-creation, of a renewal of the divine image in man through a dynamic return to the exemplar. This act of spiritual conversion, of reformation, is a second turning to God from the nothingness of sin, the absence of good and being. The return to God from this region of unlikeness first brings man back to himself, where through knowledge purified by faith he begins to perceive in himself his true nature as an image of God and as a subject in humility and obedience. And through time, in what is metaphorically conceived as a journey, man struggles ceaselessly to grow in divine likeness, gradually to deepen his knowledge, to strengthen his love of God. The outer man of the senses, in a symbolic death to the world, gives way to the inner man, the site of the image, what Augustine considers the locus of the specifically human.

How foreign to the spirit of Montaigne's *Essais* is this brief outline of the dialectic of Christian conversion. The *Essais* do not consider man's relationship to God, nor are Montaigne's concerns those of sin and purification, grace and faith, the dynamics of the sinner's return. It is precisely the absence of this religious, metaphysical focus that led Pascal to condemn the essayist's *nonchalance du salut*. Yet the loss of the perfect state and of that image which marked his true nature, the accompanying displacement from the realm of being to that of becoming, to instability and change are the very elements which distinguish *De l'amitié*. And Montaigne will strive through the essays to renew that image, to read through the opacity of his thoughts and actions to an essential self, which, like Augustine's image, is indelibly imprinted in the soul. He never seems to doubt that in the world of becoming the self exists to be known, or rather to be sought through the very flux and mutability that obscure it. In the phrase that follows the statement that La Boétie alone enjoyed his true image (and since their union made the friend another self, Montaigne too enjoyed it) and carried it off—"Je me deschiffre moy-mesme, . . . curieusement"—the essayist evokes the effort to penetrate to what he will later call *la forme maitresse*, as if deciphering the secret language of the soul. As in the Christian context, the way back to the restoration of the image, to a deeper sense of one's true nature, is through self-knowledge. To the question "why man is to know himself" Augustine answers: "In order that he may understand himself, and live according to his nature."[11] For Augustine, of course, that nature is defined by its essential relationship to God, but the interest here is that the terms of this paraphrase are precisely those that will be used by Montaigne.

Self-knowledge, of course, is not exclusively a Christian focus, and strong Socratic echoes resound as Montaigne extends the cornerstone notion of the Delphic oracle, "know thyself": "Ce grand precepte est souvent allegué en Platon: Fay ton faict et te cognoy. . . . Qui auroit à faire son faict, verroit que sa premiere leçon, c'est cognoistre ce qu'il est et ce qui luy est propre" (I, 3, 15). Nor does the concept of conversion originate with the Church. The common Greek word *epistrophe*, strongly rooted in concrete usage as a physical pivoting or turning (of the body, a wheel, the seasons), allowed figurative meaning as a moral or intellectual change of orientation.[12] In the Greek translation of Hebrew scripture the sense of coming back or bringing back most often describes the Israelites' return to God; they participate in order and unity after the stiff-necked falling away in sin to alienation and multiplicity depicted concretely as geographical dispersion. *Epistrophe* could be used to signify a change in behavior, the adoption of a new style of life as in Plutarch or a flight from the tangible world toward the self, "une démarche contemplative d'où découlent l'harmonie et l'ordre intellectuel pour l'Ame du monde ou pour l'âme particulière de l'homme."[13] The concept of *epistrophe* was central to Stoicism and colored the work of Epictetus, who enjoyed immense popularity in France in the latter half of the sixteenth century. Stoic conversion consisted in a return from those exterior events over which man has no control to interior things that depend on him, ultimately to reason and will. From the instability of the tangible world, a circular movement carries man back to himself in quest of harmony with the All under universal law. Epictetus emphasizes not God but man and the equilibrium man attempts constantly to maintain between the interior and the exterior. The Stoic seeks not to eliminate exterior reality through inaction but to remain the self or to perfect the self through activity. The return to and knowledge of the self are central: "En tout ce qui vous survient, retournez-vous vers vous-mesmes, pour chercher quel moyen vous avez de vous en servir."[14]

This particular Stoic stress has a familiar ring for readers of the *Essais*. Montaigne appears to essay and eventually discard some elements, like the emphasis on the strength of will and reason; others, like the opposition of exterior and interior and the focus on the self, remain central to the entire work. But the essays are not original in this regard: like the dictum "know thyself," these were intellectual and moral commonplaces of the times, repeated in the writings of countless contemporaries. What is strikingly different in Montaigne is not only the pivotal importance given to the Delphic injunction but the primacy of *epistrophe* as the ruling pattern of the dialectic of the *Essais*. And here we are not speaking of the specific application of either Christian or Stoic conversion. On the contrary, with that eclectic attitude so common to his age, and with a view toward the exigencies of his subject, the essayist transposes and transforms aspects of his cultural heritage to suit his purposes.

Christianity converges with Stoic *epistrophe* at the point of its secularization. In mid-sixteenth-century France, Stoicism was already taken as moral philosophy, a kind of practical guide to conduct, once removed from its original metaphysical frame-work. There were those, of course, who, like Du Vair, sought to integrate it into a traditional Christian context with which it was not incompatible, but it stood perhaps more forcefully on its own, as in Epictetus' *Enchiridion,* with its clear-cut emphasis on man and the concrete life as it is meant to be lived. Given the contemporary propensity for considering man on his own without reference to God, Montaigne could draw on Stoic precepts without distorting them on the one hand or having to accommodate his general framework to them on the other.

The dramatic echoes of Christian *epistrophe* represent a stunning transposition, for the *Essais* secularize and concretize this essential religious concept.[15] Nowhere perhaps is Montaigne more humanistic—in the rather broad sense of the emphasis on things human—and nowhere is he less traditionally Christian (one is tempted to say more un-Christian) than in this critical interchange of temporal and religious terms. What we find is the traditional circle of conversion except that the original state is not union with God, the death to the world not a spiritual renunciation which begins the return to divine sanctification, the reformation not a repristinization of God's image in man, not·a re-fashioning by the celestial maker. Instead, in a purely human context where friendship functions as a kind of secular analogue to union with God, the individual himself becomes the source of his own re-creation. All the elements of the Christian fall are present: the alienation from being and participation in unity and order; the obscuring of the image of a man's true nature; the overwhelming sense of flux, mutability, fragmentation. And the return, that endless journey back toward the source of creation, the lifelong struggle to uncover that essential image, to live in conformity with a man's true nature which takes the form of the quest for self-knowledge, is the very substance of the *Essais* themselves.

Within this context, Stoic moral philosophy and de-Christianized conversion show strong resemblances. The distinct sense of *epistrophe* which forms the basis of each system—in the first instance a return to the self, in the second a return through the self to God—is obscured where man becomes the term of the circle. Montaigne's reduction of the metaphysical dimensions of self-knowledge, of life in conformity with nature, of notions of re-creation and reformation recall his readings of Stoicism. In his hands, Stoic attitudes lend themselves to the elaboration of the dialectic of the secular conversion.

V

A fundamental characteristic of the perfect union of friendship is that it is most profoundly a prelinguistic or extralinguistic phenomenon. The fusion of wills, the perfect knowledge of intention and judgment make speech and written communication superfluous. *La servitude volontaire* stands appropriately at the origin of the friendship as if a surrogate for the unencountered La Boétie and it assumes renewed prominence, in a similar role, when he dies. But while the two friends share each other's being, it has no import. In a significant transformation of the historical situation, Montaigne mutes the long physical separation that apparently dominated, choosing instead to stress presence and union. Thus the need for letters and the written word in general is obviated, just as the mystical nature of the relationship consciously subordinates the spoken word. Not surprisingly, Montaigne never mentions any exchange between them.

When presence dissolves, when La Boétie and friendship are lost and the image of the self is obscured, the effort of recovery, of reconstruction, takes place through language. Against the Divine Logos and the written word of Scripture that stand as the instruments of Christian conversion, accessible through faith and grace, Montaigne will set his own personal book of the self. As knowledge of God is found in His book, and of man's nature as *imago Dei*, so knowledge of Montaigne and the renewal of his image will be sought through the work he writes.

The nature of the task involves writing, involves exteriorization, for to be the source of one's own being means becoming one's own subject and object. And Montaigne is well aware of the *dédoublement* required; as both writer and that which is being written about, he must distance himself psychologically and esthetically: "Je ne m'ayme pas si indiscretement et ne suis si attaché et meslé à moy que je ne me puisse distinguer et considerer à quartier: comme un voisin, comme un arbre" (III, 8, 942). In an ironic analogy to God and the image He creates of Himself, the writer must construct an image to consider, since the self as subject cannot observe itself. Whereas God in perfect knowledge re-creates Himself in the *imago Dei* as an act of pure charity, the essayist is obliged by necessity to create himself through the text before he can pretend to knowledge. In writing, Montaigne imagines (projects an image of) himself acting—that is, thinking through writing: a likeness of the self which permits scrutiny and analysis, but most significantly a literary counterpart conceived in what the essayist himself calls the airy medium of words.

The seeker as writer will turn his gaze with ever-increasing intensity to fix on the very process of essaying itself. What we have tended to see as the development through the work of an ever more intimate style, as movement from the early impersonal *leçons* to self-portraiture and the concomitant effort to respond to the Delphic oracle emerges as well as a growing self-consciousness of the activity itself. A dominant concern of the essays becomes the writing of essays, the means, the medium, the mode of self-discovery. The writer is occupied not only by the actual self-portrait but by how the self-portrait actualizes, not only by what the man is but by how the man becomes.

2

The Space Occupied
and the Time Lived

"Ramenons à nous et à nostre aise
nos pensées et nos intentions" (I, 39, 242)

I

The fact that Montaigne's biography has been reconstituted from the *Essais* confirms how much information the speaker gives about himself and the social, intellectual, and political context in which he lives.[1] Quite apart from the question of its historical validity, the reader discovers in the work a broad, self-contained setting within which the speaker situates the details of his own personal history. The world of the essays spreads out as if in concentric circles from the man at the center to embrace the household, the province, the country, and even beyond Europe's boundaries, to Asia and the New World. From his fixed vantage point, the writer looks out on this world and what he sees reveals more about the observer than his object. As we seek to know the speaker, we consider him in this geographical context, one transformed by the very act of perception, refracted through the imagination and intellect. Who he is and what he does stands in relation to the space occupied and time lived, within the universe of the *Essais* themselves.

It might be argued that Montaigne merely re-creates in the *Essais* the historical world in which he lives. References both to the times ("ce siecle," "ce temps") and to the place ("nostre estat") recall the real death and destruction wrought by internal strife, the instability created by a weak monarchy and the intrigue accompanying the quest for power. Hypocrisy and treachery in the service of ambition, or in the name of virtue, characterize the picture drawn by every commentator on the age. Montaigne himself portrays this face of things in *De la phision-omie*: "Il ne se peut imaginer un pire visage des choses qu'où la meschanceté vient à estre legitime, et prendre, avec la congé du magistrat, le manteau de la vertu . . . L'extreme espece d'injustice, selon Platon, c'est que ce qui est injuste soit tenu pour juste" (III, 12, 1043). This topsy-turvy moral world brings to mind the identical contemporary vision of Agrippa d'Aubigné, expressed in *Les Tragiques* as a *monde à l'envers*:

> . . . comme au monde à l'envers
> Le vieil pere est fouëtté de son enfant pervers;
> Celuy qui en la paix cachoit son brigandage
> De peur d'estre puni, estalle son pillage
> Au son de la trompette, au plus fort des marchez
> Son meurtre et son butin sont à l'ancan preschez:
> Si qu'au lieu de la roüe, au lieu de la sentence,
> La peine du forfaict se change en recompense.
>
> [I, 235-242]

While d'Aubigné's world has deep roots in contemporary France, it is shaped by a larger poetic vision that transcends historical reality. Montaigne's setting, of course, lies entirely outside the religious and spiritual framework of the Protestant epic's cosmic scope. And this very "down-to-earth" quality, the apparent straightforwardness and objectivity of the presentation, has led us to focus more on its historicity than its function.

However the essays are read—chronologically in terms of composition or publication or in the textual layers (ABC) of the various editions—and regardless of context or subject matter, what remains constant throughout is the physical and moral hostility of the outside world, the dominance of wickedness, vice, self-interest. On the verge of self-destruction by those who claim to save her, France is racked by civil war threatening her institutions and the lives of her citizens. The wars provoke what is least attractive in man's nature: "L'ambition, l'avarice, la cruauté, la vengeance n'ont point assez de propre et naturelle impetuosité; amorchons les et les attisons par le glorieux titre de justice et devotion" (III, 12, 1043). In the name of political and religious ideology, dogmatically convinced of the absolute truth of their beliefs, Protestants and Catholics justify monstrous cruelty and murder. Treachery and dishonesty hold sway (I, 6; II, 11) in warfare and parleys while the shock waves of civil strife reverberate far beyond the battlefield to make everyone a victim. Whether on the road or at home one is never entirely safe from war's violent incursions: ". . . en mon voisinage, nous sommes tantost par la longue licence de ces guerres civiles envieillis en une forme d'estat si desbordée, 'Quippe ubi fas versum atque nefas' [when justice and injustice are confounded], qu'à la verité c'est merveille qu'elle se puisse maintenir" (III, 9, 956). As discomforting as the constant danger of pain, death, and destruction is the uncertainty of moving about in a world filled with potential, and unidentifiable, enemies. In civil war, chaos and confusion create a situation in which friend cannot be distinguished from enemy: ". . . le pis de ces guerres, c'est que les cartes sont si meslées, votre ennemy n'estant distingué d'avec vous de aucune marque apparente, ny de langage, ny de port, nourry en mesmes loix, meurs et mesme air, qu'il est mal-aisé d'y eviter confusion et desordre" (II, 5, 366).

The wars are perhaps more symptom than cause of a sickness Montaigne describes afflicting the body politic. The advent of disorder predates this particular infection, where the intended remedy only causes greater virulence: "Elle vient guarir la sedition et en est pleine, veut chastier la desobeyssance et en montre l'exemple; et, employée à la deffence des loix, faict sa part de rebellion. . . . Nostre medecine porte infection" (III, 12, 1041). It is as if the wars legitimized and made manifest the practice of vice in which man had always been engaged; the corruption and depravity of the age color every aspect of human activity. This is a time in which the practice of cruelty exceeds anything in recorded history, where atrocities abound every day (II, 11, 432). Learning is perverted ("nostre estude en France n'ayant quasi autre but que le proufit" [I, 25, 141]) and philosophy is reduced to what Montaigne calls "ces ergotismes" (I, 26, 160). That means to wisdom and virtue, which he conceives in *De l'institution des enfans* as *gay, gaillard, enjoué* (160), has become *renfroigné, sourcilleux et terrible* (160), rendered inaccessible and undesirable by the so-called philosophers. Given Montaigne's inclination to disparage philosophy and to highlight its weakness by comparison with what he suggests are natural precepts and principles, these positive terms (*gay, gaillard*) might surprise us. They derive in part from the context of *De l'institution,* which reconciles learning and nature by returning philosophy to its etymon, the love of wisdom. The times serve to pervert the task of philosophy, for its current practice is encumbered with formulas that obscure its true object. And the circle is a vicious one, for if "les choses en soyent là en nostre siecle, que la philosophie, ce soit, jusques aux gens d'entendement, un nom vain et fantastique, qui se treuve de nul usage et de nul pris" (160), then an important path to virtue is closed and corruption will breed further corruption.

The truest measure of the wickedness of the age is not that it fails to practice virtue but that it cannot even conceive of it (I, 37, 230). Montaigne disparages evidence of justice, courage, and goodness as action feigned to achieve other ends. Hypocrisy wears the mask of virtue so that what appears good is mere illusion. Those who are called good are so only in comparison with the general iniquity of the times, as Montaigne suggests through ironic hyperbole: "Il fait bon naistre en un siecle fort depravé: car, par comparaison d'autruy, vous estes estimé vertueux à bon marché. Qui n'est que parricide en nos jours, et sacrilege, il est homme de bien et d'honneur" (II, 17, 646). In this sick age those who boast of employing virtue in the service of the world either do not know what virtue is or boast wrongly (II, 9, 993). And in the absence of true virtue, in the misuse of its name, vice runs rampant. Ambitious people enter public service not to serve but to exploit (I, 39, 237). Truth has substantially vanished and, although its name still lingers, in this *monde à l'envers* it designates its opposite: "Nostre verité de maintenant, ce n'est pas ce qui est, mais ce qui se persuade à autruy" (II, 18, 666). And thus public opinion acknowledges vice as virtue.

Montaigne's picture of himself—physically separated in his tower and morally at odds with society—derives in part from the Stoic morality he adopts on occasion in the *Essais*. In the world Montaigne portrays, where strong temptations of disintegration are setting in, where the weakened social, political, and religious structures are rendered impotent or perverted, the reader senses how depending on self-reliance to allay the disquieting fears of pain and death appeals to the contemporary mind. Montaigne himself underlines this connection in *De l'institution des enfans*, where he suggests that the pupil be broken in to the rigors of exercise as preparation against the pain and harshness of the dungeon and torture rack, which threaten the good as well as the bad in such times (I, 26, 154). And although we see him essaying Stoic attitudes most frequently in the early essays, echoes reverberate throughout all three books. The emphasis on virtue and dispassion which distinguish the Stoic from society's masses characterizes the *Essais* and informs, to some extent, Montaigne's role as outsider.

Although distinction and distance between the speaker and the world remain constant through the work, the essayist's espousal of Stoicism does not. Even in the early essays his attitude cannot be characterized as uniformly Stoic: Montaigne does not adopt the specific philosophical framework from which its moral considerations derive, remaining content to draw randomly upon Stoic writers both ancient and contemporary. Villey points to Stoic expression in Book I as *livresque,* and Frame prefers to speak of Montaigne's eclecticism, stressing how Stoicism colored by Epicureanism—the emphasis on the power of human will and reason—was common to so many humanist writings of the period.[2] Indeed, a number of these early essays question aspects of Stoical humanism which lead the writer to stress man's humility and weakness in the face of the austere demands of Stoicism (I, 7, 25, 37; II, 2, 3, 11). In the vast scope of the *Apologie de Raimond Sebond* Stoicism is swept aside, along with philosophical dogmatism in general, as pretentious and misguided, but Montaigne's attitude is never exclusive. One philosophical strain may dominate others at any given time (be it Stoic, Pyrrhonistic, Epicurean), but the view is always broad and tempered, so that even in the closing essays a Stoic note is sometimes heard.

Regardless, then, of the prevailing philosophical mood, the speaker is at odds with the world in which he lives, with the times he characterizes as "un siecle corrompu et ignorant" (III, 2, 807). Long after Stoicism has faded as a dominant motif, after the speaker has abandoned the distinction between the morally superior man and the vulgar masses, between those who can will themselves virtuous and dispassionate and those who cannot, he remains in counterpoint to the historical context. This is not merely a question of a decent man criticizing the abuses of which his contemporaries are guilty to lead them to reform, for while his observations are incisive and uncompromising, their purpose is not primarily didactic.[3] Nor does Montaigne merely place himself apart to observe and comment. He stands, rather, at the polar extreme of that social world, neither smug nor superior in his opposition but keenly aware of his distance and distinctness. What the society prizes he condemns, and those qualities he seeks to nurture in himself the society finds useless: "les qualitez mesmes qui sont en moy non reprochables, je les trouvois inutiles en ce siecle" (II, 17, 646). While hypocrisy and dissimulation become a *nouvelle vertu* (647), he speaks for truth and the generous heart which "se veut faire voir jusques au dedans" (647). In an epoch where social intercourse requires care and prudence in speech, his nature is open and vigorous. When Montaigne

remarks that the times are fit for improving man only backward
("Ce temps n'est propre à nous amender qu'à reculons, par dis-
convenance plus que par accord, par différence que par simili-
tude" [III, 8, 922]), he spatializes his moral antagonism to the
world, a distancing emblematized in the isolated tower to which
he retires.

Montaigne repudiates the social world and what it represents,
and maintains this posture throughout. He denounces that world
to renounce it, he turns away from it through symbolic destruction that clears the ground for subsequent reconstruction. This
movement is both the reiteration and the extension of the para-
digmatic death that accompanies the rupture of Montaigne's
friendship with La Boétie. As if the now fragmented, alienated
soul repeatedly reaffirms its fundamental "otherworldliness,"
clearly not in any transcendental sense, for this "other" world
will be Montaigne's own creation.[4] From immersion in and
dependence on exterior things, the movement of conversion
brings about an ever-increasing reliance on the self as source of
knowledge and value. Montaigne seeks to define himself against
the world, in opposition to public ideology; he attempts to do
what others do not do, to be what others are not. Conscience,
personal nature, what he comes to call the *patron au dedans* (III, 2,
807), become the touchstone by which to judge action: "J'ay mes
loix et ma court pour juger de moi, et m'y adresse plus
qu'ailleurs" (807). Finally, he turns the hostile environment,
menacing both body and soul, to his advantage and uses it for
personal reformation, in order to accustom himself to endure
misfortune, to resist temptation, to come to rely on his own
resources: "Et me resolus que c'estoyent utiles inconveniens . . .
m'instruisant de bonne heure à contraindre ma vie et la renger
pour un nouvel estat. La vraye liberté c'est pouvoir toute chose
sur soy" (III, 12, 1045-46). This is a Stoic echo at the very end of
the essays; not a return to faith in the absolute power of reason
and the will, to philosophical dogmatism, but a reaffirmation of
the distinction between exterior and interior things, of the degree
to which the self is the source of its own being in the world.

II

The proximate geography of Europe stands essentially as negative space: distant America represents its symbolic counterpoint.[5] In a posture that recalls Tacitus' *Germania* and prefigures that of Rousseau, the essayist participates in an idealizing tradition reaching back to the classical moralists. Little is new here: the point of view and the actual details recounted can both be found in the books Montaigne read, although he lays claim to firsthand knowledge through personal contacts. The sympathetic introduction of distinctly foreign customs undermines contemporary usage and underscores its relativity. The essayist's purpose may be political, to offer social criticism; it may be philosophical as well, to heighten the sense of diversity, nourishing the pervading skepticism. But over and above these pragmatic aims the fruits of nature—her noble people or their customs—stand against European civilization corrupted by artifice as components of that tension between the natural and the artificial that strains in the world of the *Essais.*

The New World is not the only extra-European area of which Montaigne speaks: references to Asia—and Turkey in particular—considerably outnumber those to America.[6] Interestingly, these references function as do those to other countries in Europe, past or present. That is, the essayist draws from his knowledge of Turkey—a bookish knowledge, admittedly—to provide examples of praiseworthy or blameworthy conduct or customs, to point up the relative merit of familiar Occidental ways. The description of the lavish Indian suicide pyre in *Coustume de l'Isle de Cea* (II, 3) implies a universality extending the geographical scope of the essayist's argument, but its particular role is to set into relief instances of suicide recorded in Spain or Marseilles. The countries of Asia do not function in any important symbolic way. They were, perhaps, too close geographically and psychologically to Europe, too familiar as archetypal infidel (and recently very menacing) to serve as moral counterpart.

The opposite is true of the New World, idealized to function

as symbol. Unknown until modern times, and thus uncon-
taminated by the march of civilization, America stands as if at
the dawn of humanity, as Montaigne says of its inhabitants in
words borrowed from Seneca, "viri a diis recentes," men fresh
sprung from the gods (I, 31, 207). Two essays present the New
World (*Des cannibales, Des coches*); further references occur only
occasionally through the *Essais* (II, 12, 22; III, 13), but it
remains a model in counterpoint, very much like the friendship
with La Boétie. As the essayist's present ontological state has its
opposite in the distant unity of friendship, so contemporary
society finds its antithesis in remote America.

In *Des cannibales,* Montaigne insists on historical veracity by
differentiating the New World from Plato's account of Atlantis
and from the island whose discovery Aristotle ascribes to the
Carthaginians. The account of America does not serve as a myth,
as a fiction rendered verisimilar by the wit and imagination of the
cultivated mind, but as unadorned reality, witnessed by that
simple, crude eye incapable of deception: "Cet homme que
j'avoy, estoit homme simple et grossier, qui est une condition
propre à rendre veritable tesmoignage" (205). But the invitation
to accept the presentation as true is more rhetorical than real, an
effort to have the reader suspend disbelief, enter the world of the
literary work, accept its premises, its governing forces, the
general rules by which it operates. What concerns us here is not
whether Montaigne actually employed a man who had lived in
America, whether he met sailors and merchants who had made
the voyage, or spoke with three Brazilian Indians in Bordeaux in
1562. The declarations provide that framework within which the
reader understands the world he describes and its dependence
upon tensions between nature and artificiality, simplicity and
science, distance and proximity both in time and space.

Within this context, then, the New World surpasses in perfection even the most idealized models that human fancy has
conceived: "Il me desplait que Licurgus et Platon ne l'ayent eüe
[connaissance]; car il me semble que ce que nous voyons par
experience en ces nations là, surpasse, non seulement toutes les

peintures dequoy la poësie a embelly l'age doré, et toutes ses inventions à feindre une heureuse condition d'hommes, mais encore la conception et le desir mesme de la philosophie" (206). Absent are all those elements that characterize modern European life, both causes and effects of the perversity of contemporary society: "il n'y a aucune espece de trafique; nulle cognoissance de lettres; nulle science de nombres; nul nom de magistrat, ny de superiorité politique; nul usage de service, de richesse ou de pauvreté; nuls contrats; nulles successions . . ." (206). But this is something more than the simple negation of contemporary society, for the absence of lies, treachery, dissimulation, envy indicts postlapsarian man in general. The temperate climate of this preagricultural-, premetal-age society where work is unknown ("nulles occupations qu'oysives"), where illness, deformity, and the ravages of age do not exist, reinforces the Edenic dimension of the presentation. The land is not hostile but gives abundantly of its natural resources; nor does society menace the individual, for a common kinship predominates.

Potential faults are neutralized and even rendered virtues by the essayist. Barbarism is redefined, recast, and endowed with symbolic meaning to heighten our revulsion at the spectacle of European savagery rather than Brazilian cannibalism. War is ennobled by the conduct of the combatants ("leur guerre est toute noble et genereuse" [210]), for the victor seeks only to exceed his enemy in valor and virtue. Polygamous marriages are sources of harmony and order reminiscent of the ideal of Old Testament practice. And what greater value could Montaigne place on this culture than to consider its poetry anacreontic and its language reminiscent of Greek: "c'est un doux langage et qui a le son aggreable, retirant aux terminaisons Grecques" (213).

Unlike the Golden Age men of Seneca's nineteenth letter to Lucilius, whose natural ignorance of sin was to be surpassed by the acquired, practiced virtue of the philosopher, this prelapsarian state represents the lost ideal. No notion of progress, of linear movement toward a higher, more perfect practice as the Stoic claims; no sense of *felix culpa*, of a fall that allows man to reascend with a dignity heretofore unknown. The movement Montaigne implies would be circular, a return to what once was and is no longer. The past represents the social ideal, what man harkens back to and what he longs to approximate. The vision of the future, as in the case of the lost friendship, becomes the mythical past. When Montaigne enunciates the principle that informs prelapsarian perfection—that men know how to "heureusement jouyr de leur condition et s'en contenter" (210)—he introduces the very terms that will describe his ultimate desire, stated in the closing words of the essays: "C'est une absolue perfection, et comme divine, de sçavoyr jouyr loiallement de son estre. Nous cherchons d'autres conditions, pour n'entendre l'usage des nostres, et sortons hors de nous, pour ne sçavoir quel il y fait" (III, 13, 1115).

When the essayist takes up the theme of the New World again in *Des coches* (III, 6), his description has evolved in important ways, but its symbolic and contrastive function still predominates. Another part of the Americas, to be sure, and societies more technologically advanced, but similar in their practice of virtue. We are not dealing here with the same primordial state as that of *Des cannibales,* but rather with what that culture might look like after considerable advance. And what strikes the reader is that its pristine virtue has remained essentially intact. We are still near the infancy of the world, juxtaposed to the decrepit, palsied state of Europe: "Si nous concluons bien de nostre fin, et ce poëte [Lucretius] de la jeunesse de son siecle, cet autre monde ne faira qu'entrer en lumiere quand le nostre en sortira" (908).

If there is a comparison to be made between the vision of the New World and the Old, it is with the Greek and Latin cultures. Here the essayist is careful to avoid the impression of an unbroken, linear direction in intellectual and moral history. The classical moment clearly represents a summit of human achievement but Montaigne will insist on cultural relativism by stressing the value of the Egyptian and Chinese civilizations and the potential excellence of cultures unknown. Human history, like human nature, displays erratic movement: "Ce n'est pas à dire qu'elle y ayt lors employé son dernier effort [nature working in antiquity]. Nous n'allons point, nous rodons plustost, et tournoions çà et là. Nous nous promenons sur nos pas" (907). Nature's eternal potential for producing and animating fertile minds does not affect the sense of decline that emerges from the simple juxtaposition of the modern and ancient worlds. The world may not have begun in the Golden Age of Greece as Lucretius vainly attempted to suggest, just as it surely is not ending today (Montaigne finds monstrous the vanity of giving such momentous import to one's own age), but clearly these two points represent the zenith and nadir of a particular intellectual and moral tradition. And it is in this context that the relation with the Aztec and Mayan civilizations becomes meaningful. We no longer enjoy (as in *Des cannibales*) an Edenic moment that, while rooted in specific geography, exists essentially as a lyric, or perhaps mythic, state. Rather, America now bears a certain affinity with the classical world: a distant culture, removed in space as the ancient is in time, the embodiment of the highest human achievement. In military valor they stand side by side; "Quant à la hardiesse et courage, quant à a fermeté, constance, resolution contre les douleurs et la faim et la mort, je ne craindrois pas d'opposer les exemples que je trouverois parmy eux aux plus fameux exemples anciens que nous ayons aus memoires de nostre monde par deçà" (909). In pomp and magnificence— the framing theme of *Des coches*—no known work compares in utility, difficulty, and nobility with the road from Quito to Cuzco in Peru. And in moral virtue, a natural affinity: "Que n'est tombée soubs Alexandre ou soubs ces anciens Grecs et Romains une si noble conqueste . . . meslant les vertus Grecques et Romaines aux originelles du pays! . . . Combien il eust esté aisé de faire son profit d'ames si neuves, si affamées d'apprentissage, ayant pour la plus part de si beaux commencemens naturels" (910).

Clearly the supreme era of human history remains that of the classical cultures; one would not expect otherwise from a Renaissance humanist. What is striking, then, is the way the comparison embraces the Indian cultures, portraying them as a younger, simpler version of the more mature, sophisticated societies of Greece and Rome. Montaigne prizes the natural, unadorned way of life that he ascribes to the New World; in the teaching of European philosophy and the lives of its exponents he seeks out that very attitude. The outlines of the ideal philosopher which emerge from the last essays of Book III appear an amalgam of New World simplicity and Old World introspection and self-consciousness as they converge in the figure of Socrates.

The moral kinship is apparent; and, by contrast, modern Europe is found woefully wanting. The ancient world is as much its counterpoint as the New World. Whatever is good takes place "out there" in time and space, remote enough to be inaccessible, distant enough to be considered objectively and to serve as an example. As if surrounded temporally and spatially by these models, contemporary time and space press inward, hostile, menacing, negative, offering no solace, no asylum; and yet return to that other era, to another place, is impossible. Montaigne does not reject the world for a personal mysticism, nor does he stress his own superiority, as nineteenth-century Romantics were wont to do. On the contrary, he remains very much anchored in a specific historical context, situated at a precise moment, in a precise place. In fact, the evils that have seduced his contemporaries tempt him as well as he pictures himself struggling continually to resist. Montaigne's feel for the lure of glory, ambition, and vanity, his insight into the human inclination for masks and ceremony, his sense of the dangers of man's pretention to knowledge heighten his awareness of the potential range of human error but do not exempt him from it. The effort to turn away and to return to himself becomes the record kept in the *Essais*. But it is important to note that turning away from the social world involves the recognition that the lures, inclinations, and pretensions derive from man's very being; the societal whole, in this case, represents only the sum of its parts. In modern society, man is both the creator and the creation of the state of things.

The Delphic oracle, which the revered ancients heeded,

enjoined man to examine himself, finding him alone in not doing
so: "Sauf toy, ô homme . . . cháque chose s'estudie la premiere
et a, selon son besoin, des limites à ses travaux et desirs" (III, 9,
1001). The cultures of the New World, and of classical Greece
and Rome, in different ways represent examples of what man can
achieve: the first spontaneously, naturally, the second intention-
ally, through an act of will and judgment. Like the nostalgia of
the lost friendship, these models of what once was appear to
stimulate the *epistrophe*. Amelioration may be possible, or at least
the effort itself, which seems to ennoble. In the context we have
been discussing, contemporary society can be the source of
neither virtue nor knowledge, nor can it in any way provide the
source or sense of being. It can act negatively to absorb, to
swallow man, to lose him to himself, or positively to throw him
back to himself ("à reculons"). The tension, as we have said,
underlies the essayist's every move. Montaigne's veering back
toward the self, his physical retirement, the way he turns the
world to his own advantage and the reaching back to the ancient
and New World cultures appear to derive from when and where
he lives.

III

We come to the essayist's immediate space, that occupied by his
family and property. Although these details are more commonly
found in intimate journals or confessions, given the interplay
between Montaigne and his surroundings we might have expected information about family life, wife, and children. But
such details are not provided. Although mentioned infrequently
in passing, they are conspicuously missing from the substance of
the essays. It has been suggested that Montaigne cared little for
his wife, whom he apparently married in deference to his father's
wishes, or his children—six daughters, of whom all but one died
in infancy—and thus simply did not include them in the text.
While this biographical hypothesis may be so, it misleads, I

think, by devaluing the thematic and structural importance of this absence and diverting the reader's attention from it. The necessity to diminish the space occupied by the return to the self demands an exclusionary practice, one best understood in the context of his attitude toward the management of his estate.

The early Stoicism of *De la solitude* suggests that the essayist purposely separates himself from what he most dearly cherishes in order to steel himself against the pain of their loss. In that *arrière boutique* all our own, he says, we must "discourir et . . . rire comme sans femme, sans enfans et sans biens, sans train et sans valetz, afin que, quand l'occasion adviendra de leur perte, il ne nous soit pas nouveau de nous en passer" (I, 39, 241). This attitude accompanies the Stoic conversion we spoke of earlier, where the soul turns in upon itself from the outside world in its quest for self-sufficiency. As Montaigne describes the substantial nature of this movement, he leaves aside the more abstract *convertible* to forge a new word that evokes a concrete, tangible image: "Nous avons une ame contournable en soy mesme" (241). At question is not only the preparation to live without what is perishable but the task of untangling oneself from the web of relations and involvements that distract the soul from its proper focus: "C'est assez vescu pour autruy, vivons pour nous au moins ce bout de vie. Ramenons à nous et à nostre aise nos pensées et nos intentions. . . . Il est temps de nous desnoüer de la societé . . ." (242).

When Montaigne comes back to the question of the household in *De la vanité*, his tone is more informal, relaxed, less stern and demanding (one is tempted to say less Stoic). As opposed to the necessary strength of will that underlies that earlier injunction to pull back from worldly attachments, here the desire to live a comfortable and relaxed life dominates. Having found his disposition ill suited to the tasks of domestic management he seeks by any means available to lessen the burden of responsibility, to avoid the petty demands and trivial cares that prick so deeply. As head of the household, Montaigne finds his duties "plus empeschante que difficile" (949) and so he accepts any occasion for distraction;

he avoids occasions for vexations and turns away from the knowledge of things that are going badly.

Everyday annoyances threaten the peace of mind of a man who claims to seek only "à m'anonchalir et avachir" (954); equally as important is the danger of being swallowed up by the myriad responsibilities. Montaigne backs away not because he scorns the mundane but because he fears becoming a slave to his affairs ("serf de mes negoces" [954]). And, not coincidentally, when he imagines the contrasting situation, the one for which he feels himself best suited—that of living on another man's fortune— the disadvantage which comes to mind is the very same: obligation and servitude. All through the essays Montaigne recognizes the danger of becoming enslaved to attitudes, opinions, emotions, or external associations and responsibilities. Here he uses Cicero's demeaning words to characterize that condition as antithetical to the whole thrust of his efforts: "Servitus obedientia est fracti animi et abjecti, arbitrio carentis suo"—Servitude is the obedience of a broken and abject mind, lacking free will (954). The business of the household, because it is busyness (what he refers to as a life *affaireuse,* 949, 954), always encroaches on the essential preoccupation with the self.

"C'est pitié d'estre en lieu où tout ce que vous voyez vous embesongne et vous concerne" (951), and so Montaigne seeks other places through evasion both psychological and physical. When at home he attempts to distance himself from the household as he does from the world: "Je me contente de jouir le monde sans m'en empresser" (952), he says in the same context. And he voyages to block out the troublesome thoughts of management, finding that his soul more easily achieves detachment from a distance.

Montaigne travels, then, to get out from under the responsibility of his estate and analogously, he tells us, to get away from a country whose moral state he decries. But we are talking about something more than mere physical displacement, for in the context of *De la vanité* the voyage becomes more significantly a metaphor for life, and for the register he keeps of it, the essays:

"Mon dessein est divisible par tout: il n'est pas fondé en grandes esperances; chaque journée en faict le bout. Et le voyage de ma vie se conduict de mesme" (978). What the household and the world have in common is that they bear down heavily on the essayist ("Ce qui me poise le plus . . ."; "Et cecy aussi me poise" [961]) like a physical weight that impedes movement. But to live, as to travel, one must be light, untrammeled, unattached to the things that render man immobile. And so material possessions, family, friendship, public opinion, social calamity, thoughts of death are all weights to which the essayist refers in *De la vanité* and which he seeks to neutralize. As long as he is not mortgaged (*hypotheque* [966]) to anything outside himself he is free to live, to travel that interior space that leads back to the self.

This, of course, cannot prove why Mme. de Montaigne and the family are almost totally absent from the essays; it does, however, explore the implications of that absence in the framework of the essays. It seems equally significant that the two individuals on whom Montaigne dwells—La Boétie and his father—are both dead. Over and above their inherent worth, which gives them a legitimate claim to the essayist's attention, is the overriding fact that neither is there presently. They are, for different reasons, a part of that past which, like antiquity, represents the moral and intellectual good, idealized perhaps as only the past can be, viewed with a nostalgia that fixes upon yesterday as the positive counterpoint of today. Not that Montaigne severs all links with exterior physical reality or withdraws to an abstract solipsism rooted in the past, for he needs, and desires, the concrete world and the present moment. The resolution he seeks is not assured by retreat from the world, nor will it ever be satisfactorily achieved. But if he is to pursue his quest, he must move away from the world to come back to it, move toward the past to come back to the present and, most essentially, to himself in it.

3

The Rhetoric of Humility

"L'homme ne peut estre que ce qu'il est"
(II, 12, 520)

"Et quis homo est quilibet homo cum sit homo"
(Augustine, *Confessions,* IV, 1)
(What indeed is any man, seeing that he is but
a man)

I

If being and knowledge cannot be founded in the space occupied
and the time lived, there remains the possibility that man can
reason his way to truth by considering the nature of God's
universe. This is what the Spanish theologian Raymond de
Sebond demonstrated in his *Theologia naturalis*—published in
1487 and in French in 1519—which Montaigne tells us he translated in a matter of days in 1569 at his father's request. This
exercise brought him to the logic of Sebond's arguments, as he
worked them in his own language, cast them in words of his
choosing. In the *Apologie de Raimond Sebond* Montaigne comes
back to explore on his own questions of man's capacity for
knowledge.

Montaigne's longest essay occupies the physical center of the
Essais. The paradox of its content, which seems to belie the
notion of *apologia,* has attracted considerable critical attention in
an effort to explain why, outside of the first introductory pages,

what is entitled a defense reads like an attack, why Sebond's rational construct should stand while others fall before Montaigne's critical assault on reason. But the essayist's opening remarks carefully delineate a fundamental distinction that sets Sebond's effort apart from that of others and, just as significantly, from his own. What accords the *Theologia naturalis* its validity as metaphysical inquiry, we are told, is that Sebond has been guided by a profound faith conceived in the light of divine grace.

The opening argument of the *Apologie* maintains that when illuminated by the true faith that grace allows, human reason can sustain belief. Its corollary, which will form the body of the essay, contends that on its own reason is incapable of attaining truth and knowledge. Insight into the nature of things universal is thus inherently beyond human intelligence. Only if God deigns to make them accessible by bestowing form on the barren matter of human arguments through grace can man penetrate the divine mysteries to "embellir, estandre, et amplifier la verité de sa creance" (441). Man can see only if God discloses, and the knowledge acquired reflects back to embellish and amplify a prior conviction and religious predisposition. Montaigne describes an epistemological circle where man knows because he believes and believes because he knows, where both knowledge and belief are gifts from God: "Il . . . faut . . . accompaigner nostre foy de toute la raison qui est en nous, mais tousjours avec cette reservation de n'estimer pas que ce soit de nous qu'elle dépende, ny que nos efforts et argumens puissent atteindre à une si supernaturelle et divine science" (441). Because Sebond enjoyed faith and grace, his arguments are true and may even prove useful in starting the neophyte on the road to divine knowledge: "La foy venant à teindre et illustrer les argumens de Sebon, elle les rend fermes et solides" (447). Montaigne places his emphasis in the bulk of the essay—from which Sebond is, in the main, absent—on the vanity of unaided reason to impugn the religious doubters and Protestant reasoners who attack the *Theologia naturalis* and undermine traditional Catholic faith.[1] He defends Sebond by discrediting his critics and their methods although he realizes, as he explains to Marguerite de France, that this approach undercuts his own argument: "C'est un coup desesperé, auquel il faut abandonner vos armes pour faire perdre à vos adversaire les siennes . . ."(558).[2]

The statement that man rises above his earthbound station by God's grace alone returns dramatically at the end of the essay as if to frame Montaigne's consideration of reason unaided: "Il [man] s'eslevera si Dieu lui preste extraordinairement la main; il s'eslevera, abandonnant et renonçant à ses propres moyens, et se laissant hausser et soubslever par les moyens purement celestes" (604).[3] This polemical structure sets the metaphysical against the physical to provide a transcendental perspective from which to disclose the vanity of all human activity. In this regard, the *Apologie* stands as an essay apart, how dramatically can be seen from Montaigne's stunning deprecation of Socrates, that towering sage of the rest of the work: "les actions vertueuses de Socrates . . . demeurent vaines et inutiles pour n'avoir eu leur fin et n'avoir regardé l'amour et obeïssance du vray createur de toutes choses, et pour avoir ignoré Dieu" (447). In the *Apologie* Montaigne raises questions about the nature of man and his world: he concludes with man's puniness and the futility of his action, with his total dependence on God. In other essays these same questions serve as a point of departure to throw man back to himself, to stress his independence and responsibility, to determine his action. The observations on time and existence at the close of the *Apologie* underscore the vanity of the quest for being: "il n'y a aucune constante existence, ny de nostre estre, ny de celuy des objects. Et nous, et nostre jugement, et toutes choses mortelles, vont coulant et roulant sans cesse. Ainsin il ne se peut establir rien de certain de l'un à l'autre, et le jugeant et le jugé estans en continuelle mutation et branle" (601). In *Du repentir* familiar words amplify the same theme, not to belittle or devalue human endeavor but to describe its setting, to explain why Montaigne essays himself in order to depict becoming: "Le monde n'est qu'une branloire perenne. . . . Je ne puis asseurer mon object. Il va trouble et chancelant, d'une yvresse naturelle. Je le prens en ce

point, comme il est, en l'instant que je m'amuse à luy. Je ne
peints pas l'estre. Je peints le passage" (805). Comments on the
mind imposing its own forms on things in the *Apologie* underscore the problematic nature of human knowledge ("Les yeux
humains ne peuvent apercevoir les choses que par les formes de
leur cognoissance" [535]); in *De Democritus et Heraclitus* the disclosure of these forms as the mind searches and judges serves to
give the measure of the man who perceives them ("Tout
mouvement nous descouvre" [302]). Where the closing remarks
of the *Apologie* ("ny que l'homme se monte au dessus de soy et de
l'humanité: car il ne peut voir que de ses yeux, ny saisir que de ses
prises") conclude by stressing the miraculous power of the super-
natural ("C'est à nostre foy Chrestienne . . . de pretendre à cette
divine et miraculeuse metamorphose" [604]), their counterpart
at the very conclusion of the essays, in *De l'experience*, leads to the
affirmation of things human: "Les plus belles vies sont, à mon gré,
celles qui se rangent au modelle commun et humain, avec ordre,
mais sans miracle et sans extravagance" (III, 13, 1116).

The *Apologie*, then, appears in striking opposition to the body
of the *Essais,* as if the necessity of the apologetic demanded that
there be disjunction, that the essay be isolated, independent in
its perspective and its conclusions. Why at the center of the work
alone should the essayist assume and sustain a transcendental
perspective? It could be, of course, that he sought to insist on his
own religious orthodoxy as he argued the essential superiority of
faith over reason, and reaffirmed the traditional Christian values
of humility, obedience, and ignorance. Or, as some critics have
suggested, the fideism he expresses, which separates faith and
reason, may allow him to attack certain religious articles while
maintaining the posture of a believer.[4] But the difficulty with
these hypotheses is twofold: first, they are extremely difficult to
establish and, second, they displace the critical focus from the
essayist to the historical man. Given Montaigne's delight in
paradox and the eclecticism of his approach, he unabashedly
supports Christian claims with pagan sources, juxtaposes orthodox notions on the nature of man to equivocal statements on the

immortality of the soul (his remarks on Plato are also valid for the Christian position). When he posits the relativity of religion to suggest that what man takes for absolute is determined by custom, time, or place, is the reader to extend this to include Christianity? When he attacks the philosopher's proof of the existence of God by design, is this meant to undermine Christianity's use of the same argument? At differing points in the *Apologie* Montaigne emerges as a deist, a fideist, a Pyrrhonian, a relativist, both an orthodox and unorthodox Catholic, as well as an intellectual supporter of ignorance. To pin Montaigne down is to destroy him; to define his position is to create one for him. The question of his belief is fundamentally a moot one.

Clearly, the structure of the *Apologie*—its metaphysical perspective and the thrust of its argument—fulfills a rhetorical function. When he characterizes his method to Marguerite de France as extreme, Montaigne implies it is a strategy, similar to the final parry of the swordsman: "Ce dernier tour d'escrime icy" (558). That is, the position imposed by the argument becomes paramount. The debater shapes his stance to the demands of the argument; he adjusts his claims to overcome the strength—or danger—of his adversary. He thus has recourse to fable, hyperbole, preposterous stories, and the Pyrrhonian position itself. The argument cannot be read as proof of the speaker's profound personal conviction, and even less so of the historical figure behind the speaker. It serves as a defense of Sebond but functions more significantly in the framework of the structural and thematic fabric of the total corpus of the *Essais*. Here the *Apologie* discloses its centrality.

Man on his own is Montaigne's target in the *Apologie*. The specific response to Sebond's critics broadens quickly into a position that encompasses all purely human endeavor: "Considerons donq pour cette heure l'homme seul, sans secours estranger, armé seulement de ses armes, et despourveu de la grace et cognoissance divine, qui est tout son honneur, sa force et le fondement de son estre" (449). Montaigne introduced this larger scale in the opening lines, where he states that knowledge,

although great and useful, neither represents the supreme good
nor has the power in itself to lead to wisdom, contentment, or
virtue. And while his father may have received learned men in his
home as "personnes sainctes et ayans quelque particuliere inspiration de sagesse divine, recueillant leurs sentences et leurs discours
comme des oracles" (439), Montaigne records his own lack of
"faith" and uses it as a prelude to the attack: "Moy je les ayme
bien, mais je ne les adore pas." Ironically, the revered father's
attitude—which brought Sebond's book to his attention and led
directly to the translation—points up the fundamental error of
those Montaigne will upbraid: they take human reasoning for
oracular pronouncement and scholars for holy men, as if heaven
and earth were on equal footing. The hypothesis "Let us consider
for the moment man alone" sets the argument whose conclusions
are already established. Ranging over the wide spectrum of what
man has sought and claimed to know, Montaigne cites authority
after authority, heaps example upon example to insist on the
blinding vanity of human presumption and the idolatrous quest
for knowledge. In terms often angry and violent, his jeremiad
seeks to abase man who, in his folly, values learning over true
wisdom, power over humility, who mistakes the relative for the
absolute, luster for light: "Le moyen que je prens pour rabatre
cette frenaisie et qui me semble le plus propre, c'est de froisser et
fouler aux pieds l'orgueil et humaine fierté; leur faire sentir
l'inanité, la vanité, et deneantise de l'homme; leur arracher des
points les chetives armes de leur raison" (448). In his arrogance,
man exaggerates his intellectual capacity, overestimates his capri-
cious senses, and misjudges *science* as the path to happiness and
virtue. Blind to the disparity between being and becoming, he
confounds his nature—and his powers—with those of God, eternally re-enacting his primordial error. He does not find truth and
he loses himself.

   The echoes of the biblical prophets crying out against the
stiff-necked people and the New Testament evangelists preach-
ing contrition and repentance, stressing human frailty to strip
away presumption, are unmistakable. Pride, as man's original

sin, the source of his fall from grace perpetuated through time as a negative birthright, keeps him from turning back to God in humility. But as Pascal so clearly noted in the *Entretien avec M. de Saci,* the *Apologie* in its relation to the *Essais* does not humble man to point him away from himself to God; its concerns are mundane rather than transcendental. The essay's conclusions do not initiate the spiritual pilgrimage to the creator but preface man's secular journey through life: "J'aurais aimé de tout mon coeur le ministre d'une si grande vengeance, si, étant disciple de l'Eglise par la foi, il eût suivi les règles de la morale, en portant les hommes . . . à ne pas irriter par de nouveaux crimes celui qui peut seul les tirer de ceux qu'il les a convaincus de ne pouvoir pas seulement connaître. Mais il agit au contraire de cette sorte, en païen."[5] The destructive thrust reduces man to point zero, where he stands naked; yet this picture—which one might expect from Luther or Calvin—will not lead beyond man but back to him.

The recognition of human vanity pivotal to the movement of religious conversion finds its counterpart in the Montaignian framework where presumption occupies an analogous center as the archetypal obstacle to return to the proper object of attention. In the context of the *Apologie* Montaigne restates the biblical precept that man must descend before he can ascend in terms that reverberate through the entire fabric of the *Essais:* "Il nous faut abestir pour nous assagir" (492). For man to seek wisdom in the Christian context—that is, to approach God in a motion metaphorically described as vertical—he must first be humbled (rendered low, from the latin *humus,* earth, ground).[6] The secular conversion, as if taking place in a horizontal plane—in terms that absorb high-low into the broader opposition between outside and inside—demands that man's attention be brought back from outside to fix on himself. As he comes to know and acknowledge his natural limitations, man approaches worldly wisdom: "C'est une absolue perfection, et comme divine, de sçavoyr jouyr loiallement de son estre" (III, 13, 1115).

Although Montaigne purposely avoids "humility" for its religious connotations, the recognition of the boundaries of human capacity reoccurs as a motif throughout the *Essais,* for it is the absolute prerequisite to the return to the self. As the essayist focuses on self-knowledge he becomes increasingly aware of pretension and presumption as major obstacles that carry the gaze away from the self. And he circles the problem to catch what he might call its *divers lustres.* Sometimes he stresses how little man can know; at other times he juxtaposes the distorting lens of vanity as self-love to vanity as emptiness; over and again he reiterates the tendency to look away, or go away, from the self and the necessity of return. In *De la diversion* Montaigne under-lines "nostre imbecilité et bestise naturelle" (838) as he shows the mind prey both to diversion and the power of the imagination. The same notion reappears in *Des boyteux*: "Nous aymons à nous embrouiller en la vanité, comme conforme à nostre estre" (1027). The conclusion of *De la vanité* finds in man's misery and empti-ness both the explanation of why he looks outside and the corrective necessity for him to follow the Delphic injunction: "Regardez dans vous, reconnoissez vous, tenez vous à vous" (1001). And as a last example of the extent of these related threads in the Third Book, we recall Montaigne's condemnation of Socrates' "ecstases et ses demoneries" (1115) at the end of *De l'experience* and the *Essais,* and his observation that man seeks other conditions and goes outside of himself because he does not know what it is like inside.

To presumption and pride Montaigne adds curiosity as a fundamental source of human error. In the *Apologie* he assumes both Christian and Platonic stances to condemn its excesses: "Les Chrestiens ont une particuliere cognoissance combien la curiosité est un mal naturel et originel en l'homme. Le soing de s'aug-menter en sagesse et en science, ce fut la premiere ruine du genre humain" (498). Montaigne juxtaposes Augustine's statement that God is better known by not knowing to this paraphrase of Plato: "Et Platon estime qu'il y ayt quelque vice d'impieté à trop curieusement s'enquerir et de Dieu et du monde, et des causes premieres des choses" (499). Later on, in the Third Book, he again associates curiosity with that philosophical activity that leads man away from nature and himself: "Les inquisitions et contemplations philosophiques ne servent que d'aliment à nostre curiosité" (III, 13, 1073). Against the active quest that man pursues into error, which feeds his presumptuous claims to knowledge, Montaigne pictures himself passively led by the general law of the world ("la loy generale du monde" [1073]). Ignorance and incuriousness are qualities he seeks to cultivate, qualities appropriate for the well-made head: "O que c'est un doux et mol chevet, et sain, que l'ignorance et l'incuriosité, à reposer une teste bien faicte."

In the continuing parallel with Christian ideology, Montaigne draws on St. Paul to define ignorance: "Les simples, dit S. Paul, et les ignorans s'eslevent et saisissent du ciel; et nous, à tout nostre sçavoir, nous plongeons aux abismes infernaux" (II, 12, 497). Childlike innocence and humility accompany the lack of learning that guarantees salvation. And Montaigne finds his secular analogue in the Brazilian savage and in the idealized peasant who emerge through the *Essais*. Early in the work, when his position is more consistently Stoic, he distinguishes the sage from the common populace incapable of the effort of will and intellect required to confront human experience. Later on, as he turns more profoundly and self-consciously inward, Montaigne pretends to recognize in the peasant a kind of essential man, close to both physical and human nature, unspoiled by learning, simple and innocent because ignorant, spared in part because of his rural rather than urban societal life:

> La plus part des instructions de la science à nous encourager ont plus de montre que de force, et plus d'ornement que de fruict. Nous avons abandonné nature et luy voulons apprendre sa leçon, elle qui nous menoit si heureusement et si seurement. Et cependent les traces de son instruction et ce peu qui, par le benefice de l'ignorance, reste de son image empreint en la vie de cette tourbe rustique d'hommes impolis, la science est contrainte de l'aller tous les jours empruntant . . . [III, 12, 1049]

The rustic is a literary creation, of course, an idealized construct; one cannot imagine Montaigne abandoning life in his tower, his books, his writing to live as his literal counterpart. The idealization functions symbolically to express attitudes fundamental to the meaningful return to the self.

The paradox of the rationalist using reason and intellect to prove their inadequacy, of the learned claiming the value of ignorance, is common to skepticism.[7] In the *Apologie*, where the rhetorical stance requires the denigration of philosophy, erudition, books, Montaigne seeks to confirm man's inability to acquire substantial knowledge as truth. In that comfortable juxtaposition of Christian and pagan references that characterizes the essay, he evokes Socrates' learned ignorance to acknowledge the limitations of human inquiry. If the primordial state of the peasant—as a lost ideal—cannot be recaptured by the already learned, it can be approximated in the admission of ignorance, the knowledge that one cannot know: Socrates understood that the gods considered him wise "par ce qu'il ne s'en tenoit pas" (II, 12, 498). Western, cultured man has to get out from under the encumbering arrogance that makes him think he knows and the subtleties and sophistications of philosophy that obscure the face of reality. The admission of ignorance, like humility, must precede and accompany the return to the self. Montaigne's insistence throughout the *Essais* on his own lack of worth implicates him in that movement.

II

Montaigne's attitudes align him with the Pyrrhonians—those, he claims, still in search of the truth. But to regard him merely as a Skeptic is to mistake his means for his end, to misjudge his effort to delineate the proper area of human inquiry. He adopts a skeptical mode of reasoning because the view of man it offers serves his polemical ends: "Cette-cy presente l'homme nud et vuide, recognoissant sa foiblesse naturelle, propre à recevoir d'en haut quelque force estrangere, desgarni d'humaine science" (II, 12, 506). Sometimes the reader senses Montaigne's longing for peace, as in *De mesnager sa volonté* (III, 10), where he sets *branle* and *repos* in opposition to emphasize how being agitated, possessed, or carried off by ideas or passions threatens the grip on the self: "J'essaie à tenir mon ame et mes pensées en repos" (1020). But while the echo of Pyrrhonian ataraxy rings clear, his deep concern with the Delphic command of self-knowledge and his acceptance of the validity of its quest distinguish him fundamentally from the Skeptic sect. The disavowal of science and the suspension of judgment here become means to the discrediting of human pretension so that man can turn back toward himself rather than the antecedents of intellectual and spiritual tranquility. Personal calm does not derive from indifference to the external world alone; in the context of the *Essais* it emerges as a function of the secular conversion.

Montaigne uses the Pyrrhonian optic, as he uses the Christian perspective, to prepare man to meet himself. At the juncture of these ideologies, at the point where their views coincide, he points up how man blindly seeks to transcend his own nature, how he loses himself in what is alien and unnatural to him. But even as the essayist sets out all that man cannot be and cannot do, he indicates, through the now familiar process of negative definition, what he is and what he can do. By this procedure, the outlines of the object he is considering emerge. Montaigne recognized the appropriateness of his intellectual position to a situation where he sought to undermine, to posit doubt, and acknowledged this as the way the Pyrrhonians argued: "Et font estat de trouver bien plus facilement pour quoy une chose soit fauce, que non pas qu'elle soit vraïe" (II, 12, 505). If man is to turn his gaze inward, he must come to understand the inanity of looking outside; the ground must be cleared, vanity and presumption swept away, so that he can see that he can only be what he is: "L'homme ne peut estre que ce qu'il est, ny imaginer que selon sa portée" (520).

As Montaigne builds up the sense of the overwhelming

uncertainty and contradiction in which the quest for knowledge inevitably culminates, the distinct outlines of the nature of man emerge from the *Apologie*. The limitations of reason, taken as the "contrerolleuse generalle de tout ce qui est au dehors et au dedans de la voute celeste, qui embrasse tout, qui peut tout, par le moyen de laquelle tout se sçait et connoit," are clearly established: "c'est une touche pleine de fauceté, d'erreur, de foiblesse et defaillance" (541). As counterpoint to this faulty instrument blindly idolized by human pride, Montaigne sets as touchstone the irresistible force of experience and criticizes the Pyrrhonians for doubting it: "et les Pyrrhoniens ne se servent de leurs argumens et de leur raison que pour ruiner l'apparence de l'experience; . . . car ils verifient que nous ne nous mouvons pas, que nous ne parlons pas, qu'il n'y a point de poisant ou de chaut, avecques une pareille force d'argumentations que nous verifions les choses plus vray-semblables" (571). It is not merely that his *science* is vain, but that man himself inclines naturally to vanity and inanity. And if philosophical speculation leads away from truth and obscures the nature of things, listening and looking inward begins to uncover the nature of the self: "Moy qui m'espie de plus prez, qui ay les yeux incessamment tendus sur moy, comme celuy qui n'ay pas fort à-faire ailleurs, . . . à peine oseroy-je dire la vanité et la foiblesse que je trouve chez moy. J'ay le pied si instable et si mal assis, je le trouve si aysé à croler et si prest au branle, et ma veuë si desreglée. . . ." (565).

The substructure that necessitates and supports that activity and that knowledge within the human province emerges clearly. The passage Montaigne borrows from Plutarch's *Moral Essays,* "On the Meaning of ϵi," with which he closes the *Apologie*, reverberates most profoundly through the *Essais* for it establishes the conditions of the self situated in time. After pointing out that human knowledge leads to neither virtue nor happiness, in the last two-thirds of the essay Montaigne focuses most directly on the impotence of reason: "Si me faut-il voir en fin s'il est en la puissance de l'homme de trouver ce qu'il cherche, et si cette queste qu'il y a employé depuis tant de siecles, l'a enrichy de quelque nouvelle force et de quelque verité solide" (500). The depiction of this twofold folly—the quest and the assurance of its success—turns on the disparity between human aspiration and its ontological situation. Man assumes that his world admits of things solid, absolute, certain, as if there were no difference between the province he inhabits and that of true being, between himself and God. Against presumptuous illusion Montaigne posits the reality of relativity, multiplicity, and movement; the elements of its lexicon—inconstancy, instability, volubility, variability—reappear to form a major thematic pattern of the essay. Reason is "si instable et si mobile" (568), like fortune itself, "diverse et variable" (516). The senses, "incertains et falsifiables à toutes circonstances" (592), operate on exterior objects which themselves have "divers lustres et diverses considerations" (581). Human judgment is in the power of "perturbation" (568), susceptible to "agitations vehementes" (568). Little wonder that the fruits of *science* and philosophy are nothing more than "cette varieté et instabilité d'opinions" (545). When Montaigne comes to look at himself, he finds "le pied si instable et si mal assis, . . . si aysé à croler et si prest au branle" (565), given to "agitations" (566); his soul rocked by "les secousses et esbranlemens" (565) of bodily passions. The world itself contains "une infinie difference et varieté pour la seule distance des lieux" (525). And in this framework, man seeks " (la) veritable essence" (597), "la vraye essence (des) choses" (590), "une reelle subsistance" (601) as if they were accessible to him.

Thus the general characteristics of man in his world emerge, functions, as Montaigne suggests, of time and space: "Mais qu'est-ce donc qui est veritablement? Ce qui est eternel, c'est à dire qui n'a jamais eu de naissance, ny n'aura jamais fin; à qui le temps n'apporte jamais aucune mutation. Car c'est chose mobile que le temps, et qui apparoit comme en ombre, avec la matiere coulante and fluante tousjours, sans jamais demeurer stable ny permanente" (603). What is in flux is in time, below the sphere of the moon, although man yearns to escape his condition: "et se va plantant par imagination au dessus du cercle de la Lune et ramenant le ciel soubs ses pieds" (452). Fundamentally, this observation, this reaffirmation of man's proper place in the region of generation, corruption, and change, forms the basis for future activity. By exploring the geography of what lies outside man's reach, Montaigne delineates the parameters of that area within: "Les extremitez de nostre perquisition tombent toutes en esblouyssement: comme dict Plutarque de la teste des histoires, qu'à la mode des chartes l'orée des terres cognuës est saisie de marets, forests profondes, deserts et lieux inhabitables" (544). What he has asserted about the world has been confirmed by his own experience, both intellectual and physical; against abstract philosophical speculation he has posed his own concrete reasoning and the fruits of listening to and watching himself. Some readers, puzzled by the paradox of rational argument turned against reason itself, have asked how Montaigne can use the very faculty he discredits, whose efficacy he denies. But the question oversimplifies the problem. It blurs the distinction between reason's capacity for questioning and its weakness in affirming and, more importantly, it disregards that fundamental separation on which Montaigne will insist through the *Essais* between the sphere of becoming and that of being. The *Apologie* does not contend that reason absolutely fails in the realm of becoming but that it fails to operate absolutely.

Montaigne delineates man's imperfection, to be acknowledged and accepted. The hyperbole that characterizes the rhetoric of humility is designed to annihilate not man but his pride, so that he can see himself as he is and—to recast the essay's closing words—eventually suit the handful to the hand, the armful to the arm, and the stride to the reach of his legs. The negation of the *Apologie* implies affirmation, the tearing away is also an uncovering; as the bounds of the *monstrueux* are defined, those of the natural emerge. To show up the vanity of looking outward is to show the necessity of looking inward. The secular conversion turns on this axis, both away from and toward.

III

The secular conversion requires continual renewal. The motion described is not a single semicircle by which the self turns and veers once and for all back toward the point of origin but a series of circles that depict the continuing dialectic of losing and finding the self, turning and returning. The tension between the inclination to go away from the self and the injunction to come back appears most strikingly at the end of *De la vanité*, where Montaigne indicates that man's gaze tends outward naturally ("nature a rejetté bien à propos l'action de nostre veuë au dehors" [1000]) at the same time that he indicts him—in the words of the Delphic oracle—as the one thing in the universe that does not study itself first.[8] This deviation from the rule of universal nature marks the flight from the self as unnatural and so the paradox is compounded, for then man is both inherently inclined and disinclined to look at himself. While Montaigne may delight in paradox, the play here is not for its own sake; it gives the reader the sense of the endless pull and tug of conversion (as turning) re-enacted. The elusive *vraye essence* of things that human curiosity seemingly cannot resist pursuing, the attraction of fame or glory, the lure of social and political involvement, and, underlying it all, the vanity to which man is always prey threaten to carry him off away from himself, to alienate him in things exterior. Over and again, as if recognizing and reaffirming the commitment, Montaigne returns to those attitudes and desires that, as he says, mortgage the freedom of the soul: "il faut mesnager la liberté de nostre ame et ne l'hypothequer qu'aux occasions justes. . . . Voyez les gens apris à se laisser emporter et saisir . . ." (III, 10, 1004). The more he looks at himself the greater his sense of the fragile, precarious, temporary quality of return, of how easily man is diverted from the proper object of his attention. In the Third Book, for example, this is constantly on his mind; from the opening lines of *De l'utile et de l'honneste* ("Nostre bastiment, et public et privé, est plain d'imperfection" [1, 790]) to the familiar closing words of *De l'experience,* the themes of imperfection, of vanity, of escape or flight from the self resound. The lesson of the *Apologie* is a recurrent motif in the fabric of human experience.

The reenacted conversion derives from the realm of becoming, the province of time that defines the context of the *Essais*. Within the boundaries of this world set, as we mentioned earlier, below the sphere of the moon, we look for change, flux, plurality, for to speak of permanence, stability, or unity would imply transcendence beyond what Montaigne considers the properly human. The veering back to the self can never be absolute, the turning of the gaze never immutably fixed, for both the gaze and the self are endlessly moving, evolving. In this duration, Montaigne's soundings locate a series of selves, separate though contiguous, in successive moments in time. And because change itself is not absolute, the essayist will insist on continuity as well, on resemblance as on difference, as the richness of the notion "autre moy-mesme" (805) suggests in *Du repentir* (III, 2). The essayist does not lose himself in the wholly relative or cast another way, does not lose himself because he refuses the wholly relative. While the *autre* indicates change, difference, the *moy-mesme* provides the link, the sameness that survives in spite of change. Indeed, the very notion of "moving away" from the self or "coming back" to the self presupposes a sense of self that allows the coordinates of situation to be fixed, distance and direction established. Montaigne seems to suggest the existence of some underlying entity that he ends up calling the *forme maitresse* or *patron au dedans*, which reveals itself as the multifarious faces of its manifestations in time. There is no primal essay, just as there is no concluding moment. Each stock-taking, each *essai* of that continuum of selves is repetition: in each new moment a new self arises, for each new self a renewal of the basic drama created by the tension between the outward impulse and the inward urge takes place, a reenactment of conversion.

The inherent link between time and repetition comes more sharply into focus by juxtaposing the secular conversion and its spiritual counterpart. Religious salvation demands a return to

God—that is, demands transcendence of the world of becoming to eternal Being. Conversion stands as the paradoxical resolution of the dialectic which situates man at once in time and timelessness. As in the miracle of creation, immanence and transcendence meet as the soul in life is reformed in God, at the point where sinner becomes saved. While the new man remains in the world, and thus prey to its temptation, he views it henceforth from a higher perspective. Using the Augustinian model, we can speak of a point of origin, a moment of initiation, although it is clear that it has duration and that we are speaking of a gradual growth in divine likeness, of a journey with a fixed destination in God.

To the extent that conversion is situated in the realm of time—the secular turning wholly, its religious analogue partially—it involves the difficulty of keeping the gaze fixed on the proper object of attention: the self or God. The concluding chapters of Book X of Augustine's *Confessions,* like the essays of Book Three, rehearse the ever-present dangers of distraction and diversion even while affirming the conversion that transcends them. But the differences are fundamental, for the converted Christian has also moved beyond time. He is mutable in himself but firmly established in God; anchored in the source, he draws his new life from it. As man is reformed, he moves irresistibly toward absolute resolution by the motive force of charity, possessing God through knowledge. The questions of who, what, and where he is are eternally answered. And so we can speak of conversion in the singular, as the completion of a unique circle by which man re-turns to Himself, by which he recovers his true image.

Religious conversion then, is a spiritual change in a return to God, a unique journey with clear direction and termination, a gradual revivification, the fusion of mutability and permanence of God's likeness through Scripture, the divine written Word. The secular conversion by contrast is an ethical and intellectual reorientation, a turning whose concreteness Montaigne chooses to stress: "Nous avons une ame contournable en soy mesme" (I, 39, 241). It is a question of concentration on the self, and the reader takes note of a gradual delineation of the lines of its image. Montaigne, too, suggests that his movement is voyage, but the routes traveled are as diverse, as directionless, as endless as life itself. Here Montaigne arrives at the fusion of change and continuity through his written word, the book of the self.

PART II
THE BOOK AS SOURCE

4
The Primacy of the Book

"nulle science ne se peult acquerir sans livre où elle
soit escrite" (Sebond, *La théologie naturelle,* p. xi)

The continuing analogy in counterpoint between religious and
secular conversion extends to the axes on which those movements pivot, to the book as instrument of return. Here Scripture
serves as the archetypal book, the text through which man gains
divine knowledge. But it is important to note that Western
cultural tradition as a whole is fundamentally bookish, that with
the notable exception of the oral philosophy of the early Greeks,
knowledge has historically been transmitted through books and
learning acquired by reading. The extraordinary literary and
philological activity of Renaissance Europe, its assumption that
truth is contained and communicated in the written word,
reaches back across the centuries to find its antecedents in the
priestly castes and sacred books of the pre-Christian Near East
and Egypt.[1] Thus the importance of libraries from the great col-
lection at Alexandria to the modern templelike structures where
Western man maintains the storehouse of his accumulated
knowledge. Montaigne's reverence for books in general and his
preoccupation with his own in particular derive profoundly from
this tradition. Reader and writer come together in the *Essais* to
reaffirm the primacy of the Book.

I

Christianity, Professor Curtius suggests, gives the book its highest consecration. Elaborating on the Judaic tradition, which held that the first five books of the Old Testament were given directly by God to Moses at Sinai, making reading and study of His word man's appointed task, Christianity became a religion of the Holy Book. Scripture was considered the sacred text, informed and inspired by the divine presence; like Christ, it was the Word incarnate, the juncture of letter and spirit. All necessary knowledge, sacred and profane, lay within this encyclopedic text; both the precepts governing man's moral and spiritual life and knowledge of God Himself were to be sought there. This did not mean, of course, that the Bible was self-evident or that reason alone opened up scriptural meaning. The elaborate system of exegesis which characterized biblical study through the Middle Ages distinguished the letter and the spirit of the text (its body and soul) to uncover deeper levels of meaning through allegorical, tropological (moral), and anagogical (mystical) interpretation. Prayer and the holy life were considered necessary to the understanding of Scripture in its mystical sense: for Origen, the "interior man" needed to grow for the secrets of God's text to become accessible.

From the archetypal notion—Christ as the model, written by the Holy Spirit at the Incarnation, and Scripture, the Logos incarnate in the flesh of the holy text[2]—Christian tradition extended the book metaphorically to be the record of God's presence in the heart and mind of man, in his life and his world. Medieval church fathers spoke of the conscience as a book, written in the memory by each person "pour être confronté au jour du jugement, avec le livre des vivants, dont l'Apocalypse a parlé."[3] In the book of the heart was written what God had inspired the writers of the holy books to record: the conviction of man's misery, his need for God, his union with Him through Christ. The book of experience contained the life of the interior man, his thoughts, the movement of his soul, and his aspiration

to God. The Mosaic law, the prophets, and the Gospel that mark
the road to salvation were called collectively the book of the way.
Written in the nature of things and in its forms was the book of
the world.

This last book—in its analogical relationship to Scripture—
concerns us most profoundly because it provides the thesis for
Sebond's natural theology and the antithesis for Montaigne's
Essais. The world, as Sebond sees it, contains indelible marks
made by God, readable like the Bible itself:

> Dieu nous a donné deux livres, celuy de l'universel ordre des
> choses ou de la nature, et celuy de la Bible. Cestuy-là nous fut
> donné premier, et dés l'origine du monde: car chaque creature
> n'est que comme une lettre, tiree par la main de Dieu. De façon
> que d'une grande multitude de creatures, comme d'un nombre de
> lettres, ce livre a esté composé: dans lequel l'homme se trouve,
> et en est la lettre capitale et principale. Or tout ainsi que les lettres,
> et les mots faicts des lettres font une science, en comprenant tout
> plain de sentences et significations differentes, tout ainsi les
> creatures joinctes ensemble et accouplees l'une à l'autre emportent
> diverses propositions et divers sens, et contiennent la science, qui
> nous est necessaire avant tout autre."[4]

All that man needs to know, indeed all that man can know—
"la sapience et la science de nostre salut"—resides in the configurations of the natural universe as knowledge existing from
the beginning of time that he must rediscover. Sebond describes
a world of corresponding signs, bound together and informed by
the eternal Godhead to point horizontally through their associations and relationships to each other and vertically to the
ultimate Signified.[5] Absolute marks written on the face of the
earth and of human experience, God's own imprint made for the
very purpose of revealing Him: "a ceste cause bastit elle [divine
intelligence] ce monde visible et nous le donna comme un livre"
(p. xi). The act of acquiring knowledge of man and God is an
assimilative rather than a creative process; it requires the delineating of given truths, symbolically expressed as reading.

Sebond distinguishes between the natural and the written sign

by insisting on the primacy of the book of nature. For reasons
that appear essentially pedagogical, the learned professor and
theologian sweeps away the traditional learning program to make
true knowledge ("ceste science, qui est une fontaine de verité
salutaire" [p. vii]) accessible to all men:

> Et n'est besoing que personne laisse à la lire ou apprendre par
> faute d'autre doctrine: car elle ne presuppose ny la Grammaire,
> ny la Logique, ny autre art liberal, ny la Physique, ny la Méta-
> physique, attendu qu'elle est la premiere. . . . Par ainsi ceste
> doctrine est commune aux laics, aux clercs et à toute maniere de
> gens: et si se peult comprendre en un mois et sans peine. Il ne
> la fault apprendre par coeur, ny en avoir des livres: car depuis que
> elle est conceuë, elle ne se peult oublier. [p. vii-viii]

Metaphysical egalitarianism that not only promises salvation but
adopts the very vocabulary (*doctrine, science, livre, sapience*) of the
program it seeks to replace. But perhaps more important than its
accessibility is the infallibility of the text of creation; the only
prerequisite demanded is divine grace: "nul ne peut veoir de soy,
ny lire en ce grand livre (bien que tousjours ouvert et present à
nos yeux) s'il n'est esclairé de Dieu et purgé de sa macule
originelle" (p. xi). The book of nature, Sebond insists, cannot be
falsified, erased, or incorrectly interpreted. Even the heretics
cannot misunderstand its meaning, so clear and imposing are its
signs. It is as if to read were to know, naturally, intuitively,
absolutely, without reasoning and the secondary process of commentary and interpretation: "Elle [la doctrine] ne se sert d'argumens obscurs, qui ayent besoing de profond et long discours:
car elle n'argumente que par choses apparentes et cogneuës
à chacun par experience, comme par les creatures et par la nature
de l'homme" (p. viii). Man appears to enjoy his primal relationship to nature, where what is apparent, is.

If man is totally at home among natural signs, he finds the
written word opaque, more reluctant to give up its truth.
Language resides within this universe of evident correspondences, but as enigmatic symbol, ambiguous and multilayered,
the words themselves no longer unequivocally expressive. Sebond

sees Scripture—which he clearly accepts as God's own book, traced in His hand—resisting the discovery of its essential meaning. The written word does not impose its truth on the reader but rather allows myriad interpretation and even heretical reading. The formal learning required to approach Scripture appears to compound the occasions for error.

In this total network of interlocking signs, Sebond stresses the superiority of the accessible and the self-evident over the obtuse, the natural over the intellectual, the intuitive over the discursive. The truth of the book of nature complements that of Scripture, in fact gives its reader all that is found in the holy book; it teaches man, Sebond tells us, to know unerringly and with great certainty what is prescribed, contained, and ordered in the Bible. Moreover, it serves as a key to the sacred writings of the Church fathers: "ceste doctrine ouvre à un chacun la voye à l'intelligence des saincts docteurs: voire elle est incorporee en leurs livres (encores qu'elle n'y apparoisse point) comme est un Alphabet en tous escrits. Aussi est-ce l'Alphabet des Docteurs: et comme tel il le fault premierement apprendre" (pp. vi-vii). It is as if the signs were arranged in an ever-increasing order of difficulty, like alphabets superimposed one on another: creatures marked as so many letters combined to disclose God's primordial truth, which in turn are letters read to open up the holy books, in turn the signifiers of that unique truth which is God. Truth is confirmed and reaffirmed in symbols deriving from a unique signified as man uncovers divine omnipresence. But as we have seen, for Sebond the first step suffices: the book of nature alone teaches man all he needs to know.

To the metaphorical book of nature and literal sacred writings, Sebond has added yet another book, his own, the transcription into the written mode of the original *liber creaturarum*. Truth, whose immediacy and certainty he attempted to characterize by repeated use of the metaphor of sight ("ceste doctrine apprend à tout homme de veoir à l'oeil sans difficulté et sans peine la verité" [p. vi]), he paradoxically casts in the more equivocal signs of language. An interpretive layer is superimposed on the primal text, one with the potential to bring the reader simultaneously closer to and further from it. Sebond's book requires learning where the book of nature required none: the *Theologia naturalis* presents demonstrations and proofs based on reason where the book of the creatures imposed itself naturally. The visible—whether literal or figurative—and the expressible may be irresistibly intertwined, but Sebond's transposition from one form of language to another appears to give up a measure of accessibility for theology.

II

Montaigne does not speak explicitly of the book of nature when he discusses Sebond in the *Apologie,* but the implications of this central—and unnamed—metaphor reverberate outward from this physical and intellectual axis of the *Essais.* The concept of *liber naturae,* the universe it presupposes, and the truth it renders possible become the point from which Montaigne moves to establish the book of the self as the primary text of man's knowledge. As we have seen, the record he keeps in the *Apologie*—and throughout the essays—of man's inability to decipher that larger book helps him to turn his gaze inward, to elaborate his own text.

The essayist himself justifies our excursion into Sebond's *Theologia naturalis* through the references that incorporate it into the world of the *Essais.* As he sets about to translate the *Prologue*—where Sebond justifies his method—Montaigne came across the concept of the book of nature and the special significance assigned to it. His reading of these opening pages is more than a translation or interpretation, for he transformed—one might even say deformed—important aspects of Sebond's exposition. He changed Sebond's doctrine from *necessary* to *useful;* instead of teaching man to know *infallibly* what is contained in Scripture, it now gives him *great access* to the understanding of Scripture. The translator modified the view that his doctrine teaches *all the truth* necessary to man, to state that it teaches "the truth as far as it is possible for natural reason to do so."[6] These textual alterations apparently stemmed from religious considerations, from the desire to reduce Sebond's exclusive reliance on the book of nature and to soften his assertion of its superiority over Scripture, both views for which the *Theologia naturalis* had been placed on the Index from 1558-59 to 1564 and for which the *Prologue* remained condemned from that point on. At the same time, and here looking back from the context of the *Essais*, the modifications betray an intellectual discomfort with Sebond's position, a sense that the book of the creatures is not that easy to read, that its meaning is not clearly accessible or self-evident. When the essayist stands in his own universe, nature as a book is no longer open to him.

Intellectually, Montaigne inhabits a world dramatically opposed to Sebond's, a region encompassed below the circle of the moon, secular, self-contained, posited as autonomous, as man's own ground. This is the fideistic hypothesis based on the separation of faith and reason that we consider characteristic of much of Renaissance humanism. Within these boundaries Montaigne redraws for himself, that purifying grace that illuminated Sebond's insightful reading of the book of nature simply does not shine. The polemical framework of the *Apologie,* where man labors entirely on his own, pictures the text of the world as illegible; the apparent meanings of God's imprint on the universe remain hidden.

Montaigne further underscores man's essential alienation from his world by affirming a remark, ascribed to Plato, that nature is an enigmatic poem (Plato had actually meant that poetry was by nature enigmatic). The notion is elaborated, recast in the metaphor of painting and again in words borrowed from Cicero: "Ay je pas veu en Platon ce divin mot, que nature n'est rien qu'une poësie oenigmatique? comme peut estre qui diroit une peinture voilée et tenebreuse, entreluisant d'une infinie varieté de faux jours à exercer nos conjectures." ("Latent ista omnia crassis occultata et circumfusa tenebris, ut nulla acies humani

ingenii tanta sit, quae penetrare in coelum, terram intrare possit"
[536]—All those things lie hidden and enveloped in such thick
shadows that no human genius is keen enough to be able to
penetrate into heaven or descend into the earth.) While we may
hear a distant echo of the Greek notion that the gods express
themselves in cryptic form, the passage implies that meaningful interpretation is virtually impossible. For the Platonist,
nature as poetry or painting—an analogous aggregate of symbols—occupies an inferior rung in the order of being, three times
removed from the only true reality, the eternal, unchanging
realm of Ideas. This art reproduces images of appearances, of the
ever-changing, mutable world of the senses. When Montaigne
affirms the words he puts in Plato's mouth, he suggests that
nature, like the work of art, is a pale imitation, a distorting
reflection that leads only to uncertainty and ambiguity. Rather
than the primordial text bearing God's direct imprint, nature
becomes a distant copy, incapable of revealing knowledge and
truth. The metaphor accounts for nature's inherent impenetrability, for its veiled and shadowy faces and the variety of false
lights it gives off.[7] Sebond's picture of a universe filled with
symbols that lead back to their referent-author gives way to the
world as obscure signs removed from their source, cut off from
what they signify; they cannot point to any reality beyond themselves, they stand fundamentally as their own end. In Platonic
terms, and in the framework of the *Apologie,* to be preoccupied
with this "poësie oenigmatique" is to lose oneself in the tran-
sitory world of appearances. For Montaigne, in the *Essais* as
a whole, this text as its own end becomes a primary object of
attention.

Montaigne confirms the pejorative status of poetry (analogously strengthening his view of nature) by characterizing philosophy
as "une poësie sophistiquée" (537). Immediately following his
comments on nature as a "poësie oenigmatique," he reduces
philosophy to an imitation of what is already art, removing it
even further from the source of truth. Drawing on the contemporary literary vocabulary, the essayist distinguishes between

the real and the imaginary, between the *naturel* and the *estranger*, to describe philosophy's *fictions* as *forgé(es)*, *inventées*, untrue however *vraysemblable*. In the sixteenth century, *fiction* was a pejorative term associated with *feinte, mensonge, hypocrisie*;[8] to use it in reference to poetry provides an indication of the degree to which that art was considered dissimulation and the poet a counterfeiter.

In the universe Sebond describes, discursive reasoning and speculation—what is there called natural theology—has a legitimate function, indeed a necessary one as the instrument of truth. Montaigne's world renders that activity mere exercise, for it does not permit language to function essentially—that is, to uncover and disclose the hidden relationships among things. In these passages in the *Apologie*, the philosophical text, by its own admission, bears no necessary fundamental relationship to that which it seeks to explain: ("elle nous donne . . . les choses qu'elles mesmes nous aprend estre inventées" [537]). If language resides in the world as part of the nature of things, even if it no longer stands by itself as the unequivocal mark of its referent—as we imagine Hebrew functioning before Babel—it might function analogically, metaphorically, to approximate truth. Interpretation and commentary, as if turning round and round the object in question, might elucidate by saying things that are similar to it, as if the thing as sign could be cast and recast in parallel languages and so give itself up to apprehension.[9] But Montaigne's discussion here does not appear to permit such a reading.

Montaigne's argument emphasizes the distance separating man from truth, the impotence of his rational, discursive efforts. "La philosophie nous presente, non pas ce qui est, ou ce qu'elle croit, mais ce qu'elle forge ayant plus d'apparence et de gentillesse" (537): if concepts give the appearance of truth, if they seem plausible, like the epicycles, eccentrics and concentrics that astrology calls to its aid, then philosophy is satisfied that it has done all that it can. But Montaigne carefully distinguishes this from truth. We are not in an Aristotelian setting where the mimetic process improves upon material reality, revealing the universals embodied in the particulars of nature. Nor is this that imitative art—whose truth derives from its verisimilitude—which is a way of learning, of gathering the meaning of things. The fictions described are merely imaginary constructs, consistent with the general sixteenth-century intellectual and literary tradition that reduced Aristotelian imitation and verisimilitude to the benign state of simple copy and possibility—by ignoring their philosophical underpinnings—at the same time as it superimposed a Platonic structure that tended to transform them altogether by equating seeming truth with untruth, imitation with dissimulation.[10] The Platonic context Montaigne shapes in this passage, for example, absorbs the verb *inventer* (from the latin *invenire,* come into, find) used by the defenders of poetry to suggest its capacity for finding out or uncovering the true nature of things, to render it the equivalent of fiction, that is, made-up.

Montaigne joins philosophy and poetry in a pejorative union that inverts a relationship dating from antiquity and perpetuated through the Middle Ages into the Renaissance. From early Greek discussions of Homer's truthfulness through Plato's depreciation of poetry to the allegorical readings that disclosed the wisdom of the *Iliad* and the *Aeneid,* the classical world debated the connection between poetry and philosophy. And in spite of the intellectual weight of those who disagreed, the identification and fusion of these two disciplines survived. In the *Roman de la Rose* writing poetry is called "travailler en philosophie"; this medieval expression was extended through the sixteenth century in what has been variously named scientific, philosophical, or cosmic poetry. Drawing the requirements from classical antiquity that the poet be learned with encyclopedic knowledge and be inspired (this is particularly striking in Ronsard's case), contemporary literary opinion endowed poetry with the power to disclose the associations between man and the universe, to uncover the secrets of nature. From Scève's *Microcosme* to Du Bartas' *Semaine—*

including works by Peletier du Mans, Baïf, Belleau, Lefèvre de la Boderie—philosophical poetry brought together the universal corpus of knowledge prized by the humanists in a compendium meant to reveal truth. Here the written text clearly provides a reading of other signs and symbols, a deeper understanding of cosmic reality. Commentary, interpretation, allegory, and metaphor function as analogous, interlocking languages within this totality to open up the real nature of things.[11]

Montaigne's rejection of the popular Renaissance concept of man as microcosm undermines the entire structure of associations on which this view of reality, and the book of nature, are based. When the essential resemblances are considered mere images—that is, when the linguistic level breaks away from the interlacing network—words no longer mean more than they say. To treat the microcosm as another fiction is to suggest that the universal correspondences have dissolved or, what amounts to the same thing, that man can no longer read his way to them:

> Vrayement ils [philosophers] ont eu par à raison de l'appeler le petit monde, tant ils ont employé de pieces et de visages à le maçonner et bastir. . . . Ils en font une chose publique imaginaire. C'est un subject qu'ils tiennent et qu'ils manient: on leur laisse toute puissance de le descoudre, renger, rassembler et estoffer, chacun à sa fantasie; et si ne le possedent pas encore. Non seulement en verité, mais en songe mesmes, ils ne le peuvent regler . . ." [537]

And this particular image recalls a bad painting, one that renders a known and familiar object unrecognizable, which deceives rather than enlightens. We sense here not only the diminishing of the book of nature to mere literature but also the degree to which art—linguistic or visual—is trivialized to the purely representational. A good painting becomes a good copy: "nous exigeons d'eux [painters] une parfaicte et exacte representation des lineamens et des couleurs, et les mesprisons s'ils y faillent" (538).

III

In the world Montaigne describes, the book of nature is impenetrable, the source not of truth but of philosophical discourse—mere words—which man has mistaken for substantial knowledge. God's other, primal book, Scripture, suffers the same consequence. As we saw earlier, the essayist does not question the validity of the divine texts; he confirms that faith and grace can provide illumination and suggests that truth resides in the books, discernible with the transcendental key. But for man on his own, that man Montaigne considers throughout the essays, all languages—metaphorical or literal—resist penetration. To seek comprehensive understanding, to demand certainty, to expect to discover what is essential is to misjudge both the power of the seeker and the nature of the medium. And so Scripture shares with other books the potential for misreading, for arbitrary interpretation, for ambiguity: "Combien de querelles et combien importantes a produit au monde le doubte du sens de cette syllabe, Hoc! ['Hoc est corpus meum']" (II, 12, 527). And again in *De l'experience* (III, 13), as he decries man's propensity for sterile commentary, Montaigne cites the confusion to which reformist views have given rise: "J'ay veu en Alemagne que Luther a laissé autant de divisions et d'altercations sur le doubte de ses opinions, et plus, qu'il n'en esmeut sur les escritures sainctes" (1069).

With the essential texts closed to him, it is both paradoxical and comprehensible that the essayist surrounds himself with books: paradoxical because the nature of man and of his language subjects these books as well to interpretation and misapprehension; and understandable in terms of cultural heritage, intellectual milieu, and his own compulsion for knowledge. We picture Montaigne, the humanist, as he would have us see him, studying, writing, reading in his tower library: "Là, je feuillette à cette heure un livre, à cette heure un autre, sans ordre et sans dessein, à pieces descousues; tantost je resve, tantost j'enregistre et dicte, en me promenant, mes songes que voicy" (III,

3, 828). The breadth of his reading infuses and animates the text of the essays and provides him with quotations. At the same time, Montaigne describes an evolution in his relationship to books roughly analogous to the movement of the *Essais*: "J'es-tudiay, jeune, pour l'ostentation; depuis, un peu, pour m'assagir; à cette heure, pour m'esbatre; jamais pour le quest" (829). He depicts himself moving away from books as a means to wisdom and, we understand, toward himself and his own book as its source.

The belief that knowledge and wisdom derive from books is a central element of Montaigne's cultural background, as we mentioned earlier. All through the Middle Ages and into the Renaissance scholars poured over works of authoritative authors, seeking first as readers to rediscover and to assimilate given facts and established truth and then, as writers, to integrate and re-present the corpus of knowledge. The voracious humanist appetite for classical literature (fed by the invention of printing) and the intensity of philological analysis to restore and assure the integrity of these texts mark a particularly active period in this continuum. New editions of Latin works and new translations of Greek works abound. Commentaries and glosses expound and interpret, applying techniques of historical and textual criticism to works of history, philosophy, archeology, poetry, theology, mathematics, medicine, and Scripture.[12] And all this activity was animated by a profound self-consciousness, by a sense that through the knowledge uncovered in these texts modern man was deepening his comprehension of the world. Reading, study, and writing represent the highest activities of the mind, books the basis for learning.

The historical Montaigne is most clearly a man of books and it has become a commonplace to speak of his books as his friends and to describe the essays as conversations with the great writers of antiquity.[13] Villey has painstakingly documented Montaigne's reading, reconstructed his library, and pointed out both the variety and the quantity of the source material that makes its way into the *Essais*. Comparison with the writings of Seneca and with

Amyot's translation of Plutarch indicated to Villey that the form
of Books I and II resembled the popular and widespread
Renaissance genre of *leçons*, collections of maxims and aphorisms
that disseminated the teachings of the ancients. This study led
him to characterize the structure of the *Essais* as an evolution
from the early, impersonal reflections of Montaigne's reading to
the richly embroidered personal self-portraiture of the later
essays.

The essayist in the text acknowledges the strong presence of
books, and in the early essays insists on their dominance: "Je
m'en vay, escorniflant par cy par là des livres les sentences qui me
plaisent" (I, 25, 136). His own book, he tells us in speaking of
Seneca and Plutarch, is "massonné purement de leurs despouilles"
(II, 32, 721). The question of borrowing or imitating and of
expressing what is one's own—notions crucial to the validity of
the self-portait—is here cast as a discussion of education which
serves as a metaphor for the writing of essays. The unnamed
students of *Du pedantisme* and the ideal pupil of *De l'institution
des enfans* bear the same relationship as the essayist to the
accumulated knowledge (the books) of the past. Questions of
what one learns and how one learns, of one's ability to assimilate
the tradition without being absorbed by it, of making knowledge
one's own, of the function of memory all indicate that the essayist
is a perpetual student and the student a potential essayist.
Montaigne's opening pages on education (II, 26), where he
speaks of his own book and his borrowings, bring together the
essayist's concern that he be visible through his acquired learning
("Je ne vise icy qu'à découvrir moy mesmes" [148]) and the student's obligation to make knowledge his own; the essay concludes on the same note: "il ne faut pas seulement loger chez soy,
il la faut espouser" (177).

The early essays neither completely coincide with the superficial pilferings Montaigne describes in *Du pedantisme* (as if the
essayist himself surrendered to his overwhelming pedantic inclination) nor are they identical with the later, more richly
personal texts. But to admit that differences exist between the

early and late essays is not inevitably to condemn large sections of Books I and II; it is rather to suggest the possibility, or even the necessity, of movement and change in human life. We are not speaking of movement from bad to good as the writer learns his craft, or even of a shift from impersonal commentary on reading to personal observations of the self, for the personal is everywhere, to a greater or lesser degree, and the self is everywhere the fundamental object of discovery: what shifts is the screen on which the self is projected.[14] The essayist first interacts with ideas acquired through reading, through contact with what contemporary culture considers the highest achievements of the human intellect. The insights to be gained, the experience to be drawn from worlds removed in time and space, enrich both his private and public life. From military strategy to the practice of virtue, the myriad aspects of human activity, of human drives and inspirations, spread out before him. The essayist chooses his subjects, paraphrases, quotes, comments, acknowledging his procedure, often keeping precise references to his borrowed material to himself as if to highlight its content rather than its source. The presentation of these ideas and their continual interplay with the essayist's own comments build up a vision of the world in which the meanderings of that mind we follow, the personal intellectual journey we accompany, unfolds. And the reader watches Montaigne turn more profoundly and more self-consciously inward as the book of the self absorbs those of others, as the writing and reading of his own book becomes the fundamental source of knowledge. The essayist cannot come back to concentrate on himself until he has gone out to others and to the world; he cannot compose his own book to gain knowledge of himself without first encountering traditional book knowledge.

Books, then, represent Montaigne's starting point, but the recurrent circular patterns in which his movement participates is neither smooth nor uninterrupted. Some of the shorter essays of Book I which appear entirely derivative—examples and anecdotes interspersed with occasional reflection—are followed by others in which the essayist draws his material from his own experience.

The distinction emerges for example, in the First Book if we compare essays 5-6-7 with 8: *Si le chef d'une place assiégée doit sortir pour parlementer; L'heure des parlemens dangereuse;* and *Que l'intention juge nos actions* with *De l'oisiveté.* Clearly the emphasis shifts from the outside world to the self, but the reader recognizes the two sides of the same coin. Consideration of military strategy reveals the way men think and act, raises questions of judgment, honor, trust, and the worth of one's word. It allows the essayist to compare ancient times with his own ["Quand à nous . . ." (I, 5, 26); "Mais . . . nos façons sont entierement eloignées de ces reigles" (I, 6, 28)] and to talk about himself in this context: "Je me fie ayseement à la foy d'autruy" (I, 5, 27); "Mais le philosophe Chrisippus n'eust pas esté de cet advis, et moy aussi peu" (I, 6, 29). Montaigne takes up the subject of intention (I, 7) to explore questions of obligation, of promise, to examine again the giving of one's word. When in *De l'oisiveté* he speaks almost exclusively of himself in a highly personal way (as if on furlough from military service), the content seems to derive directly from a quotation of Lucan ("Variam semper dant otia mentem" [I, 8, 33]—Ever idle hours breed wandering thoughts), as if the essayist were merely embroidering on a borrowed idea. The point, of course, is that Montaigne is never entirely dependent on books just as he is never entirely free of them. Nor does he look to be. The world and his experience of it are refracted through books just as his own person and his experience of it will be refracted through his own book. We witness continual comment on the world juxtaposed to and interspersed with comment on the self. In this duality lies the paradox of self-discovery, the search for the self (as if it existed) which at the same time forms that self through the process of borrowing and assimilation (as if it did not previously exist).

Although Montaigne does not always speak explicitly of himself, that self is always speaking. The interplay between the assimilation of others' ideas and the expression of his own reveals aspects both of human nature and of his particular nature. What the essayist discovers about man bears directly on his sense of himself and determines the degree to which he accepts or attempts to move away from his own propensities and inclinations. He is eclectic in the choice of his subject matter and in his attitudes toward it. He poses ideas and assumes views as if they were lenses through which aspects of human life become apparent and then he replaces them with other positions. Montaigne shares points of view with writers of the past but takes no system as his own. As we follow the essayist through his text, the coincidence between what the world looks like and what he looks like in it grows paradoxically stronger and weaker. Montaigne will attempt to show that he is at the same time of the world and distinct from it.

Throughout the *Essais* Montaigne sustains the play between what we are calling the outside world—both a man in his particular culture or society and man in general, that "humaine condition" of which he speaks—and his interior self, although the emphasis appears to change. Roughly speaking, it appears that at first he writes as if looking at "l'humaine condition" will reveal something of each man while in Book III he chooses to stress the corollary that "chaque homme porte la forme entiere de l'humaine condition" (III, 2, 805), that one discovers humanity by looking at oneself. The examination of the broad questions of man's customs, of death, pain, and poverty, discloses the predominance of variety, diversity, inconstancy, and relativity. Montaigne's look at man situated in time (I, 11, 24) reveals the inclination to subordinate the present to things past or future. In *De la solitude* (I, 39) he explores that social, gregarious instinct that seems a part of human nature, which is part of his own nature, and in this case seeks to move away toward what appears a repossession of the self: "il se faut sequestrer et r'avoir de soy" (239). All of these observations build up the overall picture of the world in which the individual man resides: traditional knowledge acquired through books, considered and assimilated through a book. Reading, Montaigne might say, provides food for thought, thought that delineates the general nature of man and his world, thought that discloses a particular man's nature.[15]

IV

Paradoxically, the man of books pretends to be totally ignorant—
"ce ne sont icy que resveries d'homme qui n'a gousté des sciences
que la crouste premiere" (I, 26, 146)—and he devalues book
learning: "Fascheuse suffisance, qu'une suffisance purement livresque" (152). Throughout the *Essais* Montaigne denounces writers
and bemoans a culture burying itself under its own verbosity:
"tant de paroles pour les paroles seules" (III, 9, 946). In *De
l'experience* he speaks out against interpretive commentary, against
that proliferation of literature about literature: "Il y a plus affaire
à interpreter les interpretations qu'à interpreter les choses, et plus
de livres sur les livres que sur autre subject: nous ne faisons que
nous entregloser" (III, 13, 1069). Montaigne censures the
Western intellectual tradition as it was being practiced, as it had
developed from antiquity through the Middle Ages. The gloss
that sought through commentary and analysis to penetrate to the
heart of the text, to reveal its truth, becomes an instrument of
doubt and ignorance: "Qui ne diroit que les glosses augmentent
les doubtes et l'ignorance, puis qu'il ne se voit aucun livre, soit
humain, soit divin, auquel le monde s'embesongne, duquel
l'interpretation face tarir la difficulté" (III, 13, 1067). Like the
book of nature, as if inherent in any system of signs, written
language stands as fundamentally impenetrable.

In *Des livres,* Montaigne comments on fable and myth, as if
purposely to allow for multiple layers of meaning in a text and
thus to legitimize symbolic interpretation as an instrument to
truth. But his observations belie this conclusion, for although as
in Scripture an original "meaningful" text may exist, it does not
unfold in the parallel language of analysis: "La plus part des
fables d'Esope ont plusieurs sens et intelligences. Ceux qui les
mythologisent, en choisissent quelque visage qui quadre bien à
la fable; mais pour la pluspart, ce n'est que le premier visage et
superficiel; il y en a d'autres plus vifs, plus essentiels et internes,
ausquels ils n'ont sçeu penetrer; voylà comme j'en fay" (II, 10,
410). All through the *Essais* Montaigne recognizes an intel-

lectual and spiritual distance that separates him from things outside, a space that makes them alien—that is, essentially unknowable. He stresses at once an object's varied faces, the relativity of his own point of view, and the inclination to accept the surface for the center, to take the part for the whole. Things may have being, just as a text may have meaning, but the conjunction of the viewer's (reader's) weakness and the opacity of the medium of existence frustrates understanding. Thus Montaigne will claim that his opinions give the measure of his sight, not the measure of things. Truth lies buried until the Author chooses to disclose the meaning of the symbols; but that lies outside the world of the *Essais*.

Montaigne turns often to the subject of books (and his own reading), looking at it from varied points of view, considering it in the contexts of pedantry, education, *science*, diversion, philosophy. He expresses a range of attitudes that distinguishes knowledge from wisdom, what is borrowed from what is one's own, and, most significantly, the books of others from the *Essais*. Truth and knowledge do not reside in the accumulation of books, nor is true learning acquired by appropriating their contents, by memorization: "Nous ne travaillons qu'à remplir la memoire, et laissons l'entendement et la conscience vuide. . . . Nos pedantes vont pillotant la science dans les livres, et ne la logent qu'au bout de leurs lévres, pour la dégorger seulement et mettre au vent" (I, 25, 136). Reading matter should be a means rather than an end, something to be used rather than merely possessed; true knowledge cannot be taken over from the outside, from others, but rather must be built up from inside the self. And in the richness of Montaigne's continued juxtaposition of *esprit* and *âme* as man's learning faculty, we see the fusion of intellect and conscience, of knowledge and wisdom, as the highest human achievement.

Books, then, are double-edged, a source of good or what the essayist calls "un dangereux glaive" (II, 25, 140), depending on the use made of them. Montaigne appears to describe two positive ways of acting on books that appear ultimately to be two aspects of a single notion: a movement out toward them in an effort to appraise the author's manner and to measure his judgment and a bringing in of the books, an attempt to make foreign matter one's own. This second activity, when abused, describes that tradition we have discussed, which he has pictured as appropriation through memory, as a well-stuffed head, as an acquisition rather than a natural possession. As if overcoming that distance that keeps man and things apart, Montaigne pretends not a mere juxtaposition that brings the two nearer in physical space but a transformation of things to surmount an epistemological separation. Once inside, the thing loses its former (unknown) identity and becomes part of the absorbing organism, a process described by the metaphor of eating: "C'est tesmoignage de crudité et indigestion que de regorger la viande comme on l'a avallée. L'estomac n'a pas faict son operation, s'il n'a faict changer la façon et la forme à ce qu'on luy avoit donné à cuire" (I, 26, 151). The source of meaning is thus displaced from things to the self, which absorbs and reconstitutes being in its own terms.

In this sense, Montaigne refers metaphorically in *De l'institution des enfans* to the book of experience or of the world: ". . . tout ce qui se presente à nos yeux sert de livre suffisant" (152); "Ce grand monde . . . c'est le miroüer où il nous faut regarder pour nous connoistre de bon biais. Somme, je veux que ce soit le livre de mon escholier" (157). This is not at all analogous to Sebond's book of nature, to configurations of meaningful symbols that are read and interpreted to discover truth. Truth does not reside outside, in signs, but inside in relation to the touchstone of the self. The world of experience, whether lived physically or refracted through books, offers ideas, attitudes, opinions, and positions as the raw material to be absorbed and refashioned in one's own image—that is, according to one's nature.[16] This is not a creation *ex nihilo* but a reshaping of pre-existent matter, involving at the same time the outward movement of appraisal and evaluation and the inward pull of absorption and assimilation. In the famous metaphor of the bee, Montaigne brings the two movements together to describe the ideal education and, we understand, the ideal of his own activity, the molding of judgment: "Les abeilles pillotent deçà delà les fleurs, mais elles en font apres le miel, qui est tout leur; . . . ainsi les pieces empruntées d'autruy, il les transformera et confondera, pour en faire un ouvrage tout sien: à sçavoir son jugement. Son institution, son travail et estude ne vise qu'à le former" (152). The outside world becomes a function of individual or personal truth, and the background against which that truth can itself be judged. This is the book of the world as mirror, where the student as essayist finds the reflection of the proper object of study, himself: a never-ending continuum of absorption and reflection, of re-forming judgment and disclosing it, of taking ideas in and trying them out, of exploring the world to discover the self.

Montaigne describes the parallel processes of education in terms transposed from poetic imitation and invention. We recognize the same interplay that characterized the theory and practice of the Pléiade between homage paid to traditional learning (or stylistic achievement) acquired from the ancients and emphasis placed on personal or individual expression. When du Bellay speaks of enriching the French language through imitation, as the Latins did with Greek, he uses the metaphor of food so frequent in Montaigne: "se transformant en eux, les devorant, et apres avoir bien digerez, les convertissant en sang et nourriture . . ."[17] Ronsard pictures himself in "Hylas" as a bee gathering pollen from flowers to make something of his own:

> Mon Passerat, je ressemble à l'abeille
> Qui va cueillant tantost la fleur vermeille
> Tantost la jaune: errant de pré en pré
> Volle en la part qui plus luy vient à gré,
> Contre l'Hyver amassant force vivres.
> Ainsi courant et feuilletant mes livres
> J'amasse, trie et choisis le plus beau,

> Qu'en cent couleurs je peints en un tableau,
> Tantost en l'autre: et maistre en ma peinture,
> Sans me forcer j'imite la Nature.[18]

Imitation and invention are at the same time complementary and in opposition, the first providing stylistic and contextual raw material, the second requiring a particular talent to personalize the acquisition, to avoid being overwhelmed or engulfed by it. The artist of worth achieves an equilibrium between the two forces; the mediocre one, like the poor student who memorizes, never goes beyond mere expropriation: "Nous autres naturalistes estimons qu'il y aie grande et incomparable preferance de l'honneur de l'invention à l'honneur de l'allegation" (III, 13, 1056). Montaigne immeasurably enhances the import of this process by giving it ontological significance. What for the Pléiade governed the making of poetry now informs the shaping of man. But it is crucial to our understanding of the *Essais* to appreciate that this shaping remains fundamentally and inextricably rooted in the realm of literature. The composition of the book, the essayist maintains, is the realization of himself, and the dialectic of imitation and invention the source of both text and self.

Repeatedly the essayist directs the reader's attention to this interplay between borrowing and inventing. Conspicuously, in such essays as *Du pedantisme* (I, 25), *De l'institution des enfans* (I, 26), *Consideration sur Ciceron* (I, 40), *Des livres* (II, 10), *Sur des vers de Virgile* (III, 5), *De la phisionomie* (III, 12), and *De l'experience* (III, 13), he points up the dominance of one or the other side, stressing his debt to others as he deprecates his own contribution, or minimizing it to highlight the originality of his book. Montaigne maintains that he speaks in others' words to compensate for the weakness of his own ("je fay dire aux autres ce que je ne puis si bien dire" [II, 10, 408]) or, in a more positive casting of the same idea, paradoxically to express himself better ("je ne dis les autres, sinon pour d'autant plus me dire" [I, 26, 148]). Some sources are named, others alluded to, most slip unnoticed into the fabric of the text. Some borrowings, he says, are so well known they do not have to be cited; others are purposely unattributed as Montaigne toys with his critical readers, daring them to distinguish Plutarch's or Seneca's words from his own. In *De la phisionomie* he appears to deny all significance to this material, picturing himself as having simply given in to current fad: "Certes j'ay donné à l'opinion publique que ces parements empruntez m'accompaignent. . . . Je m'en charge de plus fort tous les jours outre ma proposition et ma forme premiere, sur la fantasie du siecle et enhortemens d'autruy" (III, 12, 1055).

Whatever the emphasis, Montaigne insists throughout the *Essais* that the myriad quotations and paraphrases are not put on to conceal or disguise him, to dazzle or deceive his reader. Against whatever is borrowed, he sets what he calls at one point "du mien, et . . . ce qui est mien par nature" (III, 12, 1055), which seems to include what is originally his as well as what he has acquired and made his own. In this context, he suggests that had he been strong enough to resist the force of contemporary style, he would have never borrowed at all: "si je m'en fusse creu, à tout hazard, j'eusse parlé tout fin seul." This is an extraordinary statement, and a quite impossible position, given the intellectual context in which he lives—that is, writes—and the fact that his own notions of the self and the way it is shaped depend precisely on this interaction and absorption we have been describing. But at the same time, it serves to underline that crucial distinction between exterior and interior so dear to the Stoics and to subordinate what is not the self—and that includes books—to what is the self, and its book. Montaigne's experience when he confronts another, when he seeks to judge and to measure what is properly its own and what is not, reflects his own relationship to his words in the *Essais*. The essayist takes up this problem in *De l'art de conferer*: "Le subject, selon qu'il est, peut faire trouver un homme sçavant et memorieux; mais pour juger en luy les parties plus siennes et plus dignes, la force et beauté de son ame, il faut sçavoir ce qui est sien et ce qui ne l'est point, et en ce qui n'est pas sien combien on luy doibt en consideration du chois, dis-

position, ornement et langage qu'il y a fourny" (III, 8, 940).
What he looks for in others—"Et tous les jours m'amuse à lire en
des autheurs, sans soin de leur science, y cherchant leur façon,
non leur subject" (III, 8, 928)—is exactly what others should
look for in him: "Qu'on ne s'attende pas aux matieres, mais à la
façon que j'y donne" (II, 10, 408). Existence demands interaction between the self and the outside world, as we have seen,
but interaction involves the risk of being possessed or overwhelmed, of being carried off—that is, of losing the self to what
is outside it. The question of literary borrowing functions as an
analogue to this epistemological and ontological situation, to the
question of constituting the self, to that of coming to know it,
and others. We see Montaigne attempting to acknowledge what
is not his, to recognize what is properly his own, to sort out what
belongs to him and what is borrowed. And because the extent to
which the borrowed material becomes one's own reveals the
measure of the man, what the essayist assimilates is at once open
and hidden, discernible and inconspicuous, so that, as he judged
Tacitus, he can himself be judged: "J'ai principalement considéré
son jugement" (III, 8, 941).

V

In *Des livres* Montaigne divides his reading into two groups,
using the familiar Horatian lexicon to characterize certain books
as "simplement plaisans" (II, 10, 410) and identifying others
"qui mesle[nt] un peu . . . de fruit au plaisir, par où j'apprens
à renger mes humeurs et mes conditions" (413).[19] In Book III
he returns to the subject once again to maintain a similar distinction, referring to books that serve as *jouet(s), passe-temps,* to
provide pleasure and diversion ("pour m'esbatre"), while affirming that "l'ame s'y exerce" (III, 3, 829). But there appears an
unmistakable shift in emphasis as Montaigne now insists that he
rarely uses books ("Je ne m'en sers, en effect, quasi non plus que
ceux qui ne les cognoissent poinct" [827]), and that when he

does it is exclusively as a pastime: "Si quelqu'un me dict que c'est avillir les muses de s'en servir seulement de jouet et de passe-temps, il ne sçait pas, comme moy, combien vaut le plaisir, le jeu et le passetemps" (829). His earlier references suggested that he learned from books, that their study ameliorated the quality of his life. The verb *apprendre* in the quotation from *Des livres* extends the didactic function of *conseiller* that he asserted in *De la solitude:* "Je n'ayme, pour moy, que des livres ou plaisans et faciles, qui me chatouillent, ou ceux qui me consolent et conseillent à regler ma vie et ma mort" (I, 39, 246). Here Montaigne reads certain books to gain instruction, as he says of Plutarch and Seneca, "leur instruction est de la cresme de la philosophie" (II, 10, 413). Later, as he generalizes about books in *De la phisionomie,* he clearly refutes their instructional value: "Les livres m'ont servi non tant d'instruction que d'exercitation" (III, 11, 1039). Man does not need learning (*doctrine*) to live at ease, and even the wisest authors contain little more than vain subtleties and verbal quibbles. Books have been trivialized into sources of "mere" exercise or entertainment: "Tout ce qui plaist ne paist pas" (1040).

The Horatian *utile-dulci* remains a valid way of speaking of Montaigne's attitude toward books if we understand both the growing emphasis on the delightful and the evolving sense of the useful. While in *Des livres* he divides his reading into the "simplement plaisans" and that which mixes "un peu . . . de fruit au plaisir," by the Third Book the essayist appears to have collapsed his categories to suggest that when he reads at all it is for pleasure, and that pleasure by its very nature is useful. This dominant note concludes *De trois commerces* (with its emphasis on reading as diversion), and reflects the theme of "se rassoir . . . et sejorner" which informs the essay as a whole. As an accompanying motif throughout the *Essais,* Montaigne takes roundly to task those books which pretend to do more or which are presumed to do so: "je ne sçay comment il advient . . . qu'il se trouve autant de vanité et de foiblesse d'entendement en ceux qui font profession d'avoir plus de suffisance, qui se meslent de vacations lettrées et de charges qui despendent des livres, qu'en nulle autre sorte de gens" (II, 17, 659). The recurring critique of the pretentiousness of writers and of the usefulness of books reaches a kind of crescendo at the end of the work in *De la phisionomie* and *De l'experience* where Montaigne appears to separate books from life by opposing them to nature and to experience: "Il ne nous faut guiere de doctrine pour vivre à nostre aise" (III, 12, 1039). As in *De trois commerces,* the value of books lies not in their actual use but in their availability; they can provide relaxation when things more real, more alive, and more natural are not accessible.

But reading for pleasure, which Montaigne chooses to stress, does not obscure the fundamental role that books continue to play in the *Essais.* The very pages where he minimizes book learning and describes himself as rarely picking up a book bristle with material drawn from his reading. The wealth of quotations and literary borrowings and allusions belie his posture as a casual reader. In the disparity between what the essayist says and what he does we read the significance of his attitude. Montaigne's stance assumes a rhetorical value to indicate a fundamental transformation in the use of books—from *instruction* to *exercitation*—and, most importantly, to signal the subordination of all other books to his own.[20]

Montaigne rejects the Western tradition of book learning, but books themselves remain the focal point of learning. His insistence on his lack of memory and his celebration of ignorance—his own and of primitivism in general—are symbolic attitudes rather than important biographical details. They represent the negation of that tradition, the starting point for its radical revision. What is in books does not constitute knowledge; rather, as we suggested earlier, their content has been neutralized and has itself become a means to knowledge. The distinction between the self and the world outside (other things) assumes prominence as Montaigne interiorizes the object of study to fix primarily, or rather exclusively, on the self: "Ce sont icy mes fantasies, par lesquelles je ne tasche point à donner à connoistre les choses, mais moy" (II, 10, 407). The function of books has shifted; Montaigne does not learn from them, he learns through them.

Specific book content, like the subject matter Socrates takes up with his students and, as the essayist would have us believe, like that of the essays themselves, assumes a random importance since anything may serve as a source of exercise: "[Socrates] empoigne la premiere matiere comme celuy qui a une fin plus utile que de l'esclaircir, assavoir esclaircir les esprits qu'il prend à manier et exercer" (III, 8, 927). Montaigne depicts his reading as a stimulus to his own thought, as raw material for his mind to work on, as the starting point of an activity that is the writing of essays itself. In his library where he works, he tells us, "je feuillette à cette heure un livre, à cette heure un autre, sans ordre et sans dessein, à pieces descousues; tantost je resve, tantost j'enregistre et dicte, en me promenant, mes songes que voicy" (III, 3, 828). The pregnant "en me promenant" depicts both Montaigne's physical movement about the room and, more essentially, that of his mind acting on and reacting to his books, involved in that *agitation* and *chasse* that are man's proper quarry (III, 8, 928). The two movements are brought together to endow books with spatial dimension, to turn them into planes over which the mind roams: "Tout lieu retiré requiert un proumenoir. Mes pensées dorment, si je les assis. Mon esprit ne va, si les jambes ne l'agitent. Ceux qui estudient sans livre, en sont tous là" (III, 3, 828). The record of that motion is that of being itself: "estre consiste en mouvement et action. Parquoy chascun est aucunement en son ouvrage" (II, 8, 386). Reading and thinking, writing and self-discovery converge in the book of the self, where Montaigne is.

5

The Range of Words

"Il y a prou loy de parler par tout,
et pour et contre" (I, 47, 281)

"Nos gens appellent jugement, langage" (III, 4, 873)

The absorption and assimilation of the sensible world and its
reconstitution through the founding of the self takes place in that
process of imitation and invention that describes Montaigne's
interplay with books. The words of the books he reads, which
embody culture, and their verbal structures in which human
history appears to reside are refracted through his individual
consciousness to fashion both himself and what we must now call
his world. This act of transformation is simultaneously one of
negation and of creation, one in which making or doing first
means undoing, a process in which all literature seems to
participate if we understand it as the interaction between
experience and imagination, between the raw material of reality
and the creative power of the human mind. And it is precisely
this literary quality that interests us, for both the old and the
new, the past and the present, the world of others and that of the
self are located in the book, in its language, in the word.

I

Although Montaigne belittles and berates contemporary practice
for the amount of writing it has produced, in a perverse way

books have always engendered other books. This activity becomes particularly furious in times of social and political disorder, periods that appear to coincide with intellectual decadence, with what he calls "l'affinement des esprits" (III, 9, 946), which accompanies the exhaustion of substantive creative élan: "Quand escrivismes nous tant que depuis que nous sommes en trouble? quand les Romains tant que lors de leur ruyne?' (946). But if texts spawning texts is a sign of the intellectual and, one senses, moral corruption of the age, it also points significantly to basic difficulties inherent in man's quest for knowledge, to a situation symptomatic of his alienation from truth and of the distance separating him from both the means to and the objects of knowledge.[1]

Montaigne's critique of philosophical inquiry in the *Apologie* questioned the capacity of rational discourse to penetrate to truth. The comparison of Sebond's book of nature and the essayist's "poësie oenigmatique" uncovered radically different structures described in terms of attitudes toward language. Against a view that considered the word's kinship to inter-related signs and symbols, and their referents, Montaigne posed its independence or autonomy, the relativity of its signifying function, the arbitrary, made-up nature of its meaning that he conveyed by the notion of poetry. When he explicitly distinguishes names from things in *De la gloire,* he draws on Sebond's chapters on the name of God but inverts the original implication. Sebond differentiates between words and things to suggest how the glory of the divine name augments while His being remains absolute: "Le nom est hors de la chose, il n'est pas la chose, mais il la marque et signifie."[2] But he seeks to stress the link between what he calls "le nom de Dieu acquis" and God Himself; God's works, stamped with His name, "laissent en nostre coeur la notice et ressemblance de Dieu avec son nom et sa gloire" (351). God's name is also "sensible, visible et ouyble, contenu en voix ou en escrit. . . . Il represente le vray nom de Dieu, et . . . il le signifie proprement et vivement" (352). And over and above these *noms acquis* is God's essential name, coeternal with His divinity: "ce nom là c'est l'estre. . . . C'est le nom universel qui contient tous les autres en soy, et qui les enclost et comprend."

Montaigne's oft-cited lines take up Sebond's point of departure: "Il y a le nom et la chose: le nom, c'est une voix qui remerque et signifie la chose; le nom, ce n'est pas une partie de la chose ny de la substance, c'est une piece estrangere joincte à la chose, et hors d'elle" (II, 16, 618). But the example of the increasing glory of God's name that follows serves only to introduce the subject; the essay places exclusive emphasis on the disparity between verbal attributes and the nature of things. The network of signs described by Sebond in which words function as a correlative language—contained in the notion that God's works are His name—assumes an arbitrary, accidental status as Montaigne absorbs the question of language into the larger framework of his distinction between the inside of things and what is outside. The specific, sublunar context reduces Sebond's concern with the divine name to raise questions about human glory and to stress the gratuitous nature of reputation. If, like God's acquired name, a man's glory may increase while his being, pictured as "estans indigens et necessiteux au dedans" (618), remains unchanged, then we must recognize the fundamental difference between what man is and how he appears, between what is exterior and what is inherent. Montaigne seeks to turn the reader's (and his own) attention inward from seeking the approbation of others: "Ce n'est pas pour la montre que nostre ame doit jouer son rolle, c'est chez nous, au dedans, où nuls yeux ne donnent que les nostres" (623). Against *contenances* he sets *coeur,* (625), against *cette vie fantastique et imaginere* lived in public esteem, *nostre vraye vie et essentielle* (628), against *honneur, conscience* (630).

In this dynamic of internal-external, language functions as part of the outside.[3] Because it "floats free" of any essential relationship with its referent it participates in the world of appearances as a part of what things "look like." As if language were located in the sensible world, apprehended by the eye or ear like color, shape, sound, accidental qualities susceptible to misunderstanding. Montaigne repeatedly reinforces this impression by juxtaposing the visual act as a metaphor of the intellectual. Speaking in *Des Livres* of reading intensely, which, he says, "esbloüit mon jugement, l'attriste et le lasse," he suggests a more relaxed, informal approach, "tout ainsi que, pour juger du lustre de l'escarlatte, on nous ordonne de passer les yeux pardessus, en la parcourant à diverses veuës . . ." (II, 10, 409). Even a man's name is not an essential part of him, *une marque particuliere*: "je n'ay point de nom qui soit assez mien: de deux que j'ay, l'un est commun à toute ma race, voire encore à d'autres. . . . Quant à mon autre nom, il est à quiconque aura envie de le prendre" (II, 16, 626).[4]

The three elements that comprise Montaigne's world—the self, things (les choses), and words (les mots)—interrelate in a way that is both tenuous and tentative. Things, both physical and intellectual, whether laid hold of by the senses or the mind, exist essentially apart from the self, impenetrable both because of the weakness of the viewer or seeker and because of their own opacity. Montaigne's richly varied use of *lustre* shows up both sides of this epistemological dilemma. Things have a diversity of lights or faces which cause (or allow) them to be taken first in one way then in another. In *De Democritus et Heraclitus*, the essayist speaks of the "cent membres et visages qu'a chaque chose" (I, 50, 302); in *Comme nous pleurons et rions d'une mesme chose*, "chaque chose a plusieurs biais et plusieurs lustres" (I, 38, 235); in *Des livres*, "les subjects ont divers lustres et diverses considerations: c'est de là que s'engendre principalement la diversité d'opinions" (II, 10, 581). And as a last example, in *De l'experience* Montaigne refers to the difficulty of pinning down action: "Non seulement je trouve mal-aisé d'attacher nos actions les unes aux autres, mais chacune à part soy je trouve mal-aysé de la designer proprement par quelque qualité principalle, tant elles sont doubles et bigarrées à divers lustres" (III, 13, 1077). At the same time Montaigne's insistence on the mind's natural infirmity makes man himself responsible, since he tends to look at things "par quelque faux lustre" (II, 10, 410). In *Nous ne goustons rien de pur,* for polemical reasons things are pictured as simple to underscore man's propensity for rendering them complex and obscure: "la foiblesse de nostre condition fait que les choses, en leur simplicité et pureté naturelle, ne puissent pas tomber en nostre usage" (II, 20, 673). Montaigne depicts the lively and restless mind probing, seeking to penetrate, to understand and, one senses, to control, and then losing itself in the multiplicity of perspectives it assumes: "Il n'est pas besoin d'esclairer les affaires si profond-ement et si subtilement. On s'y perd, à la consideration de tant de lustres contraires et formes diverses" (675). And, finally, the mind divests things of their qualities and characteristics to impose its own peculiar and personal imprint on them.

Somewhere in the space separating the self from things—and here, we understand, other men are as things distant—language would function ideally to render the world intelligible, to create meaningful order. Such of course is not the case, as we have seen, since signs remain approximate, apart from substantial reality in the world of accidental existence. Yet man has been inclined to delude himself, to confound words and things, to treat the surface as substance. As the agent of this delusion, reason plays both on man's need to know and on his gullible imagination and exploits the abstract nature of language, which allows it to be freely manipulated. Montaigne recognizes the persuasive power of the verb, its image-evoking force and man's propensity to take words for reality, an error that is compounded by the difficulty of verifying their professed truth: "je ne me puis garder, quand j'oy nos architectes s'enfler de ces gros mots de pilastres, architraves, corniches, d'ouvrage Corinthien et Dorique, et semblables de leur jargon, que mon imagination ne se saisisse incontinent du palais d'Apolidon; et, par effect, je trouve que ce sont les chetives pieces de la porte de ma cuisine" (I, 50, 307). Montaigne takes advantage of the multiple meanings of *discours* to use it both as reason-reasoning and as language-conversation; this links the faculty or act and its instrument of expression and suggests, etymologically, that random, directionless movement associated with error (*errare*). Men build worlds with words, they erect verbal (immaterial) constructs that the listener, and often the speaker himself, mistake for substance. In *Des boyteux* Montaigne examines how words are confused with truth: "Nostre discours est capable d'estoffer cent autres mondes et d'en trouver les principes. . . . Il ne luy faut ny matiere ny baze; laissez le courre; il bastit aussi bien sur le vuide que sur le plain, et de l'inanité que de matiere" (III, 11, 1027).

The image-evoking or persuasive capability of language excites the imagination to conjure up things without any necessary correlation with reality. In the sixteenth century, the imaginative faculty was closely linked with the senses and thus was subject both to being deceived and to creating its own distortions; Montaigne reiterates this all through the essays, particularly in *De la force de l'imagination* (I, 21). The poet was, of course, a primary example of one who made, or perhaps more precisely made-up, things with words, using his imagination to form his work, relying on his words acting on the reader's imagination to evoke a picture whose resemblance to nature was considered one of the objects of art.[5] Here lies one of the bases for the mistrust of poetry, its equation with lies and untruth and the reason the vocabulary used to describe it—*feindre, fiction*—carried weighty pejorative overtones, as we mentioned earlier.[6] Speaking of history, Montaigne differentiates between imagining or making up and giving a true representation in precisely these terms; in fact, he explicitly chooses the one over the other when describing an account of Xenophon: "Et son bon disciple, feignant ou recitant, mais à mon advis recitant plustost que feignant les rares perfections de ce grand Cyrus" (III, 10, 1016). When operating in the realm of words, the distinction is not always apparent; without a substantial touchstone, the reader can choose to believe something as true and at the same time affirm its tentativeness and his own uncertainty: "à mon advis." When Montaigne seeks to underscore the ambiguity or impenetrability of nature and philosophy, to stress man's inability to read through to truth, he refers to them as poetry.

The impact of Montaigne's metaphor becomes more striking

when we regard poetry in the contemporary framework of rhetoric from which it was considered to derive. The late fifteenth- and early sixteenth-century treatises on poetry are well known as the "arts de seconde rhetorique," but even as the word "poetry" assumes prominence to indicate an important shift in emphasis from concentration on rhyme schemes to broader questions of style, its ties to the art of "premiere rhetorique" remain firm.[7] In the *Art poétique françoys* (1548) Sebillet affirms the resemblance of the orator and poet, distinguishing between them on the basis of meter alone: "et sont l'orateur et le poëte tant proches et conjoinz, que semblables et egauz en plusieurs choses, different principalement en ce que l'un est plus contraint de nombres que l'autre."[8] The theories of the Pléiade, whether expressed by Du Bellay, Peletier du Mans, or Ronsard, echo similar views, which suggest little difference in the aims and techniques of the two arts. In the lexicon of the poetic act (invention, disposition, elocution), in elements of style (decorum, ornament, tropes, and figures), and in poetry's desired end (to move its audience, to persuade) we recognize its debt to rhetoric and the contemporary inclination to affirm the kinship.

The sound manipulation of language in the presentation of *arguments,* the valid expression of conceptions "invented," was grounded in the Renaissance notion—derived from the rhetoricians of antiquity—which emphasized the link between words and things, between form and content. Whether considering the relationship of the work to that which it imitated (nature or model authors) or to its effect on the audience, the integrity of the *res-verba* pairing demanded that words serve as faithful, what we might call substantial signifiers. The particular expression with which words invested things had to be appropriate.[9]

Underlying this insistence one glimpses the contemporary sense of the real space separating words from things, of the accidental mode of language, and of the potential for disparity and disjunction.[10] From the purely aesthetic perspective, the *res-verba* couple serves as a standard for literary judgment, a way of determining whether a work is good or bad by comparing expression to invention. Paucity of expression or its over-exuberance, for example, seems to upset the equilibrium in which words and things apparently must exist to fulfill the purpose of their union. Montaigne rebukes Cicero for the imbalance that prizes eloquence to the detriment of conception: "Fy de l'eloquence qui nous laisse envie de soy, non des choses" (I, 40, 252). Rather than serving to embody and to transmit ideas, attitudes, and insights, Cicero's language operates on its own, as an end in itself. Neither the original conception nor the image evoked in the reader's mind corresponds to the medium, for the words betray and deceive.

The activities of both poet and orator, then, by the very terms used to describe and to judge them, highlight Montaigne's concerns with language, as essayist, and seeker of the self. Whether focusing on the unscrupulous orator who strives will-fully to abuse his audience, the poet whose feigning can be fiction, the liar, or the lawyer, the essayist goes beyond esthetics and literary judgment to raise questions of human conduct, of virtue and knowledge. When he takes Agesilas' definition of rhetoric for his own, he affirms that this art perverts the ideal *res-verba* relationship: "Un Rhetoricien du temps passé disoit que son metier estoit, de choses petites les faire paroistre et trouver grandes. C'est un cordonnier qui sait faire de grands souliers à un petit pied" (I, 51, 305). Things intellectual and elements of physical reality as well—what man can see and touch—are subject to the distorting potential of language: "ceux qui masquent et fardent les femmes, font moins de mal; car c'est chose de peu de perte de ne les voir pas en leur naturel; là où ceux-cy [the rhetoricians] font estat de tromper, non pas nos yeux, mais nostre jugement, et d'abastardir et corrompre l'essence des choses" (305). Words can be made to function as a mask, as a surface to veil truth, to distort what Montaigne calls the real nature of things; here, at least, where he seeks to point up how language is abused, Montaigne implies that valid expression might render it accessible.

While the ideal may be to express and to communicate the

"essence des choses," Montaigne will insist most often on that
space of which we have spoken and on the abuses of those who,
like the rhetoricians and poets, deal in what he calls the airy
medium of words (II, 6, 379). *De l'experience* stresses the
inadequacy of words to things and castigates the lawyers, judges,
theologians, and philosophers for playing on the disparity to
spread error and confusion. When he speaks of the dissension
created by Luther's opinions, Montaigne underlines the divorce
between language and conception and the inability of words to
express ideas unequivocally, to capture and convey meaning:

> Nostre contestation est verbale. Je demande que c'est que nature,
> volupté, cercle, et substitution. La question est de parolles, et se
> paye de mesme. Une pierre c'est un corps. Mais qui presseroit:
> Et corps qu'est-ce?—Substance,—Et substance quoy? ainsi de
> suitte, acculeroit en fin le respondant au bout de son calepin. On
> eschange un mot pour un autre mot, et souvent plus incogneu.
> [III, 13, 1069]

Language cannot correspond to the endless diversity of human
experience, physical and mental, and thus limited tends to
generalize, to infer similarity and resemblance that distorts.
Single words refer to various things, contain several meanings,
and instead of precision give rise to ambiguity, multiple meaning. Rather than pinning things down to reveal them, words
point to myriad faces that confound. As abstract signs they are
continually susceptible to refinement, continually in need of
interpretation, but always in the same medium, as paraphrase,
commentary, definition which themselves merely extend the
process. Language cannot render the world intelligible nor can it
impose meaningful order; as Montaigne says in Virgil's words,
"Sed neque quam multae species, et nomina quae sint,/Est
numerus" ("Mais il serait impossible d'en énumérer toutes les
espèces et d'en dire tous les noms" [*Georg.*, II, 103; III, 13,
1076]).

    Words give rise to words, texts to texts, while truth and
knowledge remain distant and inaccessible. Throughout the

Essais Montaigne consistently places responsibility on man, on his proud yearning for the absolute, on his curiosity and the fallibility of his intellect, and, in the context we have been discussing, on the weakness of reason's medium of operation. To speak of the failure to know is to indict all the books that pretend to explain. As preparation for death, or *les inconveniens naturels* (III, 12, 1039) of life, philosophical discourse offers bodiless subtleties, verbal quibbles: "quand je me trouve au propre, je sens que ma langue s'est enrichie, mon courage de rien." In the growing maze of his linguistic constructs the seeker loses his way, as if he were unaware that words are inadequate to the expression of things, that by their very nature they lead to ambiguity and equivocality. And in another of those passages in which Montaigne affirms the real existence of things as opposed to intangible language, he pictures the distortion of nature itself: "Et en ont faict les hommes comme les parfumiers de l'huile: ils l'ont sophistiquée de tant d'argumentations et de discours appellez du dehors, qu'elle en est devenue variable et particuliere à chacun, et a perdu son propre visage" (1049). The outside world of surfaces, in which words participate, betrays the writer's intentions and the object of his quest.

In his own writing Montaigne experiences this disparity between words and conception or intention. He finds that language operates in ways that give written works an autonomy beyond their authors' designs, and in this context he admits the difficulty of knowing and distinguishing his own work for what it is: "L'ouvrage, de sa propre force et fortune, peut seconder l'ouvrier outre son invention et connoissance et le devancer. Pour moy, je ne juge la valeur d'autre besongne plus obscurement que de la mienne" (III, 8, 939). Montaigne also confesses that he ventures mental and verbal sallies that he mistrusts and does not believe: "Moy qui suis Roy de la matiere que je traicte, et qui n'en dois conte à personne, ne m'en crois pourtant pas du tout: je hasarde souvent des boutades de mon esprit, desquelles je me deffie, et certaines finesses verbales, dequoy je secoue les oreilles; mais je les laisse courir à l'avanture" (943). When he places

certain activities or accomplishments beyond the natural human
capacity, Montaigne speaks of *saillies,* stressing the separation of
body and soul and the consequent separation of the man from his
work, whether his achievement be the attitude of Stoic grandeur
or the words of poetic genius: "Nostre ame ne sçauroit de son
siege atteindre si haut. Il faut qu'elle le quitte et s'esleve, . . .
qu'elle emporte et ravisse son homme si loing qu'apres il
s'estonne luy-mesme de son faict; . . . comme . . . les poëtes
sont espris souvent d'admiration de leurs propres ouvrages et ne
reconnoissoient plus la trace par où ils ont passé une si belle
carriere" (II, 2, 347). The echoes of neo-Platonic divine fury are
unmistakable in the description of the artist being carried off,
allowed privileged insight to produce something that must be
considered apart from him, as not essentially his. The poet
himself confesses that these *saillies poetiques* "surpassent sa suffisance et ses forces, et les reconnoit venir d'ailleurs que de soy"
(I, 24, 127). Montaigne clearly recognizes the value of such
inspired poetry and in fact uses the same vocabulary to describe
this superior art ("la bonne, l'excessive, la divine . . . poésie")
and its effect on him: "Elle ne pratique point nostre jugement:
elle le ravit et ravage. . . . Dés ma premiere enfance, la poësie
a eu cela, de me transpercer et transporter" (I, 37, 232). But he
refuses this *ravissement* that he calls madness, precisely because it
exceeds judgment and reason, moderation and proportion, which
characterize wisdom. He must also reject it since its source lies in
fragmentation: the work stands as alien to its maker.

II

That the relative or accidental mode of language occupies Montaigne's attention depends on a paradoxical correlative he appears
to affirm that written language functions as the repository of
reality, as the medium through which things most significantly
assume being. On the one hand, words by their very nature exist
apart from things and, on the other, they contain those things, or

rather stand for them in a meaningful way. Montaigne seems to acknowledge the validity of language, however imperfect, as the peculiar medium of human expression—that is, as the external representation or revelation of interiority. Words apparently can bear a man's imprint, they can be expressive: "c'est le seul util par le moien duquel se communiquent nos volontez et nos pensées, c'est le truchement de nostre ame" (II, 18, 667). From this angle, the repeated use of *discours,* bringing together the rational and the discursive, reinforces the sense of language as reason's distinctive instrument. We appreciate Montaigne's anger at those who would upset this precarious equilibrium, so susceptible to distortion and exploitation, because so much depends potentially on the fragile relationship between words and things (actions, objects, concepts).

When Montaigne explains how he comes to write in *De l'oisiveté* (I, 8), he describes a movement from reflection to writing, one that implies a change from incoherency to form, from tumultuous agitation to a more ordered, and traceable, motion. He maintains that he writes in order to review the ineptness and strangeness of the mind's activity; what he puts down in words becomes indelible. His mental meanderings assume concrete, tangible form so that they no longer slip, ephemeral, through the grasp of his awareness. Accompanying this setting of thought, Montaigne indicates that written language permits a bridling or containing of the mind in action: "L'ame qui n'a point de but estably, elle se perd: car, comme on dict, c'est n'estre en aucun lieu, que d'estre par tout" (32). In the spatial metaphor the essayist prefers, the mind is pictured either in disordered commotion or moving toward a fixed goal or point of reference, either lost or able to be located, and the distinction appears to depend on whether it is musing or writing. The inchoate, shifting nature of reverie gives way to the word fixed on the page, perhaps through the self-conscious deliberation that accompanies that setting of thought. Between the ideal calm and repose Montaigne sought in retirement and the reality of the mind's turmoil in idleness ("faisant le cheval eschappé" [33])

Montaigne discovers a process where movement can coincide with purpose, where agitation becomes *exercitation*. As he casts his thought through the essay, language provides a mode of being that renders the mind accessible.

When Montaigne states that words are the single instrument of communication of will and thought, he implies that we can know people or things only through language. He uses books to discover the qualities of the author: "Et tous les jours m'amuse à lire en des autheurs, sans soin de leur science, y cherchant leur façon, non leur subject. Tout ainsi que je poursuy la communication de quelque esprit fameux, non pour qu'il m'enseigne, mais pour que je le cognoisse" (III, 8, 928). He notes Plutarch's presence in his writing, discernible to the careful reader: "Les escrits de Plutarque, à les bien savourer, nous le descouvrent assez, et je pense le connoistre jusques dans l'ame" (II, 31, 716). When he considers Tacitus' history at the end of *De l'art de conferer* (III, 8), Montaigne evaluates the usefulness of its form, the appropriateness of its style, the sincerity of the historian's views and their validity, and draws from his reading a feeling for his stature as a man. Primarily what interests the reader is the quality of the writer's judgment ("J'ay principalement consideré son jugement" [941]), evident both in what Tacitus says and what he does not say. His reluctance to speak of himself, for example, appears a fault: "le n'oser parler rondement de soy a quelque faute de coeur. Un jugement roide et hautain et qui juge sainement et seurement, il use à toutes mains des propres exemples ainsi que de chose estrangere" (942). Montaigne's bias is obvious here and his criticism predictable. Of consequence is the presupposition that the man as writer (that is to say, the evidence of his judgment) resides in the words of his text, present, approachable, and accessible, for this notion lies at the very heart of the book of the self.

If Montaigne castigates rhetoric's abuse of language, which makes verbal fantasy appear real, he appreciates poetry's capacity to render things more pointed and vivid than reality itself. In his comments on style in *De la vanité* (III, 9) he extends poetic vigor and verve to prose, suggesting that the best discursive writing too can mold language into what we have called the repository of reality: "la meilleure prose ancienne (et je la seme ceans indifferemment pour vers) reluit par tout de la vigueur et hardiesse poetique, et represente l'air de sa fureur" (995). While not directly inspired by the Muses, this prose expresses the effect of its frenzy in the leaps and gambols that Montaigne will make a part of his own work. But we might wonder here as well if in his picture of poetic furor where, as he says, the poet himself is utterly poetic and the original theology and the first philosophy are poetry, Montaigne does not harken back to a utopian moment when word and thing coincided, when language embodied reality in the poetic expression which was "l'originel langage des Dieux" (995). While that time is forever past, its echoes reverberate in Virgil's *Aeneid,* where Montaigne experiences the full force of Eros: "Tout asseché que je suis et appesanty, je sens encore quelques tiedes restes de cette ardeur passée. . . . Mais de ce que je m'y entends, les forces et valeur de ce Dieu se trouvent plus vives et plus animées en la peinture de la poesie qu'en leur propre essence,

> Et versus digitos habet.
> [And verses have fingers to excite]

Elle represente je ne sçay quel air plus amoureux que l'amour mesme" (III, 5, 849).

In *Sur des vers de Virgile* Montaigne juxtaposes sex and love to its poetic expression in his comments on the nature and function of poetic language. Nowhere in the work is he more anatomical in his description of sexual matters, including personal ones: "Certes, elle [la nature] m'a traitté illegitimement et incivilement,

> Si non longa satis, si non bené mentula crassa . . .
> [But if the penis be not long or stout enough]

Et d'une lesion enormissime" (887). Nowhere does he discuss the sex act more fully to underline it as a vital human principle.

"Tout le mouvement du monde se resoult et rend à cet accoup-
plage: c'est une matiere infuse par tout, c'est un centre où toutes
choses regardent" (857). And, paradoxically, nowhere is the
essayist's current experience more literary, but at the same time
nowhere does language appear more effectively to contain and
communicate reality. Like the Eros of the *Aeneid,* substantial,
alive, and animated, and Venus, never more beautiful than in the
painting of poetry, Lucretius' vision of the goddess strikes Montaigne as corporeal. He weighs (*ruminer*) the verses to find an
eloquence "nerveuse et solide, qui ne plaict pas tant comme elle
remplit et ravit, et ravit le plus les plus forts espris" (873). In
this context of lovemaking, *remplir* and *ravir* function as erotic
metaphor to evoke a reader physically ravished and carried off by
the words. Montaigne attributes vigor to the language ("plein et
gros d'une vigueur naturelle"), life to the expression ("vifve"),
and flesh and bone to the words ("de chair et d'os" [873]). And
the ability to invest language with real life he credits to the
author's quality of mind. In a fundamental equation where *bien
dire* is juxtaposed to *bien penser, jugement* to *langage,* and *beaux mots*
to *plaines conceptions* (873), Montaigne places the writer and his
work in apposition so that language embodies judgment, indeed
stands as signifier of it. In this context eloquence becomes a
measure of intelligence, the exteriorization of interiority.

All this is not to suggest that Montaigne prefers literature to
life or that he finds books an adequate surrogate for engaging
physically in sex. He makes this perfectly clear in the opening
pages of the essay when he declares that age alone has caused him
to seek pleasure through the exercise of his imagination: "Que je
me chatouille, je ne puis tantost plus arracher un pauvre rire de
ce meschant corps. Je ne m'esgaye qu'en fantasie et en songe,
pour destourner par ruse le chagrin de la vieillesse. Mais certes il
y faudroit autre remede qu'en songe: foible luicte de l'art contre
la nature" (842). And when he concludes the parenthesis on
writing which he had opened to expand on his reaction to
Lucretius, he proposes to leave books aside and speak more
"materiellement" (about love). At the same time, the power he

ascribes to poetry in particular and to the potential of language in general remains real and the capacity (and often the legitimacy) of the imagination to vivify the inner emotional life undeniable: "à un corps abattu, comme un estomac prosterné, il est excusable de le rechauffer et soustenir par art, et, par l'entremise de la fantasie" (892).

What Montaigne borrows from the utopian ideal is the potential of language to point beyond itself in a meaningful way. Words apparently always threaten to fly off on their own, to be signs without substance, and we have seen how they can evoke visions whose truth is purely verbal. Whether Montaigne notes Virgil's ability to render love more vividly than the thing itself or pictures the mind ransacking the storehouse of words and figures to express itself, we see him ascribing to language the capacity to represent what is, to contain or give body in a way that is more real than any other mode of being.

In *Du démentir* (II, 18) the essayist extends and makes explicit the sense of his earlier remarks in *De l'oisiveté* which inferred that where reflection by itself opened the mind to shapeless, disordered activity, putting his thoughts on paper allowed order and purpose to be introduced. Musing is set against writing, as is idleness against what we might call practice (*exercitation*), an activity that alone offers the possibility of a fixed goal, which shapes and forms thoughts to make them discernible, recognizable, susceptible to evaluation and judgment. Rather than the mind whirring aimlessly in convolutions that fade like so much smoke, its axis becomes an established subject, its traces are imprinted on the page. In his essay on giving the lie, Montaigne affirms that the written word can impose order: "Aux fins de renger ma fantasie à resver mesme par quelque ordre et projet, et la garder de se perdre et extravaguer au vent, il n'est que de donner corps et mettre en registre tant de menues pensées qui se presentent à elle. J'escoute à mes resveries par ce que j'ay à les enroller" (II, 18, 665). Hyperbole serves to make the point that order and purpose—the very qualities lacking in the musing of idleness—emerge through writing: fancy even dreams with uniformity and intention. The written word provides direction and keeps the mind from getting lost, but perhaps most importantly Montaigne suggests that thought changes its mode of being as it passes from a purely mental to a recorded form. Ephemeral and gossamerlike, existing only to vanish without a trace, beyond the control of will, thought assumes a kind of concreteness, a materiality that Montaigne expresses repeatedly as body (*corps*). This metaphor exceeds its linguistic function to become the central truth of the book of the self. If thought is anywhere—which seems to mean that it can be gotten hold of—it is where it materializes in written language. Montaigne does not deny the existence or the reality of the purely cognitive, just as he never doubts the existence of the self he seeks to uncover. He merely imagines it as indefinable and impenetrable until exteriorized through the written word. *Donner corps* and *mettre en registre* are the same act.

Montaigne pictures the literary invention of his preferred classical authors in terms that differ from his own. When he equates language and judgment in *Sur des vers de Virgile* (III, 5) he imagines Horace, for one, possessing a distinct conception, seeing clearly and deeply into the thing and then casting about for the appropriate expressive language. Here the thought— vivid, insightful, qualitatively sound—merely seeks articulation equal to it: "Il [Horace] voit plus cler et plus outre dans la chose; son esprit crochette et furette tout le magasin des mots et des figures pour se représenter" (873). We do not sense from this that the mind's activity is completed through writing; words get it out, exteriorize it, make it communicable. Interior concepts, full and solid, call for solid expression, as simple thoughts simple words: "Gallus parle simplement, par ce qu'il conçoit simplement."

While this description seems inappropriate to Montaigne, as we have seen, it does again reinforce the view of language's capacity to act as the repository of reality, the medium where things significantly reside. Whether, as in the case of Horace, the thought process precedes the writing that seeks to express its achievements or whether, as in the essayist's own case, the thought process itself is what the words express, the mind and its activity are found and judged in language. But it may well be, we should add, that Montaigne's own procedure is not as dramatically opposed to that of Horace as this discussion might imply. He is, as we will see later, artist as well as essayist, and the writing of essays will often resemble what Horace, Gallus, and Plutarch do, as Montaigne seeks to find suitable expression— both in vocabulary and figures of speech—for insights and concepts already apparently grasped. He will bend the language to his needs and compose metaphors that conform to his intention. But whether looking to exteriorize thought or thinking itself, whether communicating concepts or the act of conception, Montaigne will treat his text as consubstantial to himself. Citing verses from Marot's *épître* to Sagon, he notes the superiority of the stinging poetic lash over its physical counterpart: "Et si ces verges poétiques . . . s'impriment encore mieux en papier qu'en la chair vifve" (II, 18, 665). And when he comes to speak of himself, he will emphasize his real presence in his words: "Je m'estalle entier: c'est un *skeletos* où, d'une veuë, les veines, les muscles, les tendons paroissent, chaque piece en son siege. . . . Ce ne sont mes gestes que j'escris, c'est moy, c'est mon essence" (II, 6, 379). He inhabits his book to such an extent, he admits at one point, that he hesitates to erase what he has written; in rubbing out the words he would leave nothing of himself: "Si je portoy le rasoir par tout où cela m'advient [where he is not sure of what he originally meant], je me desferoy tout" (I, 10, 40).

III

Montaigne expresses his concern with the capacity of words to hide what is and his confidence in their ability to enclose and disclose it in *De l'art de conferer* (III, 8), for these opposing inclinations in tension dominate the drama of discussion. Framing his presentation by commentary on his own activity, in terms that turn the practice of discussion into a metaphor for the writing of essays, Montaigne links speaking, writing, and living in order to raise questions at once intellectual and moral. His effort to know and judge others, and himself, focuses irresistibly on language as the unique medium of the soul to consider its use and abuse as a matter of intention and will. To pervert dialogue and debate is to sin, in a real sense, against truth: "Noz disputes devoient estre defendues et punies comme d'autres crimes verbaux. Quel vice n'esveillent elles et n'amoncellent. . . . Nous n'aprenons à disputer que pour contredire, et, chascun contredisant et estant contredict, il en advient que le fruit du disputer c'est perdre et aneantir la verité" (926). As he emphasizes truth, Montaigne appears to mean both the validity of the argument and the degree to which a man's words—as faithful indicators of his thought and action—can be used to measure his judgment and the strength and beauty of his mind. He separates objective truth about the subject, or the empirical world, from what the quality of the polemic reveals about the interlocutor or, in this case, about the self: "Quand vous gaignez l'avantage de vostre proposition, c'est la verité qui gaigne; quand vous gaignez l'avantage de l'ordre et de la conduite, c'est vous qui gaignez" (927).

Characteristically, Montaigne devotes as much space to verbal dissimulation as to disclosure, to express the force of that inclination, to set off what ought to be by delineating what ought not. While he notes, as we saw earlier, how language can go off on its own, beyond the intentions of its user, he aims at those who willfully hide behind words. Whether in the case of the intellectual cowards who, fearing correction, "parlent tousjours avec dissimulation" (924) or the *maistre(s) es arts* who dazzles and dupes with book learning, or even that of the essayist himself caught up in the heat of debate ("J'ay autrefois employé à la necessité et presse du combat des revirades qui ont faict faucée outre mon dessein et mon esperance" [936]), the disparity between what a man says and what he is predominates. Social and political position are exploited to lend import to words of little merit, just as people impute wisdom and knowledge to the powerful by reason of rank alone. The appearance of a man, or of his speech, can conceal proper value and true worth; as Melanthius said of Dionysius' tragedy, "Je ne l'ay . . . point veuë, tant elle est offusquée de langage," and as the essayist proposes to those who judge the great, "Je n'ay point entendu son propos, tant il estoit offusqué de gravité, de grandeur et de majesté" (935). Office, and the dignity attached to it, can result wholly from good fortune just as successful action can derive purely from chance; by giving weight to his words they conceal the man behind. Montaigne stresses the fortuitous to point up the difficulty of determining the inside by the outside of things.

Cutting through *sottise* and *bestise,* separating out the pedants and the powerful, Montaigne characterizes the common perverters of truth as *ineptes* to express their foolishness or stupidity and highlight their lack of skill or aptitude for that *art* he describes. The truth of which he speaks emerges not from the acquisition of learning but from its quest, not from the accumulation of knowledge but the way it is sought. While the essayist recognizes the validity of propositions and arguments established through discursive reason, as we saw earlier, he maintains a clear distinction between pursuit and possession: "nous sommes nais à quester la verité; il appartient de la posseder à une plus grande puissance" (928). Here, of course, are the echoes of the *Apologie* and countless other references throughout the essays to man's inability to attain full knowledge. But here, as well, what we might call the dialectic of failure becomes itself the source of another kind of knowing. From matter, which concerns truth and the world, Montaigne will turn to manner, which concerns the discovery of self. The quest remains man's most fundamental activity, one coincidental to his nature: "L'agitation et la chasse est proprement de nostre gibier: nous ne sommes pas excusables de la conduire mal et impertinemment; de faillir à la prise, c'est autre chose" (928). Although resolution is impossible, the quest is not abandoned as fruitless; rather, modified by the sense of its relativity, it becomes itself the object of scrutiny. The truth to which Montaigne continually refers will slide between that of subject matter, which appears an essential condition to the proper conduct of the hunt (its aim if not its goal), and that of manner, speaking genuinely oneself and recognizing the validity of the other's position. Depth of insight and soundness of argument come together with sincerity of expression and submission to truth as indicators of the quality of that mind which, in a characteristic Montaignian circle, is at once the means and the end of pursuit.

The mind in movement expresses itself in discourse, here pressed, challenged by an ideal interlocutor, a nameless Socrates. Montaigne establishes the principle of learning through counterpoint and negative example as the heart of discussion: "Il en peut estre aucuns de ma complexion, qui m'instruis mieux par contrarieté que par exemple, et par fuite que par suite" (922). Contradiction and criticism stimulate self-examination, lead to self-correction and the acknowledgment of truth. Martial terms depict the necessary clash, the vigorous confrontation essential to successful debate: "Si je confere avec une ame forte et un roide jousteur, il me presse les flancs, me pique à gauche et à dextre. . . . La jalousie, la gloire, la contention me poussent et rehaussent au dessus de moy-mesmes" (923). Strength, virility, and vigor determine the quality of this fencing match (927) and of its outcome or victory (925, 927). Nowhere in the essays is Montaigne more the soldier than in *De l'art de conferer,* nowhere do we see him so energetically a partisan of military activity. A metaphor, of course, on the part of this most unmartial man, but one that performs multiple duty: it sets opposition and contradiction as the axis of discussion; it expresses the dialectical nature of learning and the discovery of truth. It also characterizes true debate and the proper use of language as action, distinct from languid rhetorical argument: "Il nous faut fortifier l'ouie et la durcir contre cette tandreur du son ceremonieux des parolles. J'ayme une societé et familiarité forte et virile, une amitié qui se flatte en l'aspreté et vigueur de son commerce" (924).

Just as strikingly, the military metaphor, and particularly that of fencing, highlight the sense of debate as exercise, practice, as self-referential movement: "Le plus fructueux et natural exercice de nostre esprit, c'est à mon gré la conference" (922). What matters here is the quality of the action itself. In fencing, as the sportive analogue of battle, the point is to test one's powers— although the fencer can win or lose the match, it's how he plays that counts. Montaigne's debater proceeds in similar fashion; subject matter thus becomes of secondary importance to the way it is handled, as if it merely offered an occasion to set the mind working. Montaigne pictures Socrates focusing on the arguers rather than the argument, on their impertinence rather than that of their art: "Il empoigne la premiere matiere comme celuy qui a une fin plus utile que de l'esclaircir, assavoir esclaircir les esprits qu'il prend à manier et exercer" (927). The products of the mind are important as indicators, signs that point to its quality, as Tacitus' history reveals the judgment Montaigne considers.

The analogy between the art of discussion and the writing of essays—with that emphasis on *exercer* appropriate to both—is sharpened by Montaigne's praise of discussion in familiar Horatian terms as sweet and useful, as if it were a literary act. To the line where he speaks of *conference* as the most fruitful and natural exercise of the mind, he adds, "j'en trouve l'usage plus doux que d'aucune autre action de nostre vie" (922). Debate is treated as a verbal artifact, a form purposely constructed with language, similar in mode to other types of literary expression. As a creation of its interlocutors, it has its precepts and principles whose proper application determine the nature of the thing composed. Montaigne's *art* of the title of the essay appears both to move discussion closer to the other arts (as producing artifacts) and to indicate that there is a skill to its practice. And the verbal construct bears the imprint of its maker, which can be considered and judged as a measure of the quality of his mind. In this instance, the common and often critically overworked Montaignian antithesis between nature and art must be modified. Montaigne describes discussion as artificial, self-conscious, to be acted out according to certain rules, demanding particular abilities as if it were a war game or sport. Here art serves not in contrast but as a complement to nature, as the means through which the nature of a man makes itself apparent. When he describes the necessary order of discussion, Montaigne uses the arguments of shopboys and shepherds as a model to characterize the results of a disinterested concern with the subject and the conversation (as opposed to the self-interest of the sophisticated rhetors and scholars): "Ce n'est pas tant la force et la subtilité que je demande, comme l'ordre. L'ordre qui se voit tous les jours aux altercations des bergers et des enfans de boutique, jamais entre nous" (925). The simple or natural, thus idealized, provides a dramatic counterpoint to the abusive conduct of the learned. Practiced, it turns into an art where alone it can be said to exist. The natural viewed as ideal, self-consciously approximated through artifice, describes a paradox central to the *Essais*. We will take up the relationship between nature and art, history and literature as they affect both the person and activity of the narrator in a later chapter.

Montaigne subsumes the essential elements of discussion under the notion of *ordre*, which he introduces through his example of the natural. The word itself is repeated in successive sentences, twice in the quote cited above and once in the preceding line: "Tout un jour je contesteray paisiblement, si la conduicte du debat se suit avec ordre." The immediate context suggests that order means thematic continuity, which Montaigne expresses as movement along a road: "Mais leur tumulte et impatiance [that of the shopboy and shepherd] ne les devoye pas de leur theme: leur propos suit son cours" (925). To get off that road (*detraquer, devoyer*), to wander from it through stupidity or guile, is to detour from the right direction and undermine the very purpose of the movement. And for valid discussion to move appropriately, the interlocutors themselves must have a correct manner: "A quoy faire vous mettez vous en voie de quester ce qui est avec celuy qui n'a ny pas ny alleure qui vaille?" (926). A vigorous, even tumultuous discussion, one marked by impatient interruption, conforms to order if the interlocutors listen to each other and, one gathers, if they speak sincerely (or as Montaigne says, bravely, where "les mots aillent où va la pensée" [924]) and acknowledge truth: "Je festoye et caresse la verité en quelque main que je la trouve." When an answer or comment is not to the point, things become "trouble et des-reglée" (925), the form is obscured, the road lost.

Order, it appears, is what the art of discussion allows. Montaigne defends the self-conscious accent on form as compatible with the integrity of content in an observation that actually understates their relationship: "On ne faict poinct tort au subject, quand on le quicte pour voir du moyen de le traicter" (926). But he has just posed the natural as ideal and so will appear to temper the concern with means by speaking of a natural way, one of sound understanding as different from the artificial scholastic way of the inept. Interest in overall shape or direction of the argument is legitimate; overemphasis of particular formal aspects, of figures, delivery, or "la closture dialectique de(s) . . . clauses" (926) is perverse. Clearly, truth is only pursued where the correct form permits order, where sincere expression, the acknowledgment of valid argument, and appropriate response hold sway. The notions of order, of roads and gaits, involve the "how" of discussion, determine its manner or shape and, not coincidentally, the manner of the interlocutors, for, as we have seen, the truth that emerges touches both the subject and those who pursue it. And this last, of course, is of greatest concern to Montaigne, the seeker of self-knowledge.

From as early in the essays as *De l'oisiveté,* the sense pervades that form and order are fundamental to any mode of being (or expression) which pretends to accessibility. In the cultural tradition of the essayist, as it derives from the Greeks, order is intrinsically preferred to disorder, harmony or unity to discord, and Montaigne builds on these antitheses to make form the instrument of self-knowledge. With allowances made for leaps and gambols of his thought (and style), for the spontaneous, natural tone of his presentation, we see Montaigne's idiosyncratic use of the terms as he insists that what he does (that is, thinks

and writes) has form and order. Random motion in which the
mind loses itself, like the confused and disorderly discussion,
must become essays (or debate) with subjects where the mind, to
try itself out (*exercer*), assumes a form that allows its progress to
be considered and judged. When Montaigne speaks of this
exteriorization, he uses the terms *ordonner* and *renger* (II, 6, 378)
to describe how he comes out; when he praises Socrates for what
we might call the evenness of his gait, he puts it in these familiar
terms: "le pris de l'ame ne consiste pas à aller haut, mais ordonnéement" (III, 2, 809). And when commenting on Perseus, he
finds in the disordered, flighty, and erratic character of his mind
the reason why "il n'estoit cogneu ny de luy ny d'autre quel
homme ce fust" (III, 13, 1077). Order characterizes both the
highest quality of the mind's activity and the form that renders it
accessible. As we speak of debate and discussion, it is the mark of
personal achievement: "quand vous gaignez l'avantage de l'ordre
et de la conduite, c'est vous qui gaignez" (III, 8, 927).

Two basic difficulties in his enterprise concern Montaigne.
The first is the natural inclination to formlessness, apparent in
the problems of conducting a proper discussion, which must be
overcome if truth of any kind is to be served. Hence the "art" of
discussion, the formulation of certain conditions and conduct,
and the correlative notion that it is a skill to be learned and
practiced. The essayist does not underestimate the effort required, for example, to admit the validity of another's argument,
or to resist insult or anger; the space devoted to the variety of
"propos vains et ineptes" (930) and to the number of "ineptes
ames entre les sçavantes" (931) serves as a measure of the
problem. Montaigne's own movement through *De l'art de conferer*
both underscores the dilemma and points the way out of it. We
see him functioning as his own Socrates, first taking a hard line
against *sottises,* then coming back to question his certainty that he
is right: "Or quoi, si je prens les choses autrement qu'elles ne
sont?" (928). He criticizes his impatience with views other than
his own and recognizes his personal *sottise*: "Combien de sottises
dis-je et repons-je tous les jours, selon moy" (929). In a dialectic

that parallels that of the proper discussion, Montaigne debates aspects of discussion itself, declaiming a position, examining and finding fault with it, showing how critical judgment must consider both the other's position and one's own: "j'entens que nostre jugement, chargeant sur un autre duquel pour lors il est question, ne nous espargne pas d'une interne jurisdiction" (930). Here he overcomes a certain rigidity of attitude and by admitting its weakness sustains that form through which the self can be known. Alone, and obliged to play both interlocutors, Montaigne must constantly be on guard against his own egotism, his own need to be right. The success of his venture depends on the ability to consider and judge himself as if another: "Je ne m'ayme pas si indiscretement et ne suis si attaché et meslé à moy que je ne me puisse distinguer et considerer à quartier: comme un voisin, comme un arbre" (942).

The second difficulty, which involves evaluation and judgment of the "other," is more subtle, more complex than the first, for which an art can be proposed and practiced. However strong the inclination to disavow criticism, to protect ego with insult, that bent, one senses, can be pulled back in the other direction, the art can be learned. Not by everyone, perhaps, but surely the sincere and brave man can seek to do so, however imperfectly, always aware that the tension between dissimulation and disclosure is at play. In this case, the control of language that is central to successful discussion depends on the individual; in the second difficulty, where one confronts the words of another, language and its control appear more alien and remote. Here the discussion must function as valid sign or signifier of the man behind, for the degree to which the words embody that man determines the ability to know him: "pour juger en luy les parties plus siennes et plus dignes, la force et beauté de son ame, il faut sçavoir ce qui est sien et ce qui ne l'est point . . ." (940). The principle of making things one's own underlies the activity of Montaigne's student in *De l'institution des enfans* (cf. p. 151, for example) and defines the essayist's own relation to his cultural tradition, as we have seen. Here we have the reverse of the medal, the essential effort to determine what in that which a man says and does is borrowed and what is a part of him: "La plus part des hommes sont riches d'une suffisance estrangere. Il peut advenir à tel de dire un beau traict, une bonne responce et sentence, et la mettre en avant sans en cognoistre la force. . . . Il n'y faut point tousjours ceder, quelque verité ou beauté qu'elle ait. Ou il la faut combatre à escient, ou se tirer arriere, soubs couleur de ne l'entendre pas, pour taster de toutes parts comment elle est logée en son autheur" (936). The interlocutor must determine how far what is said is understood, whether it is possessed or only held in keeping.

In these observations drawn from experience, designed to elaborate on the strategy of discussion, Montaigne appears to concentrate on subject matter and on the degree to which it has been mastered. The stupid borrow good ideas and then expose themselves by timid and inept handling: "Ils n'osent luy [the matter] changer d'assiete et de jour, ny l'enfoncer" (937). The ability to manipulate borrowed material, to go into it deeply, are precisely what the tutor demands of his student: "Que ce qu'il viendra d'apprendre, il le lui face mettre en cent visages et accommoder à autant de divers subjets, pour voir s'il l'a encore bien pris et bien faict sien" (I, 26, 151). Like experience, which must be *digerée* and *alambiquée* (31) to be meaningful, learning has also to be taken in and assimilated. The interlocutor, like the reader of history books, must be able to acknowledge the laudable lessons drawn from the storehouse of memory, but mainly his concern is whether what Montaigne calls "ces recitateurs et recueilleurs" are themselves laudable.

Knowledge of the other appears as well to be based on considerations of form and its relation to matter; here we come back to Montaigne's emphasis on manner: "nous sommes sur la maniere, non sur la matiere du dire. Mon humeur est de regarder autant à la forme qu'à la substance" (928). These lines subordinate truth of subject almost completely to the way it is presented: "Tout homme peut dire veritablement; mais dire ordonnéement, prudemment et suffisamment, peu d'hommes le peuvent." But more often Montaigne slides from one to the other as though either or both could be revelatory. We have seen him suggest that the interlocutor try to "feel out" the degree to which an idea belongs to its author, perhaps through his use of *taster* implying something of the difficulty of this endeavor. When the matter is clearly foreign, one must look to formal elements: "en ce qui n'est pas sien (il faut savoir) combien on luy doibt en consideration du chois, disposition, ornement et langage qu'il y a fourny" (940). In evaluating "quelque belle invention en un poëte nouveau," contemporary notions of invention indicate that the seeker considers the conception embodied in the poem, the thought as expression.

In the final analysis, the handling of both content and form comprises that manner that reveals mind and judgment. The depth of understanding of the matter, the appropriateness or beauty of the expression, the overall unity and shape of the piece—oral or written—are signs of interiority. The seeker must always be on the offensive, probing to sort out the part played by chance, or by trappings physical, intellectual, or verbal to measure what has been contributed personally. The reticent or cowardly man will protest that he is not in his work or that it does not embody him as he really is, claiming that it is unfinished or was done in fun; Montaigne insists to the contrary: "Or . . . laissons donc ces pieces, donnez m'en une qui vous represente bien entier, par laquelle il vous plaise qu'on vous mesure" (939). But however much he believes in the capacity of the verbal artifact to embody what is, he continues to stress the difficulty of penetrating it, of reading it for what it is. And the evaluation of one's own work—which Montaigne evidently considers the highest mark of judgment—is no easier than that of others: "je m'aperçoy qu'on faut autant à juger de sa propre besongne que de celle d'autruy; non seulement pour l'affection qu'on y mesle, mais pour n'avoir la suffisance de la cognoistre et distinguer" (939). To look upon the self as *chose estrangere, chose tierce* (942) is a prerequisite for self-judgment and knowledge, but this separation into observer and observed distances or alienates the self,

"out there." What one says and does, then, when looked at in
this way, is no more intimate or accessible than the actions of
another. And this inherent problem of self-reference compounds
those which are intrinsic to the artifact fashioned of language.
The work on its own may outstrip the inventiveness and knowledge of the artisan (*l'ouvrier*) and so cloud the degree to which it
is representative: "Pour moy, je ne juge la valeur d'autre
besongne plus obscurement que de la mienne: et loge les Essais
tantost bas, tantost haut, fort inconstamment et doubteusement"
(939). Or, as if inspired by poetic frenzy, the writer, as we
mentioned earlier, may produce things over which he has had no
control or which he finds foreign: "Moy qui suis Roy de la
matiere que je traicte, et qui n'en dois conte à personne, ne m'en
crois pourtant pas du tout: je hasarde souvent des boutades de
mon esprit, desquelles je me deffie, et certaines finesses verbales,
dequoy je secoue les oreilles" (943). Montaigne will try to
overcome this by depicting himself in diverse postures, by building a composite within which what is representative and what is
not can be sorted out. But his final words in *De l'art de conferer*
confirm the vague and imperfect nature of overall judgments:
"Tous jugemens en gros sont láches et imparfaicts."

IV

Montaigne and his reader are then left at the very heart of the
paradox of language. On the one hand, it can function as the
repository of reality, as that mode in which things most significantly assume being, where the form of that being makes
them accessible and, on the other, it can obscure the knowledge
of what is. Meaning that is not intended can be imposed on
words or they themselves can foster faulty interpretation; language can be willfully manipulated or inadvertantly misused, in
any case impeding its function as meaningful sign. As Montaigne uses this medium to test out his judgment, as he seeks
here the means to self-knowledge, he appears to become increas-

ingly aware of the difficulties and progressively involved with responding to them. The man of books is keenly aware of writing just another book and so sets his own in relation to others'. As writer and seeker of the self he confronts the airiness of language, its instability and ambiguity; as artist he attempts to fashion the medium to his advantage. How the book of the self becomes the source of the self remains his prime concern and ours.

6

Singularity and Substance

"Quel que je soye, je le veux
estre ailleurs qu'en papier" (II, 37, 784)

"Chascun est aucunement en son
ouvrage" (II, 8, 387)

I

Montaigne's tendency to speak disparagingly of the *Essais* appears to acknowledge his own insignificance and theirs and to admit that in the end his book differs little from those he so vehemently criticizes. He characterizes his borrowing of ideas and quotations as thefts (I, 25, 136; I, 26, 147) and his writing as *crotesques* (I, 28, 183), *fagotage* (II, 37, 758), *ravasseries* (III, 9, 926), and *fricassée* (III, 13, 1079) to express the variety and diversity he seeks to communicate, but pejoratively, to belittle their worth. Calling the work *une marqueterie* (III, 9, 964) provides a concrete correlative to its patchwork form; Montaigne then disparages its quality by the addition of *mal joint.*[1] And however positively we explain the well-known "excremens d'un vieil esprit" (III, 9, 946)—its physicality, its intimacy— we cannot escape its depreciatory effect. If Montaigne sees his effort as less corrupt or less dangerous than some because it is less audacious—, or in terms of the *Essais,* less presumptuous—it nonetheless casts him among the useless and inept scribblers who ought to be restrained by law: "Mais il y devroit avoir quelque coërction des loix contre les escrivains ineptes et inutiles, comme il y a contre les vagabons et faineants. On banniroit des mains de nostre peuple et moy et cent autres" (946).

In part, this self-deprecating posture derives from the place and function of Montaigne's speaker in the world he describes. His self-professed humility acknowledges man's lowly state and the futility of his desire for certain truth and knowledge. All along, the speaker affirms the emptiness of human activity, intellectual and physical, both explaining and justifying that particular path he himself has chosen toward self-knowledge. In the opening lines of *De la vanité*, which is understandably rich in disparaging remarks, Montaigne repeats Ecclesiastes' blanket condemnation of the vanity which his own writing exemplifies: "Il n'en est à l'avanture aucune plus expresse que d'en escrire si vainement. Ce que la divinité nous en a si divinement exprimé devroit estre soingneusement et continuellement medité par les gens d'entendement" (945). At the essay's conclusion he confirms his point of departure, but with qualifications: while inanity and nonsense dominate, Montaigne hesitatingly suggests that the man who recognizes it in some sense rises above it. His uncertainty coincides with the tentative posture demanded by his subject, but what emerges clearly is that within that context the essayist's own activity—his quest for self-knowledge and his confession of inadequacy—however vain, has become a virtue, perhaps the only one of which man is capable. "C'est tousjours vanité pour toy, dedans et dehors, mais elle est moins vanité quand elle est moins estendue" (1001). The extended analogy, which associates traveling, writing essays, and living, depicts Montaigne as aware of the human condition and his own, as able to accept and admit it, live with and even enjoy it and thus, in a manner of speaking, transcend it. In the closing lines of the *Essais* he uncharacteristically allows the possibility of absolute perfection, and a measure of divinity, if man rightfully enjoys his being: "C'est une absolue perfection, et comme divine, de sçavoyr jouyr loiallement de son estre" (III, 13, 1115). The recognition and acceptance of

his nature is the necessary prerequisite, as the lines quoted from
Amyot's Plutarch indicate:

> D'autant es tu Dieu comme
> Tu te recognois homme.

Montaigne's attitudes involve both participation and differen-
tiation. He resembles other men, and the essays other books,
because they participate in *la sottise* and *la vanité* which, after all,
is man's lot: "C'est un objet plein de mescontentement; nous n'y
voyons que misere et vanité" (III, 9, 1000). From a didactic point
of view, he makes this his primary lesson—as we saw in our discussion of the *Apologie*—for recognition and confession are the first
steps in what we might call Montaignian redemption—that is, the
movement back to the self, toward that "absolue perfection"
which is virtual divinity. At the same time the essayist places
himself and his book apart, as different from and, one cannot help
feeling, superior to the efforts and achievements of others. In the
opening lines of *De l'affection des peres aux enfans* (II, 8), where
Montaigne denigrates the *Essais* as "cette sotte entreprise" (385)
and acknowledges it as a wild, fantastic venture, these very
qualities serve to set it off, to guarantee its originality:

> Madame [d'Estissac], si l'estrangeté ne me sauve, et la nouvelleté,
> qui ont accoustumé de donner pris aux choses, je ne sors jamais à
> mon honneur de cette sotte entreprise; mais elle est si fantastique
> et a un visage si esloigné de l'usage commun que cela luy pourra
> donner passage. . . . Me trouvant entierement despourveu et vuide
> de toute autre matiere, je me suis presenté moy-mesmes à moy,
> pour argument et pour subject. C'est le seul livre au monde de son
> espece, d'un dessein farouche et extravagant. Il n'y a rien aussi en
> cette besoingne digne d'estre remerqué que cette bizarrerie: car à un
> subject si vain et si vile le meilleur ouvrier du monde n'eust sçeu
> donner façon qui merite qu'on en face conte. [385]

By sheer weight alone, these disparaging remarks exceed the essayist's usual modest posture. The words affirm his humility and
ignorance and go beyond, through exaggeration, to underscore
and highlight difference. If it were a *relatively* unusual work, or a

simply mediocre one, or if the raw material had been redeemable, the *Essais* would have fallen in the same category as most other books, would have been, as Montaigne says of Diomedes' volumes on grammar, "tant de paroles pour les paroles seules" (III, 9, 946). As it stands, this book is so strange and eccentric, so bizarre, that it is not only remote from common usage, it is the only one of its kind in the world. That the writer has taken himself as his argument and subject makes the work unique, worthy not of blame or of neglect but of note, and of praise. Hyperbole functions rhetorically to make the words mean more than they say.

Montaigne insists that his book stands alone as having broken new ground, and we understand that its singularity and its value derive from the very "stupidity" of the idea of speaking of oneself, the very "ordinary" nature of the subject. In *Du démentir* he distinguishes the *Essais* from *all* other books in precisely these terms: this is a work "d'une occupation propre, membre de ma vie; non d'une occupation et fin tierce et estrangere comme tous autres livres" (II, 18, 665). Contrasting dramatically with his previous remarks, there is nothing critical or tentative in Montaigne's view of the *Essais* here. In a tone clear and firm he underlines its evident superiority, referring condescendingly to the third-hand, extraneous purpose of every other work. This, in spite of the essay's emphasis on humility, which it elaborates and extends from the preceding *De la praesumption*. Throughout, we will see the essayist's self-denigrating remarks take on a positive value consistent with this affirmation of originality. With quotations from Horace and Perseus he affirms the modesty of his goal and his subject: "Les autres ont pris coeur de parler d'eux pour y avoir trouvé le subject digne et riche; moy, au rebours, pour l'avoir trouvé si sterile et si maigre qu'il n'y peut eschoir soupçon d'ostentation" (664). That he himself has never accomplished great feats, that he is, from all appearances, a man like any other remains a recurrent motif. Montaigne never suggests that his achievements, intellectual or other, justify their presentation; on the contrary, he takes pains, as we have seen, to reassert his nullity, to underline his commonness. But these statements reveal

their other side: they ward off the criticism of self-aggrandize-
ment and enlarge the potential import of the essays. By considering himself to be just another man, Montaigne gives extended
validity and broad applicability to the task undertaken and the
nature of his insights. The more personal his stance, the more
appropriately universal his remarks.

Self-presentation, and its justification, contradicts his admission in the opening lines of the essay that only the great ought to
speak of themselves: "Il méssiet à tout autre de se faire cognoistre,
qu'à celuy qui a dequoy se faire imiter, et duquel la vie et les
opinions peuvent servir de patron" (663). Montaigne escapes the
incongruence by distinguishing between the public and private
purpose of a work, by insisting that the essays' intent is less ambitious, more intimate: "C'est pour le coin d'une librairie, et pour
en amuser un voisin, un parent, un ami, qui aura plaisir à me
racointer et repratiquer en cett' image" (664). He never poses
himself explicitly as model; speaking consistently in the terms
found here of providing some personal memento after his death, he
echoes the words of his preface: "Je l'ay voué [his book] à la com-
modité particuliere de mes parens et amis: à ce que m'ayant perdu
(ce qu'ils ont à faire bien tost) ils y puissent retrouver aucuns traits
de mes conditions et humeurs. . . ." ("Au lecteur," p. 3). This
personal goal, some critics have suggested, characterizes Montaigne's earlier essays, where his idea is that of self-portrayal; they
see the scope broadening into the quest for self-knowledge in the
Third Book and in the later additions to the first two.[2] The
essayist's own late remark that he sometimes writes "non sans
dessein de publique instruction" (665) and, more dramatically,
the familiar affirmation of universality in *Du repentir* appear to
confirm the shift from private to public realm: "On attache aussi
bien toute la philosophie morale à une vie populaire et privée que à
une vie de plus riche estoffe: chaque homme porte la forme entiere
de l'humaine condition" (III, 2, 805). Montaigne outgrows his
modest aims (although protesting his modesty) as he recognizes
the larger implications of his work.

This notion of evolution, of the growth and development of the essayist and his work, or perhaps more precisely of the essayist *through* his work, can be meaningful if it is not oversimplified. We must understand that Montaigne never simply portrays himself and never simply seeks self-knowledge; the two activities coincide in a way that makes the portrait the instrument of the quest and the quest the source of the portrait. Questions of image, of being, of self are raised early and continue through the *Essais,* as we have seen. Similarly, the book is never just individual or private and then general or public, as one exponent of this change paradoxically admits: "Il est à peine besoin d'ajouter . . . que la pratique des Essais avait en 1580 dépassé la théorie exposée dans l'avis *Au lecteur* et dans le présent essai [*Du démentir*], et que déjà Montaigne étudiait l'homme en général."[3] And at the end of the essays, in the Third Book, for example, where Montaigne speaks in the universal terms quoted from *Du repentir,* we might consider his purpose as most profoundly personal, for here he seeks through writing to externalize himself, to find and found his existence. The difficulty with the private-public movement is that it derives for the most part from what the essayist himself says of his intentions, and leads easily to an interpretive fallacy. The writer in the *Essais* is a literary figure, as we have emphasized; what he says he is doing and what he does are not necessarily identical. We have seen him taking stances dictated by the specific context of a given essay and, in terms of the question we are addressing, we have seen how modesty and humility become thematic imperatives to which he must respond. In *Du démentir* Montaigne's manner is unassuming, his comments on himself as the subject of his book belittling. Yet the overall framework created through the *Essais,* the ideas and actions esteemed and praised, clearly set his book apart. Montaigne never explicitly says his book is better than all others, only that it is different. But he does not have to.

In *De l'exercitation* Montaigne affirms the originality of his enterprise and justifies his self-presentation: "Nous n'avons nouvelles que de deux ou trois anciens qui ayent battu ce chemin; et si ne pouvons dire si c'est du tout en pareille maniere à cette-cy, n'en connoissant que les noms. Nul depuis ne s'est jetté sur leur trace"

(II, 6, 377). The novelty is not that he presumes to speak about himself—although his argument anticipates or responds to criticism on this account—but that he dares to speak only about himself. Saints, philosophers, and theologians present their own experience, and Montaigne finds fault with Tacitus in *De l'art de conferer* for his reluctance to do so, "car le n'oser parler rondement de soy a quelque faute de coeur" (III, 8, 942). The towering Socrates provides the precedent, the archetypal rationale for the endeavor: "Dequoy traitte Socrates plus largement que de soy? A quoy achemine il plus souvent les propos de ses disciples, qu'à parler d'eux, non pas de la leçon de leur livre, mais de l'estre et branle de leur ame?" (378). The humble acceptance of man's nature demands expression: "Par ce que Socrates avoit seul mordu à certes au precepte de son Dieu, de se connoistre, et par cette estude estoit arrivé à se mespriser, il fut estimé seul digne du surnom de Sage. Qui se connoistra ainsi, qu'il se donne hardiment à connoistre par sa bouche" (380). Montaigne desires that the *Essais* be seen as a unique book, the only one extant, the only effort of its kind since antiquity.

The same position resounds clearly in *Du repentir* (III, 2) where, from the opening lines, he differentiates himself from "les autres [qui] forment l'homme" as one who "le recite et en represente un particulier" (804). The philosophical truth of each individual's relationship to the human estate in general guarantees that both the procedure and the findings have universal validity. Once more Montaigne proposes himself as the first to do what he is doing: "Les autheurs se communiquent au peuple par quelque marque particuliere et estrangere; moy le premier par mon estre universel, comme Michel de Montaigne, non comme grammairien ou poëte ou jurisconsulte" (805). He sets himself apart from *les autheurs,* as if to suggest that he is not an author in the traditionally accepted sense, that his book is not like any other.

The same assurance of singularity characterizes his responses to the rhetorical questions he asks himself, as if looking to the objections of his reader-interlocutor: Is it reasonable to offer the crude product of nature to a world accustomed to art? Is it reasonable to construct a book without knowledge and art ? His answers ring positive and absolute: "jamais homme ne traicta subject qu'il entendit ne cogneust mieux que je fay celuy que j'ay entrepris, et qu'en celuy-là je suis le plus sçavant homme qui vive; secondement, que jamais aucun ne penetra en sa matiere plus avant, ny en esplucha plus particulierement les membres et suites; et n'arriva plus exactement et plainement à la fin qu'il s'estoit proposé à sa besoingne" (805). The extended negation denies all but Montaigne, setting him apart, and above. As if to temper his words somewhat, he adds that this achievement depends on nothing more than the fidelity he brings to it; but that too is extreme, expressed in the superlative: "la plus sincere et pure qui se trouve."

Montaigne softens his confident assertions of uniqueness with familiar avowals that his work is entirely without *science* and *art,* that his memory is faulty, that he might have profited from knowledge if he had had any, that after all, he speaks only as a man, "enquerant et ignorant" (806). He has, of course, prepared the way for working around the apparent contradictions, not by resolving them but by dulling their edges. He claims to know his subject better than any other writer for he is the first to write exclusively about himself. He asserts as well that philosophical knowledge or culture (*science*) is not necessary to understand so intimate a subject as the self, and from that point of view he can justifiably allege ignorance. If *art* means artificial, he avoids it purposely, whatever the social custom. But whether claiming accomplishment or acknowledging the difficulty of his task ("Il n'est description pareille en difficulté à la description de soy-mesmes" [II, 6, 378]), Montaigne affirms that he has taken the proper road. Acknowledging the nature of man, and his own as he seeks to speak of himself faithfully and as completely as possible, the essayist can pretend success without betraying his recognition of limitation or his humble stance. Compared to those others yearning for things cosmic, agitated by a curiosity and pride he considers overweening, Montaigne depicts his concern with as lowly a creature as man as modest indeed. While the philosophers seek transcendence—in *De la praesumption* he imagines them perched on the epicycle of Mercury (II, 17, 634)—he pictures himself operating at ground level ("Moy qui ne manie que terre à terre" [III, 13, 1106]), both in terms of his subject matter and his aspirations. And from this self-conscious abasement, from this knowledge of what he considers the real nature of things he draws a special sense of personal worth: "Je me tiens de la commune sorte, sauf en ce que je m'en tiens: coulpable des defectuositez plus basses et populaires, mais non desadvouées, non excusées; et ne me prise seulement que de ce que je sçay mon prix" (II, 17, 635).

Historically, of course, it is reasonable to attribute Montaigne's humility to custom—following a classical tradition—whereby writers wishing to hide their intentions, or avoid the charge of professionalism, issued modest disclaimers.[4] One could regard it as the expression of Montaigne's own uneasiness about venturing into print, a feeling progressively though never completely replaced by confidence and self-assertion. But once again we have left the *Essais* for an extrinsic explanation when theme and structure within provide meaning. In terms drawn from Socrates—whose presence looms ever larger across the three books—and reminiscent of religious conversion—whose centrality we have examined—Montaigne through the *Essais* inverts accepted values to impose a new order: what the world esteems is debased, and what it vilifies is redeemed. Passed over as unworthy, Man becomes the sole valid object of attention, knowledge of this lowly creature the highest pursuit. The recognition of ignorance becomes wisdom as paradox abounds in the juxtaposition and interplay of two contrasting orders. Modesty and singularity come together at the heart of the book of the self.

II

Montaigne's effort to differentiate his book from all others aims at that vast body of writing whose questionable worth he underscores so forceably in the opening pages of *De la vanité* and of *De l'experience*. He does not belittle those valuable books he cites in *Des livres*—for example, the poetry of Homer and Virgil, certain dialogues of Plato, sections of Seneca, the revered Plutarch— although he readily criticizes aspects he considers weak or objectionable. Nor does he seek to minimize what he has gained from the scores of other books he has read: pleasure and diversion or the exercise of his mind as he explains in *De trois commerces* (III, 3, 829). But among the countless written pages and the endless words, the worthwhile books are as a handful and Montaigne envisions loose and stammering tongues smothering the world. He takes to task books that are words for the sake of words (III, 9, 946), those where eloquence outweighs content (I, 40, 252), books about other books (III, 13, 1069), and fiction in the guise of truth (the "poësie sophistiquée" of the philosophers [II, 12, 537]). When he speaks of his own writing, he contends that it is more than mere words or impressive style, that it is legitimately self-referential and, above all, that what it presents is real. As Montaigne insists on the novelty, and necessity, of making himself his subject, he affirms that author and book coincide to express truth: "Icy, nous allons conformément et tout d'un trein, mon livre et moy. Ailleurs, on peut recommander et accuser l'ouvrage à part de l'ouvrier; icy, non: qui touche l'un, touche l'autre" (III, 2, 806). The well-known "livre consubstantiel à son autheur" (II, 17, 665) is perhaps the richest expression of the book's authenticity, for it implies a physical union transcending mere resemblance. In *De l'exercitation* (II, 6), in lines quoted earlier, Montaigne uses anatomical vocabulary to describe the *Essais* where, he says, he exposes himself entire: he speaks of it as a *skeletos* whose veins, muscles, and tendons are clearly apparent. In spite of the death-evoking *skeletos* (from the Greek, withered, dry), whose use jars ironically with Montaigne's emphasis on the living, or lifelike presentation, the image functions to imply corporality: "Ce ne sont pas mes gestes que j'escris, c'est moy, c'est mon essence" (379). The book is not merely words nor, the essayist maintains, is it merely a book. Repeatedly he insists that his own efforts could not be further from writing as it generally goes, as he says in *De la ressemblance des enfans aux peres,* "Je suis moins faiseur de livres que de nulle autre besoigne" (II, 37, 784). The attempt to distinguish himself from other writers echoes again as a prime concern.

Montaigne is keenly aware of the paradox of a writer claiming, in fact, not to be a writer, of a literary self-portraitist (or seeker) arguing that whatever he is he wants to be elsewhere than on paper. His insistence on the novelty of his approach, on his unique penetration into the matter, on the identicality of author and subject, sets him apart as a writer of special note. But writer he remains, subject to the criticisms leveled at all practitioners of the literary mode, victims all of the familiar connotations of working in the airy medium of words. Montaigne seeks to overcome these connotations by persuading his reader that, in the final analysis, he has *made* something rather than *written* it, that like the artisan— the nature of whose efforts can be physically confirmed—he has fashioned a tangible work whose existence is readily verifiable. Troubled by the traditional divergence between thought and expression, action and word, author and text, which undermines the validity of his portrait and the efficacy of his quest for self-knowledge, the essayist argues that here *escrire* is *faire,* saying both making and doing. The common disparity between appearance and reality, reflected in linguistic terms as the opposition of what a man alleges and what he is, must be reduced if the work is to fulfill its multiple purpose. Montaigne argues for the concrete "thing-ness" of the *Essais,* as if to remove it from the abstract intellectual realm to that of sense experience, where its relationship to its model, or what it purports to represent, can more readily be determined. Unlike other books composed of language that floats free from reality and, in effect as fictions, lie, this book speaks true; it is, its author implies, not words but substance.

Montaigne's distinction between *escrire* or *dire* and *faire* comprises a recurrent theme in the *Essais* and, although shaped in various ways, the opposition is constant, whether considering the action (*dire, écrire: faire*), the elements (*paroles: choses, faits, gestes*), or the medium (*langage: matière*). In *Du pedantisme* he is concerned that his ideal student learn early to differentiate between language and deed, that education deal with life, not with words. With characteristic hyperbole Montaigne condemns the tendency of book learning to become pedantry by praising the practice of virtue and martial valor at the expense of *science* and the *arts*. Echoing his own activity in terms that he later uses to describe it, the essayist extols doing over saying or hearing: certain of the ancients sought to put their children "au propre des effects, et les instruire, non par ouïr dire, mais par l'essay de l'action, en les formant et moulant vifvement, non seulement de preceptes et parolles, mais principalement d'exemples et d'oeuvres, afin que ce ne fut pas une science en leur ame, mais sa complexion et habitude" (I, 25, 142). Learning is best carried out by doing, by testing; it is a shaping of the individual, the acquisition of knowledge through experience. Here doing is seen as making, as action fashions judgment and character, as it molds and gives substance to being. The analogy with the essayist is unmistakable, with his emphasis on *s'instruire* and *amender,* on *essayer* as his means, and on the action of *mouler* and *former* the self that take place through his writing. But the comparison is implicit, the parallel unarticulated; the implications of the opposition between the realm of language and that of making and doing emerge progressively through the work to shed light on his own effort. Montaigne makes his point by playing Athens against Lacedaemon, the city where children learned to speak (*dire*) well, against the one where they learned to do (*faire*) well, where they busied themselves with words (*parolles*) as opposed to things (*choses*), where they continually exercised the tongue ("une exercitation de la langue") instead of the soul, as in Lacedaemon ("une continuelle exercitation de l'ame" [143]).

This basic antithesis informs the second of Montaigne's essays on education (*De l'institution des enfans,* I, 26), sustaining the parallel between educating and essaying, between shaping the student and writing. The opening lines, where he considers his book as a child and, however defective, claims it as his own, confirm the analogy and prelude a general interweaving of the two themes that dominate his comments on language. We find the same accent on doing rather than saying lessons ("Il ne dira pas tant sa leçon, comme il la fera" [168]), on real and natural exercises rather than written ones ("que ne choisissez vous aussi les exercitations naturelles, vrayes et non escrites" [168]). Montaigne objects to the educational program that stresses logic and dialectic whose practice he imagines fostering the separation of words from things and actions. The concentration on verbal structure alone, on eloquence as an end in itself, destroys the delicate equilibrium between form and content on which truth depends: "L'éloquence faict injure aux choses, qui nous destourne à soy" (172).

To counteract this tendency, Montaigne subordinates words to things as he examines the process of writing and speaking. Taking the literary arts and rhetoric as obvious conjunctions of thought and expression, he distinguishes between the concept as it is formed in the mind and its exteriorization or articulation. What matters in a poem, for example, is the caliber of the invention as idea, the quality of *esprit* and *jugement* manifest in it. The mental process (the act of reasoning or conception) and its product (the idea) stand independent of any compositional, or we might even say verbal, considerations, and superior to them. Using a quotation from Horace, Montaigne suggests that even in removing from poetry those characteristics thought of as properly formal— rhyme, measure, versification, and perhaps the figures and tropes as well—and in transposing the order of things the good poet will not belie himself, "les pieces mesmes en seront belles" (170). The argument or truth of the work seems not only to precede but transcend its expression as well: to one who chided him for not having written a comedy he had promised, Menander responded that it was composed and ready, that only the verses had to be added. And Montaigne adds, "Ayant les choses et la matiere disposée en l'ame, il mettoit en peu de compte le demeurant" (171).

Whatever the exact nature of the literary process, or of verbalization—and we are not provided enough detail to complete the picture—the accent Montaigne seeks to place resounds forcefully. Reminiscent of Ramus' separation of dialectic and rhetoric, of the art of reasoning well from that of speaking well, of the matter of composition from its outer form, the essayist suggests that ideas are not contingent on verbal representation, that what he calls *choses* and *matiere* exist independent of words, that, indeed, in the dialectic of expression words are selected afterward as the means to exteriorize them. According to a quote from Quintillian, stupid men reverse the proper order and seek to fit irrelevant things to their words. By analogy with the things and matter of the world, Montaigne's reference to what is formed in the mind as *choses* and *matiere* underscores its materiality, its concreteness, which contrasts dramatically with the airiness of language. Ideas are real and must dominate; "c'est aux paroles à servir et à suyvre" (171).

Paradox apparently abounds in this devaluation of outer form, in this emphasis on content, in Montaigne's sense of the reality of ideas. Repeatedly we have heard him insist that it is the manner not the matter which counts, that he reads not for *science* or *subject* but *façon* (III, 8, 928). Throughout, he evidences distrust of reason alone as a means of truth, and his frequent deprecation of *discours* as reason or reasoning seems to condemn both concepts and their expression, for in contemporary usage it could also mean language or conversation. The ideas of the philosophers are held to have distorted the true face of nature and caused man to misjudge himself and his world so fundamentally. And, finally, is it not the union of expression and content rather than their separation which ultimately determines proper style? In spite of Horace's contention about rearranging the parts, form does affect meaning.

For a number of familiar reasons Montaigne sought to exploit contradiction rather than resolve it.[5] Paradox serves to represent the meanderings of his mind, the changing attitudes and opinions that mark his passage in time; it serves as well to portray man's enigmatic nature and the complexities of life as he saw them. For esthetic pleasure and didactic impact, the paradox functions to surprise, to stimulate thought, to involve the reader actively with the text. At the same time, apparent contradictions—like the ones we have noticed—arise inadvertently from

the nature of the *Essais* and what they seek to portray, from the
fact that Montaigne looks away from a highly structured,
systematic presentation. For polemical purposes he stresses the
matter of thought to redress the formal bias, inveighing against
inappropriate speech that distorts things both in the mind and in
the world. Montaigne stresses the reality of things, in terms that
recall Ramus', their reality as they are thought in the mind. He
suggests as well that fitting words can approximate them through
speech and writing. Form is not neglected; rather, it is respected
for its proper function, for truth of expression depends on it.
Affected eloquence and pedantic manner make language an end
in itself and subordinate the real to the ephemeral. Montaigne
proposes the speech of the marketplace, the expressivity of the
soldier, to communicate a simplicity and vitality more closely
related to doing than saying, deriving not from abstract play
with words but from the concrete experience of life. Language
must be tied intimately to living, he says, just as the true mirror
of our discourse is the course of our lives.

Right reasoning is essential, for after all it is his judgment that
Montaigne essays, but in that process conception and expression
cannot be divorced. However great his emphasis on the value of
the matter alone, in the marriage of the two he as writer, interlocutor, or discussant will find his measure. At other moments,
as we have seen, he warily avoids judging the idea since he finds
it difficult to determine its true source, and he makes manner the
key to understanding. In the final analysis, the attention given to
form or manner seems to include the quality of thought as well;
the union seems indeed to be contained in the notion of *invention* as we have understood it, as the embodiment of thought in
words. Reasoning alone or eloquence alone is faulty because
partial, but Montaigne will not hesitate to stress the one or the
other for polemical reasons to correct an imbalance. Ultimately
the caliber of the man will be manifest in the quality of the
invention—in all the richness of its meaning—and the degree to
which it is his own.

That writing must communicate substance, that the value of words depends most profoundly on the reality they serve to transmit, colors Montaigne's consideration of Cicero, who in the early essays stands for disembodied eloquence. Accusing the rhetorician of attempting to gain glory by mere babble and talk, the essayist contrasts him with Xenophon and Caesar, whose deeds inform their writing: "Si les gestes de Xenophon et de Caesar n'eussent de bien loing surpassé leur eloquence, je ne croy pas qu'il les eussent jamais escris. Ils ont cherché à recommander non leur dire, mais leur faire" (I, 40, 249). Expression is clearly subordinate to performance, to valor and the practice of virtue that it merely represents. But ideas as well as action can have substance, as we have seen. Montaigne distinguishes Cicero from Epicurus and Seneca, philosophers, men of letters—literally, in this case, since each claims immortality through letter writing— but writers whose wisdom lends a literal weight to the text: "ne sont ce pas lettres vuides et descharnées, qui ne se soutiennent que par un delicat chois de mots, entassez et rangez à une juste cadence, ains farcies et pleines de beaux discours de sapience, par lesquelles on se rend non plus eloquent, mais plus sage, et qui nous apprennent non à bien dire, mais à bien faire" (252). Here reason and language come together in *discours* to communicate a wisdom whose truth Montaigne considers real and which he expresses as tangible, material. As opposed to empty letters, lacking solidity, he imagines words stuffed with meaning, as he often suggests, fleshed out. And throughout the *Essais,* words of substance—whether translating action in the world or ideas in the mind—provoke substantial response; Epicurus and Seneca teach us to *do* rather than merely *speak* well. Montaigne will insist in his own case that sense supersedes style and, again claiming singularity, that no writer as far as he knows has offered as much to take hold of or has sown his material more substantially (*materielle*) or more thickly (*drue*) on his paper. As if he were not merely saying something but making something, not merely writing but doing.

Montaigne's view of anger as a passion which carries men off, causing them to lose control of both words and deeds, evokes in his mind the disparity between what a man says and what he does. He sets the principle—"Le dire est autre chose que le faire" (II, 31, 715)—in the context of religion to explain how a wicked man can preach truth and concludes that the union of *dire* and *faire* enhances the worth of language: "C'est sans doute une belle harmonie quand le faire et le dire vont ensemble, et je ne veux pas nier que le dire, lors que les actions suyvent, ne soit de plus d'authorité et efficace" (716). Interestingly, from our point of view, he then casts the opposition in a literary framework to contrast the man who says what he thinks, who articulates personal conviction, and the one who argues a position rhetoric- ally. As in the case of Caesar, where experience informed what he said, Montaigne envisions a belief sustained with heart—like a valid idea in the mind—as something solid lending substance to the words that express it. Again, his target is Cicero, his model Seneca: "Celuy là traine languissant, . . . il ne vous donne point de coeur, car luy-mesmes n'en a point; l'autre vous anime et enflamme." Juxtaposing the experience of war and that of a deeply held feeling, Montaigne confers physical reality on the intellectual or affective life. And he carries this sense of concrete experience one step farther to include the listener or reader, excited and aroused as if brought to life (*animer*), like the very language itself: "les escrits mesmes vous sonnent."

The idea of substantial reaction forms an important part of Montaigne's distinction between philosophy and nature in *De l'experience* (III, 13). Against the false, complex, and fragmented knowledge of the philosophers, he poses the uniform simplicity of truth, the wisdom of nature, "prudence, non tant ingenieuse, robuste et pompeuse comme celle de leur invention, mais à l'advenant facile et salutaire, et qui faict tresbien ce que l'autre dict" (1073). In addition to the sense of discovery or conception that we have underlined, invention here betrays a derogatory tone suggesting something thought up, ingeniously fabricated, a fiction. Its existence is thus purely verbal and, like the empty words of the rhetorician, it cannot do anything substantial. True wisdom, on the other hand, which has its origin in nature, does what the other can only talk about. Because it has substance it is an energizing force, a source of doing and making, a guide to action.

What we see throughout, then, is Montaigne's attempt to establish the superiority of *faire* over *dire* or *escrire,* to elevate making or doing something—in the mind or in the world—over merely speaking about it. Ideas and actions come together to share a common substantiality: mental processes involve the formulation of things through conception or perception, resembling in their materiality both the objects and the actions of existential life. As Montaigne explains in *Sur des vers de Virgile,* when it comes to writing, the object's vivid and, by extension, live imprint in the mind demands words to exteriorize it, as potential form actualized by the reality of the conception: "Cette peinture [the writing] est conduitte non tant par dexterité de la main comme pour avoir l'object plus vifvement empreint en l'ame" (III, 5, 873). The activity of the mind, of judgment in particular, thus passes into a shape that is itself tangible, visible—that is, accessible.

That the reader accept this framework is essential to the validity of Montaigne's entire project. He argues that he is not merely writing but both doing and making something of substance. Based on that transfer of materiality he sets out, he claims that his book actually contains him, that he is, in the deepest sense, in the expression of his thought. The essays are the record of his *fantasies* (III, 9, 946), the picture of his *cogitations* (II, 6, 379), which in *De l'exercitation* correspond to what he calls *moy, mon essence.* This framework confirms the pertinence of the idea that the *Essais* are a self-portrait; it provides solid grounds for the assertion that they are a serious response to the Delphic injunction. Ontologically, the act of writing, and the book itself, become legitimate sources for the founding of Montaigne's sense

of being. And finally, as we have seen, no one can reproach him
for writing just another book, for wasting his time with words,
for not "doing" anything.[6]

III

Montaigne's insistence on *faire* to describe his writing does not,
in his scheme of things, render all doing equal. In *De l'exercitation* he firmly distinguishes the thought that he calls "himself,"
which he is attempting to set down, from action in the world. As
terms in the familiar Montaignian opposition between inside and
outside, the mental becomes the true indicator of particularity,
superior to exterior physical deed or accomplishment that is
dependent on the vicissitudes of fortune: "A l'adventure, en-
tendent ils que je tesmoigne de moy par ouvrages et effects, non
nuement par des paroles. . . . Les effects diroyent plus de la
Fortune que de moy. Ils temoignent leur roole, non pas le mien"
(II, 6, 379). Montaigne responds to the anticipated reproach of
others for whom action, visible and concrete, bears witness to
character by insisting that it is himself, not his deeds, that he
writes down.

The same antithesis appears in *De la vanité* where thematic
considerations demand that action again be devalued. Here,
where the words of Ecclesiastes find their response in those of the
Delphic oracle, where vanity acknowledged is vanity diminished
to some degree, modesty and humility recognize individual
action as unworthy of description. Not that thought is inherently
more representative than action, but Montaigne's action just does
not bear repeating: "Je ne puis tenir registre de ma vie par mes
actions: fortune les met trop bas; je le tiens par mes fantasies"
(III, 9, 946). Again fortune plays a role, albeit a different one, in
the qualitative distinction between thought and deeds. We must
add, of course, that *De la vanité* does not permit an exalted view
of thought either, as Montaigne indicates by his comparison with
the man who kept track of himself by studying his chamberpots.

Thought does, however, appear more intimate, more closely related to the inner man; action fulfills a subordinate function, as so much food for thought.

Montaigne turns the question over to view it from still another angle in *De la praesumption,* following his customary practice of refracting subjects through different thematic lenses. In this discussion, where modesty is particularly valued, the differential between action and thought is not qualitative (as in *De l'exercitation*) but, as a variation on the presentation in *De la vanité,* becomes a function of social position. Rather than trivialize all human activity, Montaigne pictures certain kinds of lives validating certain kinds of action. Great figures who exist on the public stage, for example, can bear witness to what they are by what they do. Montaigne does not insist that their deeds are inherently more significant than other people's. The thrust seems instead to be that acting before others, whose recognition provides or affirms a sense of being, allows an impression that stands to their person as an effective sign. Private persons, on the other hand, whose unobtrusive lives pass unnoticed, whose existences are therefore not immediately and continually sustained by the acknowledgment of others, require a medium different from action alone to determine who (or what) they are—"quels ils sont" (II, 17, 632). Montaigne uses this argument to justify self-presentation, to suggest that what looks like a presumptuous activity stems in reality from his ordinariness, that he only follows the example of Lucilius:

> Ille velut fidis arcana sodalibus olim
> Credebat libris.
>
> [Horace, *Sat.,* II, 1, 30]
> [He would confide, as unto trusted friends,
> his secrets to his notebooks.]

Inserted here out of context, Horace's literal reference to Lucilius—the father of satire—to explain his own need to practice that art becomes richly suggestive of Montaigne's own situation. For him, too, the notebooks are like friends, surrogates for the true friend lost, where he lays out his life, as he says of

Lucilius, as on a votive tablet. At the same time his presentation implies a parallel between the great figure acting and the private man writing, one that allows the essayist to compensate for the absence of an immediate audience. Writing provides a record, a means of communicating action retrospectively to the reader as onlooker, of rendering the personal public. But interestingly, the book itself becomes an "other," the very process of recording a public performance; to write in the book is to act *as if* before a friend. Although solitary, the essayist will pretend that he is not alone when he writes.

To make oneself known, or to come to know oneself, demands, then, that action be re-presented, revived through a second action, which is thought. The richness of *essayer* brings together thinking, writing, testing to make the work the central act itself. Again, in terms of the distinction between the public and private man, Montaigne implies that while action alone suffices to depict the socially prominent accurately, the common man relies on both deeds and thoughts: "Celuy là [Lucilius] commettoit à son papier ses actions et ses pensées, et s'y peignoit tel qu'il se sentoit estre" (632). But it is particularly important to establish that writing as thinking is acting in the most profound sense, and that while this acting shares the concreteness of action in the world it exceeds it qualitatively. In the essays Montaigne will present what he has done, but what he is doing stands out as his most significant and representative action.

As a footnote to this discussion we should add a word of caution about considering thought as representative. Montaigne clearly seeks to identify thinking-writing as acting and at the same time to move it away from saying, on the one hand, and doing in the outside world, on the other. The reader is asked to accept the notion that the book is more than mere words and more than fortuitous activity, that it is both substantial and deliberate. Yet Montaigne does not play down the degree to which the book is inevitably affected by the nature of language, or the intricacy of thought and the problems of deciphering its expression, nor does he belittle the role fortune and outside influences in general play in his thinking. The activity of writing, with its difficulties, itself becomes food for thought, a subject for consideration, so that the complexities of the enterprise are constantly before the essayist, and the reader as well. If thought is more representative than public deed, it is not unequivocally so, nor is it simply so. The tension between what Montaigne seeks to express and the resistance of the medium, between his desire to record thinking and thought's fluidity and impenetrability, between the effort to delineate himself and fortune's constant interference, all of this provides the drama that unfolds in the *Essais*. In the end, the depiction of that drama becomes the picture of the man.

PART III
THE BOOK OF THE SELF

7

The Life of the Mind

"La jouyssance et la possession
appartiennent principalement à
l'imagination" (III, 9, 975)

I

The opening pages of the *Apologie,* where Montaigne deals most explicitly with the *Theologia naturalis,* echo with the theme of *deus artifex,* the cornerstone of Sebond's argument of divine accessibility. In terms drawn from the *Theologia* which reach back through the God-maker metaphors of the Old Testament to their source in the demiurge-artisan of the *Timaeus,* the essayist describes the divine workman, the architect of creation, to point to the indelible mark stamped on his handiwork: "Aussi n'est-il pas croyable que toute cette machine n'ait quelques marques empreintes de la main de ce grand architecte, et qu'il n'y ait quelque image és choses du monde, raportant aucunement à l'ouvrier qui les a basties et formées" (II, 12, 446). The invisible things of God appear in the creation, through this act of exteriorization, through the materialization of the immaterial; the divine mind renders itself accessible to man—that is, substantial: "ce monde est un temple tressainct, dedans lequel l'homme est introduict pour y contempler des statues, non ouvrées de mortelle main, mais celles que la divine pensée a faict sensibles: le Soleil, les estoilles, les eaux et la terre, pour nous representer les intelligibles" (447). The presence of God and the imprint of his nature reside in the cosmos, discernible to all who truly seek Him; lack of faith, or grace, or man's imbecility alone obscure the evident relationships.

While Montaigne's use of *architecte* and *ouvrier* and the description of God as sculptor reiterate Sebond's basic formula, they curiously avoid his central metaphor of the divine author of Scripture and the book of nature. Only in his choice of *facteur* (447), which was applied to writers as well as other kinds of "makers" and in the comment "il a laissé en ces hauts ouvrages le caractere de sa divinité," where *ouvrage* and *caractere* can be interpreted as "book" and "written sign," does he offer the merest hint of that image. Did Montaigne prefer not to introduce the subject of writing and reading, whose difficulties he stresses throughout, into this context where he insists on the unequivocal relationship of God to his work and on the power of faith to discern it? Or did he desire, out of modesty or fear of blasphemy, to avoid direct comparison between God and himself as author?

Whatever the reason, and however strongly he sought to mute that analogy, it poses and imposes itself dramatically, for the topos of *deus artifex* provides Montaigne with his archetype. In general terms, as we have seen, God is the maker of the universe, the architect and sculptor of creation; the *artificium* was often broadened to painting and music as well. The essayist is also painter (II, 17, 653), artisan (III, 2, 806), and musician (III, 13, 1089) and, as we will see, composer of the book of the self in ways that parallel God's authorship of Scripture and, from a Sebondian point of view, the book of nature. In traditional Christian terms, the comparison is monstrous, inconceivable, the result of that very pride and arrogance which Montaigne so strongly chastises all through the *Essais*. But Renaissance mundanity, exalting man, articulated the analogy between God and the writer, harkening back to the special status the Greeks had reserved for the poet as one who made new things, who gave life to a new world. We find its clear expression in Jules-César Scaliger's *Poetices Libri Septem* (1565): "But the poet makes another nature and other outcomes for men's acts, and finally in the same way makes himself another God as it were."[1]

In the secular context that Montaigne delineates in the *Essais,* where he seeks to find and found being, to form and fashion himself, the role he takes on and the action he sets out ring with distant echoes of divinity. He will not claim it (except in the terms, noted earlier, at the close of *De l'experience*) nor will he speak of creation, but his authorship of the book of the self will recall the Author of the book of nature, the book of the ultimate Self. Montaigne's insistence on writing as making, his view of the book as the concrete externalization of the self, his notion of consubstantiality, of the identicality of sign and referent, evoke God's function as metaphorical writer, his creation of nature as the invisible rendered visible, tangible, intelligible, the unequivocal sign of Himself. The parallel suggests that as God is to be found in His book, so Montaigne resides in his.

The juxtaposition of secular (or literary) and religious finds explicit articulation in Montaigne's characterization of God as *facteur*: "Sebond s'est travaillé à ce digne estude, et nous montre comment il n'est piece du monde qui desmante son facteur" (II, 12, 447). Although the term clearly refers to God as creator of the universe, contemporary practice applied it as well to man as writer, author, expressing perhaps a sense of the etymological roots of poet as maker. The richness of *facteur* allows the reader to evoke God the writer and the author as maker to sustain the claim that *écrire* is *faire,* to lend to the essayist reflections of divinity.

Montaigne's image of the *Essais* as a book consubstantial with its author (parallel perhaps to God's relationship to the book of nature) further intensifies these reflections. We can, as is traditionally done, treat the notion loosely, assuming that here in the realm of literature, the domain of symbol, coessentiality or the sharing of a single substance stands roughly for equivalency, representativeness. As a weighty theological concept, however, consubstantial meant absolute and literal identicality of God the

Father and Christ the Son in their mystical union in the Trinity. Huguet notes only two uses of the term, as a noun in Scève's *Microcosme* to indicate that God "a en son fils, son Christ, son consubstancial," and as an adjective in Montaigne's figurative context. Transposed into the secular framework of the *Essais*, it brought along its precise religious connotations. Evoking the mystery of trinitarian unity, Montaigne implies that he and his book are one, that indeed he is the book and his book is he. The effect transcends the function of literature as ordinary symbol, or at least that of this particular written piece; the words do not merely stand for him as sign—however valid—but rather extend beyond the symbolic to *become* him.

This, of course, is what the essayist means to say, and yet in spite of the claim he is not the actual physical book. We might speak of the strategy or even the fiction that allows the underlying query of the essays, "who (what, where) am I" (we recall La Boétie's death and the loss of *la vraye image*), to be answered by pointing to the book, "This is I." By thus placing the text "outside" of literature, Montaigne most profoundly distinguishes it from other books, as we saw him doing earlier, as he works to overcome the impression of an accidental or "merely symbolic" relationship. And we have already noted his insistence on what we might call verbal materialism, his effort to convince his reader that the very words of the *Essais* have body, are of flesh and blood as he says. In a later chapter we will explore the question of Montaigne's substantial language with its suggestions of incarnation, its echoes of the biblical word made flesh. For the moment, let us look at his strategy of union and at the means he uses to persuade the reader of its reality. We have already examined some of the ways in which he tries to build up *écrire* into *faire*; here let us carry that line of discussion a step further, first to explore another important, related metaphor—the book as child of the mind—and then to dwell a moment on the implications of procreation as a function of the mind. If being is somehow situated in the book, then perhaps the act of writing holds the key to its form, and its disclosure. We will shift our attention from the more familiar Montaignian notion of living in the world to living through writing in the book.

II

Creation and identicality come together in *De l'affection des peres aux enfans* (II, 8), in Montaigne's discussion of a man's acts and deeds—what he has done (*faire*)—as the children of his mind: "à considerer cette simple occasion d'aymer nos enfans pour les avoir engendrez . . . il semble qu'il y ait bien une autre production venant de nous, qui ne soit pas de moindre recommandation: . . . ce que nous engendrons par l'ame, les enfantemens de nostre esprit, de nostre courage et suffisance" (399). While the main thrust of his argument delineates books as offspring, their juxtaposition to the glorious victories of Epaminondas and the statues of Phidias and Pygmalian broadens the productive scope to confer on writing both the tangibility of the figure carved in stone and the verifiability of the exploit that demands assent. Montaigne's comments touch all sides of the author-work-audience relationship to stress the coincidence of writer and book, the substantiality of the writing, and the reality of its effect upon the reader as a "monumen des Muses" (400).

The most striking statement of consubstantiality consists in Montaigne's vision of children as "autres nous mesmes" (399). While this notion found widespread sixteenth-century expression, most memorably perhaps in Gargantua's letter to Pantagruel where he speaks of his son as "mon image visible en ce monde" (*Pantagruel,* chapter 8), the essayist subordinates the more common aspect of procreation as a means to immortality to emphasize the bonds of natural affection. The children of the mind bring out "cette amitié commune des peres envers les enfans" (400), are perhaps worthier of it than their physical counterparts, for they are more noble and, significantly, more

representative: "ce que nous engendrons par l'ame, les enfantemens de nostre esprit . . . sont produicts par une plus noble
partie que la corporelle, et sont plus nostres; . . . de ceux cy
toute la beauté, toute la grace et pris est nostre. Par ainsin, ils
nous representent et nous rapportent bien plus vivement que les
autres" (400). In this uncharacteristic divorce of mind and body,
Montaigne elevates the intellectual to enhance esthetic production and, by extension, his own "child." Earlier we remarked the
absence of the essayist's family, or what might be considered the
negation of family to empty the space around him in order that
his gaze, and the accompanying quest of the self, could return
unencumbered to their primal source. Now, in the other half of
that process which is the forming and fashioning of the self, that
void can be filled with family, but one appropriate to the context.
We are, of course, juxtaposing the real and the metaphoric, the
physical and the linguistic, but this is precisely the fusion (or
confusion) Montaigne must achieve to validate his endeavor.
Here, on a level that he pretends is as real as the physical but
superior to it, the essayist reconstitutes his offspring as a guarantee of consubstantiality: "Et je ne sçay si je n'aimerois pas mieux
beaucoup en avoir produict ung, parfaictement bien formé, de
l'acointance des muses, que de l'acointance de ma femme" (401).
While we can appreciate the paradox of this paper child engendered by the man who wishes to be elsewhere than on paper, we
cannot ignore the metaphoric cornerstone on which the *Essais* are
constructed, what we have called the fundamental fiction of the
work, that of the reality of the book as man.

The notion of another self recalls Montaigne's characterization
of La Boétie in *De l'amitié*: "Le secret que j'ay juré ne deceller à
nul autre, je le puis, sans parjure, communiquer à celuy qui n'est
pas autre: c'est moy" (I, 28, 191). The death of the friend and the
ensuing loss of the sense of self underlie the essayist's effort to
portray himself, to reconstitute and safeguard himself (III, 9,
983). In the genesis of the *Essais* as it emerges from thematic and
structural elements, the need to compensate for absence domi-

nates. Montaigne seeks to replace the friend who was both another and himself or, in the terms we have been using, his own substantial exteriorization. The essays become his surrogate friend, or, perhaps, through the work he becomes his own best friend. The idea of the self as best friend surfaces in at least three different contexts: in *De la solitude* with its accent on self-suffi-ciency ("vous et un compagnon estes assez suffisant theatre l'un à l'autre, ou vous à vous-mesmes" [I, 29, 247]); in *Coustume de l'isle de Cea* where, citing Plato, Montaigne criticizes the suicide as "celuy qui a privé son plus proche et plus amy, sçavoir est soy mesme, de la vie" (II, 3, 353); in *De mesnager sa volonté* where he speaks of "l'amitié que chacun se doibt" (III, 10, 1006). While Montaigne calls nostalgically to La Boétie and articulates an un-answerable plea for someone to take his place, the writing of the *Essais* themselves betrays his understanding that he must pro-vide, and become his own other.

The several notions of the book as surrogate friend, of the self as friend, and of the book as child or other self are complementary expressions of the fundamental relationship between the writer and his work.[2] Each variant depicts the man in duplicate (since the friend or the child is considered another self) and each locates that second self in the book or, as Montaigne himself suggests in the idea of consubstantiality, identifies it *as* the book. If, in the quest for self-knowledge, man must project a self to observe, then here the *Essais* are depicted in metaphorical terms as that reflected image that must come under scrutiny. Montaigne defines the relationship between the two selves as one of simul-taneous identicality and difference: "A cettuy-cy [the child, the *Essais*], tel qu'il est, ce que je donne, je le donne purement et irrevocablement, comme on donne aux enfans corporels: ce peu de bien que je luy ay faict, il n'est plus en ma disposition; il peut sçavoir assez de choses que je ne sçay plus, et tenir de moy ce que je n'ay point retenu et qu'il faudroit que, tout ainsi qu'un estranger, j'empruntasse de luy, si besoin m'en venoit" (II, 8, 401). It is himself "out there," he pretends, and because it is "out there" it is also another; he thus confirms his existence and calls it into question at the same time. Paradoxically, the very means to self-knowledge raises obstacles to it. The self-referential perspective that provides Montaigne with the sense of being becomes the source of the tentativeness of his quest.

In the context of *De l'affection des peres aux enfans* Montaigne chooses to stress coincidence and the implications of generation. The examples of that spiritual "amitié commune des peres envers les enfans" underscore the living reality of these children, their deaths, and the reaction of their authors who chose to perish with them. His account of the dying Lucan reciting his own verses is another aspect of this effort to suggest that the child of the mind is more than a metaphor: "Cela, qu'estoit ce qu'un tendre et paternel congé qu'il prenoit de ses enfans, representant les a-dieux et les estroits embrassemens que nous donnons aux nostres en mourant" (401). When he says that what is engendered by the soul represents a man "bien plus vivement" than physical offspring, we understand that he means more faithfully, and also more lifelike, or perhaps even more alive (recalling his accent on a portrait that is *vif* in the "Au lecteur"). And when he expresses his basic concern as he speaks of his own writing in *Sur des vers de Virgile,* "Ne represente-je pas vivement," his use of *vivement* again suggests a representation both accurate and lively. The story of Pygmalion, with which Montaigne concludes *De l'affection,* exemplifies the extreme degree of affection turning into the incestuous passions that have inflamed parents with love for their children. More importantly, in this context it represents the point of fusion where analogy becomes reality, where the spiritual child—in this case already possessing a physical, "life-like" shape—becomes animated. For the sculptor, as for the authors of writings and of deeds whom Montaigne cites, the product-child was already real, as his frantic love indicates; what the gods allowed was for the love to be requited. And while the *Essais* never quite undergo the dramatic metamorphosis of Galatea, they are meant to be taken as the "coming to life" of Montaigne himself.

III

The notion that *écrire* can become *faire*, that expression can reflect thought and language embody and thus disclose man, derives in large measure from a view that affirms the reality of the life of the mind. Ordinarily, in speaking of Montaigne we emphasize his attachment to the physical world, his reliance on concrete, personal experience as the valid means to knowledge of himself and the world. The essayist confirms this reading repeatedly, reiterating his distrust of abstract reasoning, of the vagaries of the imagination and his commitment to living through things as they take place in the course of time: "Quand je dance, je dance; quand je dors, je dors; voyre et quand je me promeine solitaire-ment en un beau vergier, si mes pensées se sont entretenues des occurences estrangieres quelque partie du temps, quelque autre partie je les rameine à la promenade, au vergier, à la douceur de cette solitude et à moy" (III, 13, 1107). He eschews the powerful pleasures of pure imagination as too freely and independently provoked, and because he is "d'une constitution mixte," both mind (or soul) and body, prefers as natural those that follow "la loy humaine et generale, intellectuellement sensibles, sensible-ment intellectuels." The equilibrium and interdependence of the physical and mental sides of experiential life that Montaigne articulates in the closing pages of the *Essais* serve as a counter-point to the "humeurs transcendentes" (1115) to which man is prone, to the inclination to overrate the power and potential of the mind.

But the effort to redress this imbalance, and particularly to rein in errant imagination, must not obscure the dynamic function of that faculty. Without reviewing its multiple aspects in detail, either in the larger sixteenth-century context or in the *Essais,* we can reiterate the generally suspicious way in which imagination was viewed, both because of its propensity for lies and the made-up and its connection to the untrustworthy bodily senses.[3] Epistemologically, psychologically, and esthetically as well, as we pointed out earlier in our discussion of fiction, it carried a serious pejorative burden. At the same time, in its working relationship to reason and memory, the imagination plays an important positive role. Through its images of the sensual world, and those more abstract ideas it reproduces from memory to present to reason and judgment (which Montaigne so often calls *fantasies* as if to affirm the link between the imagination and the higher intellectual faculties and processes), imagination assists valuably in the functioning of understanding. Just as Montaigne describes reason working on imagination to restrain and dilute its power to terrorize, so he depicts the image-producing faculty in its turn acting positively, providing the mind with less fearful, more palatable pictures, as when it gives death an easy and desirable face (III, 9, 989). In *De la solitude* he suggests that imagination facilitates retirement into the self by calling up models to act as guardians: "presentez vous toujours en l'imagination Caton, Phocion et Aristides. . . . Ils vous contiendront en cette voie de vous contenter de vous mesmes, de n'emprunter rien que de vous . . ." (I, 39, 247). While Montaigne claims that his own sleep is rarely troubled by his imagination ("Je n'ay poinct à me plaindre de mon imagination" [III, 13, 1098]), he imputes to dreams the status of valid symbol: "Et tiens qu'il est vray que les songes sont loyaux interpretes de nos inclinations." And although he confesses to the difficulty of sorting them out and understanding them, although he seems to minimize their value by characterizing his own as "choses fantastiques et . . . chimeres," he does picture the imagination as a positive force, as the mediator between the hidden reality of the subconscious self and the conscious desire to know and understand.

The presentation of valuable, and valid, images to reason and judgment also underlies the individual's ability to appreciate and comprehend other men. The mobile and flexible imagination adopts attitudes and envisages situations that it imposes on the present condition of the self (as when it frightens the healthy man with visions of death, or the landlubber with sea monsters). It expands the range of possibility, changing perspective and the ways of looking at things to permit a deeper sense of that which is "other." The hypothetical shift in vantage point, the imaginary assumption of the other's outlook, creates participation in or vicarious experience of feelings, will, ideas: "Je n'ay point cette erreur commune de juger d'un autre selon que je suis. J'en croy aysément des choses diverses à moy. . . . Et croy, et conçois mille contraires façons de vie. . . . Je descharge tant qu'on veut un autre estre de mes conditions et principes, et le considere simplement en luy-mesme, sans relation, l'estoffant sur son propre modelle. . . . Je m'insinue, par imagination, fort bien en [sa] place" (I, 37, 229). All through the *Essais* we see Montaigne shifting ground in the play of antithesis he so enjoys, considering first one angle, then another. In *De Democritus et Heraclitus* he describes that movement around things that provides multiple perspective: "De cent membres et visages qu'a chaque chose, j'en prens un tantost à lecher seulement, tantost à effleurer; et par fois à pincer jusqu'à l'os" (I, 50, 302). After criticizing the art of medicine in *De la ressemblance des enfans aux peres* he puts himself in the doctors' place to imagine how they *might* have handled things: "si j'eusse esté de leur conseil, j'eusse rendu ma discipline plus sacrée et mysterieuse: ils avoyent assez bien commencé, mais ils n'ont pas achevé de mesme" (II, 37, 769). While the irony and sense of play are unmistakable, the essayist's ability to adopt this other viewpoint on an issue so close to him is striking. The depiction of the prince, ill-advised and deceived by courtiers and flatterers, in *De l'incommodité de la grandeur* (III, 7) is balanced by an appreciation of the courtiers' outlook on the dangers of speaking boldly and honestly. Montaigne acquires a greater feel for the relativity of truth by insinuating himself through imagination into the place of others; by this faculty alone does he seem able to acquire a sense of their nature and being.

What we have called the life of the mind, then, the vicarious experience of things through mental and emotional faculties, can be as powerful and positive a force as actual experience and may surpass it as a means to understanding. The imagination recalls or re-presents things separated in time and space, and this remove appears a fundamental element in the assimilation and comprehension of experience. Psychological and aesthetic distance, of course, sustain and inform self-depiction, as Montaigne notes at the close of *De l'art de conferer* (III, 8, 942) where he claims his ability to speak about himself as about a third party ("chose tierce"), to distinguish himself apart as he does a neighbor or a tree ("comme un voisin, comme un arbre"). And distance can determine his feeling for and grasp of the exterior world, as we see in *De la phisionomie* in his reaction to the religious wars: "Comme je ne ly guere és histoires ces confusions des autres estats que je n'aye regret de ne les avoir peu mieux considerer présent, ainsi faict ma curiosité que je m'aggrée aucunement de veoir de mes yeux ce notable spectacle de nostre mort publique, ses symptomes et sa forme. Et puis que je ne la puis retarder, suis content d'estre destiné à y assister et m'en instruire" (III, 12, 1046). In what we have come to appreciate as a familiar baroque metaphor, Montaigne considers the world as a stage from his vantage point as spectator to history's unfolding drama. The terms in which he describes his sense of compassion, and the Aristotelian-like admixture of pain and pleasure he feels as witness to these "pitoyables evenemens," set him further apart to emphasize both the vicarious nature of his experience and the tendency to bring it all back to his individual point of view, to personalize it in a way that transforms the event as public calamity, and supersedes it. Montaigne appears close enough to be touched by what goes on and at the same time far enough away to view it objectively and to see himself in relation to it. He rejects total absorption, with its myopic blurring, and the loss of his sense of self that accompanies being engulfed by what is exterior to him; and he avoids both total absence or strict separation and farsightedness. To experience something *as if* it were actual, as spectator to drama where one is both within and outside of the action, or in the realm of imagination that overcomes time and space, is to create a distance that renders that experience vicarious and accessible, meaningful. Through the mind and imagination Montaigne moves toward the world, and life.

IV

Montaigne's hold on the past, and his apparent inclination for it, depends on the imagination making that past present and real. What he has read or heard of, or what he saw physically, imagination allows him to revive in his mind and to experience in a deep and personal way. Again, as in the situation of the spectator, he is both there and not there, in contact and removed enough to be self-conscious. Recounting his travels to Rome, Montaigne describes the reality of the ancient heroes who people his mind: "J'ay eu plus en teste les conditions et fortunes de Lucullus, Metellus et Scipion, que je n'ay d'aucuns hommes des nostres. Ils sont trespassez" (III, 9, 996). Recognizing the evocatory power of being where the great men actually talked, walked, and supped, he contemplates their faces, their bearing, and their clothing as if they were before him. Indeed, he says that it would be ingratitude to despise the remains of such worthy and valiant men, "que j'ay veu vivre et mourir" (997). This takes place in his mind's eye, of course, played out in his imagination, but in a way that both negates time and space and acknowledges them.

The living presence of the dead and this past lead Montaigne to speak of his father (in the lines that follow those cited above on p. 996): "Si est bien mon pere, aussi entierement qu'eux, et s'est esloigné de moy et de la vie autant en dixhuict ans que ceux-là ont faict en seize cens; duquel pourtant je ne laisse pas d'embras-. ser et practiquer la memoire, l'amitié et societé, d'une parfaicte union et tres-vive." The difference between recent and distant past is nullified, both because what is gone is gone and, one suspects, because the imagination operates unhindered by degrees of time. Montaigne recognizes physical absence as distance in space and then asserts the mind's ability to overcome it so that past is rendered present and the remote given presence. This does not mean that he seeks to substitute fantasy for the difficult contingencies of existence, that in some disturbed way he cannot accept the passing of time or his father's passing. It does mean that discontinuous and fragmented reality—the flow of time and the change and transformation wrought—gains some measure of continuity, and meaning, when experience is revivified and reworked. Physical death and separation in the world give rise to what Montaigne calls a union that is perfect and very much alive in the mind. The vicarious provides transcendence of the immediate and the discontinuous.

To speak of the past and its reality is to return inevitably to the subject of friendship and La Boétie, to that long-lost perfection discussed earlier. In *De la vanité*, where the theme of absence converges with that of travel, where Montaigne explains how much better he is able to cope with the responsibilities of his household from afar, as if too close or too immediate contact were, in this case, stifling and burdensome, he himself raises the subject. True friendship, in which he claims expertise, reaches a kind of sublimity in separation:

> si l'absence lui est ou plaisante ou utile, elle m'est bien plus douce que sa presence; et ce n'est pas proprement absence, quand il y a moyen de s'entr'advertir. J'ay tiré autrefois usage de nostre esloingnement et commodité. Nous remplissions mieux et estandions la possession de la vie en nous separant: il vivoit, il jouissoit, il voyoit pour moy, et moy pour luy, autant plainement que s'il y eust esté. . . . La separation du lieu rendoit la conjonction de nos volontez plus riche. [III, 9, 977]

Physical distance is overcome, as Montaigne says, when the means of communication avail themselves, but it is more profoundly dealt with in the mind as mental or spiritual conjunction. Because the mind is forced to work harder to evoke the absent friend, intensifying the pleasure of that vicarious presence; because one attempts to live acutely enough for two and thus has a sense of tasting life more fully; because physical presence actually distracts the mind, or allows it to wander off to other things ("son assistance relache vostre attention et donne liberté à vostre pensée de s'absenter à toute heure pour toute occasion" [975]); because of some or all of these things, the enjoyment of friendship accrues in the mind. In fact, Montaigne prefaces his remarks on friendship with a sweeping statement on the role of the imagination: "La jouyssance et la possession appartiennent principalement à l'imagination" (975). To "hold on" to something, then, as we have described Montaigne's "hold" on the past, or on friendship removed in space or in time, is to live it vicariously.

What about the present? What about life as it is lived in the present, where experiential immediacy would seem to preclude the necessity of mediation through the mind? Montaigne's subject, as he describes it in *Du repentir,* is man in time, living its passage from minute to minute. He poses the possession and enjoyment of those very moments as his goal in *De l'experience*: "je passe le temps, quand il est mauvais et incommode; quand il est bon, je ne le veux pas passer, je le retaste, je m'y tiens. . . . Principallement à cette heure que j'apercoy la mienne [life] si briefve en temps, je la veux estendre en pois; je veux arrester la promptitude de sa fuite par la promptitude de ma sesie" (III, 13, 1111). All through the essays Montaigne has taken to task those drawn by an irresistible urge to skip over to the future through imagination, and here he returns to contrast his attitude with that inclination to "couler et eschapper [la vie], de la passer, gauchir et . . . ignorer et fuir." And in spite of his personal preference for antiquity and the occasional refuge he takes there ("Me trouvant inutile à ce siecle, je me rejecte à cet autre" [III, 9, 996]), he does not appear to lose himself in the past.[4]

In this context we should perhaps refer to Montaigne's emphasis on "intellectuellement sensible[s], sensiblement intellectuel[s]," for when he speaks of seizing and enjoying life in the present he intends a process and a product deriving from a clear awareness of the union of body and mind (soul). While a harkening back or a projection forward in time appears essentially a function of mind, living—as Montaigne describes it in the monumental last essay—involves a completeness that is both physical and mental. He rails against the reasoners and philosophers who would subordinate one to the other, or divide them completely: "A quoy faire desmembrons nous en divorce un bastiment tissu d'une si joincte et fraternelle correspondance? Au rebours, renouons le par mutuels offices. Que l'esprit esveille et vivifie la pesanteur du corps, le corps arreste la legereté de l'esprit et la fixe" (1114).

Given this emphasis on immediacy and on the necessary bond between body and mind which appears to elevate the physical at the expense of the intellectual and thus stress the actuality of experience, is it proper to isolate the life of the mind, as we have done thus far? In the very same context in *De la vanité* where the essayist reflects on Rome, his father, and friendship, as he notes his enduring fraternity with Pompey and Brutus, he claims that our hold on the present, like that of the past, is a function of the mind: "Cette accointance dure encore entre nous; les choses presentes mesmes, nous ne les tenons que par la fantasie" (III, 9, 996). What does it mean to say that we hold present things only by imagination? Is it an isolated comment that has little rapport with the main thrust of the *Essais*? Is it another hypothetical posture deriving from the specific framework of the essay where Montaigne tries out a perspective, an idea, and himself?

Among other things, *De la vanité* argues the value of separation and remove, as we have noted. The theme of travel, which dominates, reveals Montaigne coping more effectively with his domestic life when it is foreign to him, just as he safeguards his intellectual or spiritual life from servitude to the world by renewing his distance from it. He recognizes the value of public service but, he says, "pour mon regard je m'en despars" (952). These spatial terms he recasts in a commercial metaphor as his desire to avoid being mortgaged to others (966-68). When he is outside of France and away from the disorders of civil strife he is less disturbed by its plight or the danger to his own property, so that remoteness seems to conserve the mental well-being that close contact with this reality would upset. Traveling takes Montaigne from the narrow world of the province or the country and introduces him to a universe of varying customs and values. Removed from family and from France, he affirms his ties to a larger humanity, "postposant cette lyaison nationale à l'universelle et commune" (973). In the diversity and variety he confronts, Montaigne finds the best school for forming one's life; he comes upon different ideas and ways, and by comparison considers and evaluates his own. He looks at "other" things, "la diversité de tant d'autres vies, fantasies et usances" (973), and from abroad, in the play of continual juxtaposition of the familiar and the new, he can see himself as "other." At a distance from home, and from himself in that context, travel becomes a means to self-knowledge.

Travel is only significant, then, if one voyages in order to return, if separation is followed by reunion, movement outward by movement back. Montaigne may distance himself from the cares and woes of home, or from the social and political scene threatening to absorb him, but even as he moves away he comes back to himself. Physical remove encourages psychological distance, new perspectives on the self, reintegration. Travel must not be flight from the self but toward it, and here, of course, is its connection with the powerful concluding lines of *De la vanité*. Man's gaze, which like the traveler moves spontaneously outward, must also return to look back; the movement that can be the natural, linear escape from the self must be made to curve in a circular sweep to fix upon that self as its proper object. Man in motion, physical and psychological, contemplating where he has been, determining where he is.

Thus the conventional notion of life as a journey gains renewed vitality. Indeed, for Montaigne both life and journey involve literal movement in time and/or space from point to point—however unclear and uncertain the destinations—and both are made up of starts and stops, detours and occasional loss of way: "Mon dessein {travel plan} est divisible par tout: il n'est pas fondé en grandes esperances; chaque journée en faict le bout. Et le voyage de ma vie se conduict de mesme" (978). But more importantly, it seems, both voyage and life can be metaphorical movement toward the self and knowledge of it. Whether understood as that motion which is the return of man's gaze or its effort to follow the wanderings of the mind ("[l']alleure . . . vagabonde . . . de nostre esprit" [II, 6, 378]), Montaigne's journey toward the self takes place in the figurative space of interiority. Here separation can be a measure of flight or it can be turned to advantage to permit focus and determine perspective. In an ideal, Edenic world we would not be speaking of spatial distance; Montaigne would be at one with himself, whole and integral. The outward impulse, the imperative of conversion as the axis of the quest for the lost self, the covering of that interval back to one's own center are elements of alienation, separation, fragmentation, all part of a postlapsarian condition. Spatial distance, like time, comes after the fall. But it seems to bring with it, through the introduction of perspective, the potential for resolution.

                                    V

To speak of space and remove, in this sense, is not to suggest that consciousness detaches itself completely from the world, that it assumes an absolute perspective, one that could be compared to God's. We have seen Montaigne condemn this illusory inclination in modes ranging from the humbling tone of the *Apologie* to the positive, one might almost say spirited, conclusion of *De l'experience.* The mind working in the abstract, intellect operating dryly on its own, strikes him as both erroneous and irresponsible. The self and the essayist's consciousness of it remain always *in* and *of* the world, correlative to it. His emphasis on duality, on mind as well as body, and their union and interaction guarantees that mental operations will be grounded in concrete experience and that actual sensation will be integrated into a higher degree of consciousness. It is not enough to have an experience; as the rich implications of education suggest in *De l'institution des enfans*, it must be absorbed and assimilated if the project of forming and forging the self is to take place. And clearly we are speaking not only in terms of what Montaigne can learn from pain and his encounter with illness—perhaps the most striking of his physical experiences—but of emotional or spiritual experience, as in friendship, and of mental experience as well, as in the case of formal learning and reading. The activities of body and mind and what they undergo provide what Montaigne might call food for thought; they must be laid hold of by the understanding, worked on, apprehended and comprehended. Reason and judgment interpreting experience give it value.

In this sense we understand the nature and importance of what we have called the life of the mind: the transformation of brute experience into knowledge which does not fill the head but forms it. Individual moments must be felt, lived, and this happens only by embedding them in consciousness, when the mind's eye fixes on them, when Montaigne's thoughts come back to settle on the orchard, and on himself in it. He is fundamentally of the world, continually interacting with it, and at the same time has a perspective on it. E. B. McGilvary's description of the perspective realist, describing a way of dealing with the seemingly infinite complexity of the world, and one's experience of it, and with the desire for knowledge and order, provides us with a modern version of the Renaissance posture of *docta ignorantia* and illuminates Montaigne's own outlook:

> The perspective realist makes no claim that he can speak for the universe as it is for *itself*. He does not consider himself as an outsider looking on, a stranger, as it were, from some supernatural realm, passively contemplating a world of nature with whose goings-on he has no active business. On the contrary, he is a natural organism responding to natural stimulations and acquiring thereby such knowledge as nature thereupon puts at his disposal. This knowledge as far as he can integrate it into a system, is his

philosophy. As this knowledge and the integration of it develops,
his philosophy develops. . . . A mature philosophy for him is an
ideal never realized. He sees in part, he knows in part . . . and
that which is perfect never comes, except as a goal that lies afar
off before him.[5]

In Montaigne's case, then, living in its fullest sense demands a
doubling that is most profoundly psychological and aesthetic.
The past—both historical and personal, distant and recent—
reaches its highest level of meaning as it is relived in the mind,
rendered present. Present activity gains greatest import if Montaigne is able to step back from it as a spectator, interiorize it,
and thus experience it vicariously as a function of the mind. As if
life had to be lived twice, on two different but parallel strata, first
outside and then, as becomes more and more evident, inside the
book of the self. The journey that is life demands a third element
for completion, and one which Montaigne himself imposes to
form a triad, the *Essais.*

Montaigne establishes this association in the opening lines of
De la vanité, even before speaking explicitly of travel: "Qui ne voit
que j'ay pris une route par laquelle, sans cesse et sans travail,
j'iray autant qu'il y aura d'ancre et de papier au monde" (945).
And it is reinforced at numerous turns where diversity and
variety, vagabond movement, emerge as common denominators
of all three elements. Students of Montaigne's style have sought
to distinguish in the writing properties that the essayist attributes to his thought, and to his life, and he encourages them
himself: "Je vois au change, indiscrettement et tumultuairement.
Mon stile et mon esprit vont vagabondant de mesmes" (994).[6]
All through the essays, in fact, images of roads taken and
followed, or paths to be eschewed, serve to depict aspects of life
and thought and the experience of reading and writing. *De
l'institution des enfans* is particularly rich in this regard:

> au bout d'un long et ennuyeux chemin, je vins à rencontrer une
> piece haute, riche et eslevée jusques aux nües . . . [I, 26, 147]

Je voudrois . . . que . . . selon la portée de l'ame qu'il a en main,
il [the tutor] commençast à la mettre sur la montre; . . . quelquefois luy ouvrant chemin, quelquefois le luy laissant ouvrir. [150]

Je marche plus seur et plus ferme à mont qu'à val. [150]

This emphasis on motion, of course, derives from Montaigne's
vision of the world, and man in it, from that movement and
change which in *Du repentir* so vividly define the nature of things:
"Le monde n'est qu'une branloire perenne. Toutes choses y
branlent sans cesse" (III, 2, 804). Human life, lived in the flow
of time, appears to be an endless succession of variations and
modifications that Montaigne depicts spatially: "Nostre vie n'est
que mouvement" (III, 13, 1095). As the record of one particular
life, the essays themselves reflect existence as a metaphorical
journey; they accompany the soul in its wanderings through
time.

But, finally, the association between essays as travel and life
goes much deeper, to touch on Montaigne in quest of himself and
on his experience of reality. The *Essais* are more than a logbook of
progress and performance, more than a recording of physical and
intellectual activity. In their most profound sense they *are* Montaigne's experience, not merely the chronicle of it. It is not as if
he lives somewhere else and then writes it down in the pages of
his book, but rather that he lives most profoundly *through* the
book. What he affirms in the lines quoted earlier—"les choses
presentes, nous ne les tenons que par la fantasie"—is that the
nature of consciousness itself places him at a degree distant from
the immediate or direct contact with reality, that apprehension
by its very nature involves separation. And what we understand is
that, in Montaigne's case, what occupies the space between
actuality and apprehension are the *Essais* themselves.

8

On the Face of Things

"C'est une foible garantie que
la mine; toutesfois elle a quelque
consideration" (III, 12, 1059)

The writer's enterprise is fraught with paradox: interiority is difficult to discuss, the meanderings of the mind often barely traceable, as he frankly admits, and the medium itself at times too fluid, at times unwieldy or impenetrable. As he brings together living and writing, Montaigne apposes actual and vicarious experience, distance and immediacy, past and present. But paradox is not resolved in the *Essais,* nor does it appear to demand resolution. Although Montaigne's vision of unity and plenitude in friendship reflects the utopian ideal, his actual quest for the self does not pretend to complete knowledge or absolute selfhood; it knows and admits its limitations and seeks to operate within them. His modest aims allow contradiction precisely because they recognize contingency and eschew transcendence. Paradox abounds in the existential world, in the man and in the effort to meet that world and himself which is the *Essais.* And Montaigne absorbs it whole into the larger framework of the book to work it as he transforms writing into making and doing.

Writing as making cuts across the varied strata of the *Essais,* as a theme to persuade the reader of the book's consubstantiality with its author and as a stylistic element to embody substance through the prose. Most profoundly, Montaigne seeks to lend weight to thought and reflection, to validate the books as the medium of the life of the mind. Thinking through writing becomes significant action, which establishes the text as the concrete locus of the self. Ideas and events of the outside world, and the writer's own life there, become a function of interiority: "Il y a plusieurs années que je n'ay que moy pour visée à mes pensées, que je ne contrerolle et estudie que moy; et, si j'estudie autre chose, c'est pour soudain le coucher sur moy, ou en moy, pour mieux dire" (II, 6, 378). In this inner space that action serves to bridge the past and the present, the distant and the immediate, to provide a sense of continuity through time for the individual whose experience would otherwise remain fragmentary and discontinuous. Writing is living, Montaigne suggests in a richly ambiguous vocabulary while speaking of the essays in *De l'exercitation*: "Mon mestier et mon art, c'est vivre" (379); and again to Mme. de Duras at the end of *De la ressemblance des enfans aux peres*: "J'ay mis tous mes efforts à former ma vie. Voylà mon mestier et mon ouvrage" (II, 37, 784). As Montaigne insists on the reality of the book and the substantiality of his action, the paradoxical life of the mind itself acquires substance.

I

The central metaphor of substance is the self-portrait, introduced in the prefatory "Au lecteur": "C'est moy que je peins" (p. 3). While the meaning of the verb *peindre* may be taken broadly as "to describe," the analogy is stated explicitly in *De la praesumption*: "Je vis un jour, à Barleduc, qu'on presentoit au Roy François second, pour la recommandation de la memoire de René, Roy de Sicile, un pourtraict qu'il avoit luy-mesmes fait de soy. Pourquoy n'est-il loisible de mesme à un chacun de se peindre de la plume, comme il se peignoit d'un creon?" (II, 17, 653). The tendency to consider portrait rather loosely as verbal self-presentation, to interpret it figuratively without examining its implications as an art form, dilutes one of Montaigne's consistent accents and minimizes a principal metaphor of materialization.

The historical context invites us to place due stress on the literal portrait, for its popularity was something akin to a passion in sixteenth-century France. Although we correctly associate the genre with Renaissance painting, it did not originate there. Fourteenth-century records show that portraits were made of Jean le bon (1350-64) and of Charles V (1364-90); the Duke of Berry appears in a donor portrait and as part of a group scene in the *Très Riches Heures du Duc de Berry* (circa 1445); there are portraits in Flemish triptychs, in stained-glass windows, tapestries, funeral sculpture, in illuminations and miniatures painted on wood. But for the most part, aside from the monumental expression of Fouquet's Charles VII (circa 1445), portrait painting in France could not be considered an independent art form of any great consequence before the advent of François I (1515) and the work of Jean Perreal and the Clouets, Jean and François.[1] Drawing its initial impetus from Italian Renaissance art, which reflected the individual personality, and from the humanist revival of the classical medal and portrait bust, the genre reached its apogee in France in the first half of the sixteenth century. Although the artists who followed the Clouets were of minor importance— with the possible exception of Corneille de Lyon, most of whose work has not been authenticated—the vogue of the portrait continued unabated into the seventeenth century.

As we suggested earlier, interpreting the analogy loosely ascribes to Montaigne the effort to depict physical attributes and to delineate character traits. In this sense the *Essais* participate in a larger corpus of contemporary literature broadly considered as involving literary portraiture (Monluc's *Mémoires,* Brantôme's *Vies*, D'Aubigné's *Histoire Universelle* and *Tragiques*), differing perhaps in its self-referential focus, its exclusive concern with a single man, and its detail. Or one may look at the analogy more literally, to point to techniques in the visual arts that Montaigne seeks to approximate, as when he stresses the completeness of the self-portrait as if to lend it the spatial depth of painting: "Je me presente debout et couché, le devant et le derriere, à droite et à gauche, et en tous mes naturels plis" (III, 8, 943).[2] Or, again, critics have sought to connect themes of the *Essais* (flux, movement, change) and their stylistic articulation to elements of mannerist and baroque art.[3] But the portrait analogy relates more essentially to the nature of Montaigne's enterprise and the specific paths he has chosen to follow. It functions in the quest for self-knowledge and that effort to "composer nos moeurs," to "former ma vie"; it sheds light on the notion of consubstantiality that Montaigne seeks to impose; and it is an element in the transformation of *escrire* into *faire*, which we have considered central to our understanding of the *Essais*. Montaigne opens up levels of meaning by juxtaposing the visual, plastic art form with the verbal medium.

What is it about the portrait that Montaigne might wish to associate with the *Essais*? The desire to focus exclusively on a single man who serves as touchstone and essential point of reference for all else that is considered (Montaigne's basic claim of originality) reflects the Renaissance cult of personality and the primacy of the individual in painting. No longer subordinate to a larger, most often religious framework as a detail in the overall composition, the subject surges forward to occupy the entire canvas, as if to assert his significance. He is not alone, praying, but rather is a presence: secular man occupies center stage in a medium designed for his affirmation if not always for his glorification. The emergence of the portrait as an independent art form corresponds to the general sense of man's dignity or worth in the Catholic Renaissance in Italy and France, regardless of the multiple forms that attitude takes from Petrarch through Pico, Rabelais through Montaigne. The subject of the portrait could say with the essayist that his concern is only with himself, that to consider anything else is to go astray (III, 8, 942).

In general, humanism's keen interest in classical life nourished the vogue of the portrait, for it found in antiquity both that broad affirmation of the individual and its expression as art in the medal and the portrait bust. The Florentine Alberti was responsible for reawakening interest in medallic art, and no less a figure than Erasmus introduced it to northern Europe, with himself as subject. In Italy medals and portraits of rulers and military figures reflected the Renaissance preference for the life of action, its emphasis on personal glory and self-perpetuation; paintings of humanists expressed the esteem of learning and the sense that knowledge was a shaping force of virtue and character. Erasmus' interest in the portrait—and his own appearance—found a place in the cult of friendship that evolved from Cicero's *De Amicitia*. He and Thomas More exchanged portraits as expressions of devotion and, more importantly, as surrogates for the self. Upon receipt of a More family portrait Erasmus wrote that he would not have been better able to see his friend if he had been with him.

Fidelity to life is thus fundamental to the validity of the portrait, for it must be representative of the individual in his particularity. The quality of lifelikeness belongs particularly to the sixteenth-century French portrait, where the popularity of the chalk drawing almost overshadows oil painting. In this medium, which provided the preliminary study for the actual paintings, designs in black, red, and white chalks subordinate the elements of gesture, movement, emotional expression, and anecdote to faithful rendering through line of the model's gaze and the expression of his whole character:

> A portrait by Clouet—if to a less degree than those of his successors—is above all a "speaking" likeness. He was chiefly interested, not in attitudes and costumes, but in the human face, and he sought to record the model's features with utmost verisimilitude. But at the same time he was much concerned with the definition of contours, of the essential element, in other words, of a composition in which line was all-important. Strangely enough, this ambivalence, the dual emphasis on style on the one hand and lifelikeness on the other, was furthered by the three-crayon technique. The reduction of his means of expression to line alone fully satisfied the artist's austere concern for purity of style, while the three different chalks, by introducing color, enabled him to achieve lifelikeness and so to avoid the abstraction of a charcoal or pen drawing.[4]

Realism in this context introduces two levels of consideration, for the artist aims at a portrait faithful both to the model's physical appearance and to his character. More than an accurate copier of externals, he seeks to penetrate and express the interior man, to portray what Leonardo described in the *Notebooks* as "the motions of the mind."[5]

The notion of the coincidence of interior and exterior man reaches back to the ancient Greeks, who considered facial expression and gesture as natural signs of the movement of the spirit.[6] Aristotle held that the reading of character "rests on an assured harmony, not in the case of hearing only but other organs of sense also, between the movements within and those without."[7] The Middle Ages perpetuated this correspondence of the physical and psychological even as the conviction of man's dual nature held sway. It was understood that the visible actions and body of the outer man were essential expressions of the inner man. Leo Spitzer's study of the medieval epic points up the relationship between *le geste* and *l'émotion,* characterizing gesture as "psychophysique."[8] And, of course, the Renaissance portrait makes the same assumption and demands that the artist possess the skill of the physiognomist. In fact, from the sixteenth century on, treatises on physiognomy were part of his academic training.

The analogy of the literary portrait derives from this intellectual current and itself has roots in the writings of the Greeks. Aristotle suggests in the *Politics* that painting can go beyond outward appearances to express interiority; in his *Life of Alexander* Plutarch states his intention to penetrate to Alexander's inner self as the painter seeks to uncover the subject's character by concentrating on the face and the expression of the eyes. In a larger sense, the sixteenth century accepted the broad comparison of painting and literature which Aristotle had drawn in the *Poetics* (that human nature in action is the subject of imitation among painters as well as poets [II, 1]) and frequently quoted the saying attributed by Plutarch to Simonides that painting is mute poetry, poetry a speaking picture. And, of course, Horace's famous simile *ut pictura poesis,* which was turned around to mean "as is poetry so is painting," was often invoked to confirm the parallel between the two arts.[9]

Two distinct contemporary emphases are discernible in the affirmation of this parallel. Renaissance painters and theoreticians who articulated the notion of *ut pictura poesis* aimed at transferring to painting by association the serious role as the interpreter of human life which from Aristotle on had influenced the consideration of poetry. Certain writers, for their part, saw the significance of their art embellished when, by analogy with the portrait, they could claim for their writing the capacity to penetrate external appearance and express human interiority. Although each trend had its own dynamic, together they resulted in a closer identification of the two arts. It was perfectly natural for Erasmus to make this juxtaposition in the inscription on his 1519 medal: in Latin he says that the image has been made according to the living likeness, and in Greek that his true portrait is delineated in his written works. In this conventional apology, which becomes a display of his linguistic facility and an advertisement for his writing, Erasmus locates that inner self that is the portraitist's proper subject in his prose.

Now let us follow the line of inquiry of this section back to Montaigne and the literary self-portrait. The essayist insists on that lifelikeness that distinguishes contemporary painting, claiming at the same time that this portrayal goes beyond external appearance—what in *De l'exercitation* he calls his *gestes*— to express inner being, his *moy, essence*. Because there is both an outer and an inner man, the writer as physiognomist seeks to reproduce both human levels: he must faithfully render exterior form, which gives the portrait physical identity, which makes the subject recognizable, and penetrate to interiority to draw out and delineate character. The etymology of portrait—*protrahere*, to draw out, disclose, reveal—expresses this second fundamental function. At the close of *De la phisionomie* Montaigne recounts two anecdotes designed to show that in his own case, unlike that of Socrates, his face and bearing do indeed reveal intention and character: "Si mon visage ne respondoit pour moy, si on ne lisoit en mes yeux et en ma voix la simplicité de mon intention, je n'eusse pas duré sans querelle et sans offence si long temps, avec cette liberté indiscrete de dire à tort et à droict ce qui me vient en fantasie, et juger temerairement des choses" (III, 12, 1062). He suggests a coincidence not unlike the medieval attitude noted earlier, one that sustains the integrity of his project.

While the essayist and the reader correctly stress the value of what might be called his intellectual or spiritual life, Montaigne evidences concern for his appearance as well, for the way he *looks* to others. On more than one occasion he makes it clear that he intends his portrait to bear a striking resemblance to its subject. At this level, where the painting faithfully imitates physical traits, the verbal portrait pictures the material man and strives as well to reproduce those other characteristic qualities that distinguish him from others. The portrait as a memorial, as standing for Montaigne after death, recurs as a motif of the *Essais*:

> Je l'ay voué [this book] à la commodité particuliere de mes parens et amis: à ce que m'ayant perdu . . . ils y puissent retrouver aucuns traits de mes conditions et humeurs, et que par ce moyen ils nourrissent plus entiere et plus vifve, la connoissance qu'ils ont eu de moy. ["Au lecteur," p. 3]

> Vous y reconnoistrez ce mesme port et ce mesme air que vous avez veu en [ma] conversation. Quand j'eusse peu prendre quelque autre façon que la mienne ordinaire et quelque autre forme plus honorable et meilleure, je ne l'eusse pas faict; car je ne veux tirer de ces escrits sinon qu'ils me representent à vostre memoire au naturel. [II, 37, 783]

Of course, it is not always easy to separate those elements of a painting which represent the physical individual from those that express character. At the same time, certain distinguishing traits might bear little or no relationship to the inner man while others, like the eyes and facial expression, were held to be particularly revelatory. A good physical likeness was only considered a good portrait if it revealed interiority. In comparing

Montaigne's portrait to its visual counterpart we recognize the existence and interplay of the two levels of representation.

What we have been saying about Montaigne, then, implies acceptance of the correspondence of outer and inner man and of the potential for reading the one in the other. But while these attitudes—stemming from antiquity and reaching through the Middle Ages—endure into the sixteenth century, the period also articulates the opposite trend, which distrusts appearances and brings that correspondence into question. Here the stress is on the deceptive nature of externals and the hidden truth they traduce; rather than a gateway to interiority, appearance acts as a barrier. We have only to think of Erasmus' play of appearance and reality in the *Praise of Folly* and his insistence on the inner spiritual meaning of the Bible as opposed to the letter or "outer flesh"; of Rabelais' prologue to *Gargantua,* which capitalizes on the familiarity of the Silenus figurines to point up possible disparities between what his text says and what it means; of the towering figure of Socrates invoked over and over again in the sixteenth century to prove the disjunction of outside and inside. And, above all, Montaigne himself, who insists all through the *Essais* that things are not necessarily as they appear, undermining the very supporting structure of the portrait he draws: "ce n'est pas tour de rassis entendement de nous juger simplement par nos actions de dehors; il faut sonder jusqu'au dedans . . ." (II, 1, 338).

II

De la phisionomie (III, 12) poses this paradox in terms that weave the art of physiognomy into the larger fabric of the quest for knowledge: reading facial traits becomes the model for a number of "readings" man must do of the metaphoric faces of things. Using Socrates as the archetypal divergence of appearance and reality, Montaigne develops the fundamental opposition between *science* and *nature* which resounds through the essays to show how

surfaces deceive. Images of vision ordinarily expressive of percep-
tive reading here point up how man is taken in by external form.
Dazzled by brilliance, he misinterprets the ostentation and
artifice of *science* as valuable and solid and the simplicity of *nature*
as base and common: "Nous n'apercevons les graces que pointues,
bouffies et enflées d'artifice. Celles qui coulent soubs la nayfveté
et la simplicité eschapent ayséement à une veuë grossiere comme
est la nostre: elles ont une beauté delicate et cachée; il faut la veuë
nette et bien purgée pour descouvrir cette secrete lumiere. Est
pas la naifveté, selon nous, germeine à la sottise, et qualité de
reproche?' (1037). Man's own crude insight, his inability to
penetrate to what lies beneath the surface, converges with the
disjunction of inner and outer to throw him off the track. He
pursues *science,* which for the most part has "plus de montre que
de force, et plus d'ornement que de fruict" (1049), and forsakes
nature, profound, necessary, useful.

The metaphorical faces of *De la phisionomie* all bear the closest
scrutiny. At the most basic level—that of nature—it is a
question of reading through traits falsely attributed to what
Montaigne calls her constant and universal countenance: "Et en
ont faict les hommes commes les parfumiers de l'huile: ils l'ont
sophistiquée de tant d'argumentations et de discours appellez du
dehors, qu'elle en est devenue variable et particuliere à chacun,
et a perdu son propre visage, constant et universel" (1049).
Nature's artificial makeup does not affect her true face, nor does
it deceive the genuine physiognomist who pierces the surface to
uncover and to know her. In contemporary historical terms, the
face of things reveals a morally topsy-turvy world, as serious as it
appears; here, what looks like, is: "Il ne se peut imaginer un pire
visage des choses qu'où la meschanceté vient à estre legitime, et
prendre . . . le manteau de la vertu" (1043). On the most
personal level, Montaigne recognizes the conflicting faces of his
own political situation: "La situation de ma maison et l'acointance des hommes de mon voisinage me presentoient d'un visage,
ma vie et mes actions d'un autre" (1044).[10] The two sets of appearances are contradictory; and while in themselves they are

beyond dispute—Montaigne *does* live in Protestant country and *is*
actively loyal to the Catholic king—the implications of one are
false and the other true. Appearances require careful reading to
judge Montaigne properly.

Faces, then, can either legitimately represent what lies within
or be deceptive. Montaigne sets this paradox before his reader:
"C'est une foible garantie que la mine; toutesfois elle a quelque
consideration" (1059). The contradictory note on which he concludes the essay affirms his own multiple faces by analogy: either
"il ne sçauroit estre bon, puis qu'il n'est pas mauvais aux
meschants," as was said of the king of Sparta, or "Il faut bien
qu'il soit bon, puisqu'il l'est aux meschants mesme," as Plutarch
presented it, "en ces deux sortes, comme mille autres choses,
diversement et contrairement" (1063).[11] Montaigne's aim is not
to discredit physiognomy or the portrait but merely to point to
its tentativeness, to the common divergence of interior and
exterior, and to the necessity and the difficulty of seeing clearly.
He recognizes how the complex and subtle human personality
acting in the world eludes man's grasp: "Nous ne sçavons pas
distinguer les facultez des hommes; elles ont des divisions et
bornes malaysées à choisir et delicates" (III, 9, 992). And we
have seen him refer to the opaque depths of the mind, its vagabond movement so hard to follow. The quest for knowledge of
the self participates in the same multiplicity and paradox that
characterize all attempts to know.

The notion that things are not necessarily as they appear was
deeply rooted in contemporary consciousness and could serve
either as a basis for undermining accepted attitudes, by suggesting multiple possibilities, or for justifying the introduction of
new beliefs held to exist below the surface, or for doing both of
these things at once. In biblical hermeneutics, in the music, art,
literature, and social criticism of the Renaissance double meaning was exploited as a screening device to protect the thinker and
his ideas, as a strategy to prevent misreading by the uninitiated,
and as intellectual game. And its prevalence implies as well a
fundamental connection to the way man and the world were

viewed, as we have seen in the *Essais*. The writings of Erasmus
and Rabelais, the hermetic poetry of Scève and the popularity of
emblematic symbol, Ronsard's insistence on the poet's esoterism
and his role as *vates* all reflect, in one way or another, the varied
play of differing levels of meaning. Of course, the Middle Ages
exercised a system of multiple interpretation both of the Bible, in
which it distinguished a literal, figurative, moral, and anagogical
sense, and of secular literature, which it tended to read allegori-
cally. But the differences between the medieval and Renaissance
approaches are crucial and reflect their attitudes toward man
himself. The medieval conception of inner and outer man,
implying both separation and convergence, appears a useful
analogue to shed light on the general view of multiple interpretation. The different layers of a text seem to reflect the relationship between body and soul: though the soul's life was
considered invisible and the heart hidden, a symbolic connection
remained between body and soul that was manifest in facial
expression and other external signs. Each level exists in its own
right, with its own functional integrity, yet participates at the
same time in an interpenetrating and mutually supportive system
bound by correspondences that makes each the *sign* of what lies
beneath. The multiple strata come together for moral and
religious purposes to bring the reader, as if progressing on a
linear path, closer to God. Renaissance hermeneutics, on the
other hand, resembles the view of man that alienates inner and
outer, stressing divergence and deceptiveness.[12] Rather than correspondence among the various levels, we often find contradiction and paradox, or ambiguous meaning that is both this *and*
that. Instead of an exterior bound as signifier to the interior, the
outer layer functions independently to conceal what is within.
Multiple significance serves social, political, and aesthetic aims
and is exploited for its own sake, as intellectual play in which the
contemporary spirit obviously delights.

Few contemporary figures had a stronger sense of the variance
of outward appearance and inwardness than Montaigne, particularly in the subject that most interests him, man: "Certes, c'est

un subject merveilleusement vain, divers, et ondoyant, que l'homme. Il est malaisé d'y fonder jugement constant et uniforme" (I, 1, 9). This theme, which opens the *Essais* and reverberates throughout, frames the effort at self-portraiture and the quest for self-knowledge, for it applies most meaningfully to the essayist himself. Rather than attempt a constant and uniform judgment so incongruous to the nature of things, Montaigne depicts movement and variation, often appearing to relish the play of paradox and ambiguity which comprises what man is and animates what he does. Multiple roles, social and intellectual masks characterize *homo exterior*: what man looks like and what he is, Montaigne confirms, do not coincide, and when he comes to describe man beneath his appearances Montaigne refers to the obscure depths of elusive *homo interior*.

At the same time, the concept of portraiture demands some degree of congruity, which allows interiority to be signified by what is exterior. The portrait must, after all, be recognizable, as we suggested earlier, for Montaigne intends it to stand in his stead. Others must see him in his painting as he was in life; they must find the expressions, the attitudes, the poses representative of the character, the heart and soul, of the man they knew. Montaigne's task as portraitist, interestingly enough, bears a profound analogy to that accomplished by God through creation: "Les choses invisibles de Dieu, dit saint Paul, apparoissent par la creation du monde, considerant sa sapience eternelle et sa divinité par ses oeuvres" (II, 12, 447). This, in a purely mundane sense, is what the essayist strives to achieve: the medieval invisible heart—here secularized as mind and character—made visible through the work created (invented). The physical object, handwrought, is the *sign* of interiority.[13]

The challenge Montaigne faces is clear, given the nature of things as he sees them: if the visible is to represent the invisible, then disparity between them must be reduced. The shifting and sliding of the interior and exterior planes must somehow be stabilized enough for correspondence to occur. The strain generated by this effort is apparent everywhere in the *Essais*.

Montaigne does not attempt to impose absolute fixity or immobility nor does he bow to total variation and flux, as the situation described in *De l'oisiveté* indicates. To be faithful to things as they are he must recognize the ambiguity and paradox inherent in a world of movement and change; to portray himself—that is, reveal interiority—the signs he uses must correspond to what they signify. But resolution does not fall within this painter's province. His own powers are often found wanting; the medium resists manipulation; his efforts to reach interiority are often fruitless: "Je ne me tiens pas bien en ma possession et disposition. . . . L'occasion, la compaignie, le branle mesme de ma voix, tire plus de mon esprit, que je n'y trouve lors que je le sonde et employe à part moy" (I, 10, 40). Thus, he adds, unrehearsed speech is more representative than writing, but writing, after all, is the path he has chosen! Sometimes he writes and loses the sense of what is expressed; at other times he feels sure to have reached himself, as in *Du repentir*. And then again, in *Nous ne goustons rien de pur*, he wonders about the effectiveness of the questing mind: "Il faut manier les entreprises humaines plus grossierement et superficiellement, et en laisser bonne et grande part pour les droicts de la fortune. Il n'est pas besoin d'esclairer les affaires si profondement et si subtilement. On s'y perd, à la consideration de tant de lustres contraires et formes diverses: 'Volutantibus res inter se pugnantes obtorpuerant animi' [In weighing contradictory things, their minds became paralysed]" (II, 20, 675). Wedged between what he would like to do and what he can do, the essayist expresses the tension he experiences and the tentativeness of his enterprise by his reference to the face, the visible sign, as a weak guarantee that deserves consideration.

III

Our discussion thus far indicates that the analogy of painting in the *Essais* involves more than a loosely connected and rather banal metaphor, that indeed the concept of portrait is bound to multiple aspects of the book of the self. Nowhere is this more evident than in its bearing on the theme of materiality, to which we alluded at the opening of this chapter and to which we now return. Some observations on the modes of existence of painting and literature will highlight the centrality of Montaigne's contention that he and his book are consubstantial.

The opening pages of *Du repentir* describe that characteristic world of change and flux, of life enduring in fleeting time, of becoming rather than being so familiarly Montaignian. Within this setting the essayist locates his quest for self-knowledge in a book, a form that appears particularly suited to his task. The nature of things, as he describes them, represents the major obstacle to his success, for as *De l'oisiveté* implies, what we might call raw becoming is formless and the individual who lives it equally as shapeless: "L'ame qui n'a point de but estably, elle se perd: car, comme on dict, c'est n'estre en aucun lieu, que d'estre par tout" (I, 8, 32). There is no sense of self possible within the ceaseless turmoil of becoming. Some sort of transformation or transference has to occur to provide that self with a degree of unity and, consequently, of entity. The means chosen, as we have suggested, is the book: before Montaigne begins to write he is most profoundly nowhere.

The function of Montaigne's book recalls St. Augustine's observations on the rhythms, numbers, proportions, and, generally speaking, the rules of poetry, which transform the words of common language to impart to a fleeting multiplicity the only kind of unity, order, and stability of which it is capable.[14] This dynamic appears to inform the *Essais* themselves. As literature— and here we refer simply to that which is written—the essays involve an experience akin to that of the world itself, one rooted in temporal duration and thus perceived as variation. The writing and reading of the book take place through successive moments in time, and what is grasped is never the whole completely given but particular parts that bear a relationship to what preceded and what follows. The writer and reader move along, never at any one moment with a firm grip on anything but the partiality of the moment. What has been written or read is carried as recollection of the past, and what remains to be read anticipated—as of the future—but each succeeding present provides the only direct contact with the whole. The point of contact—what we might call the perspective—always changes and thus the sense of the whole is always changing. There is no simultaneous existence, no total presence. But arranged and shaped through the text, the words acquire enough unity to turn them into some sort of being.

There is, here, a fundamental element to keep in mind concerning the physical existence of the book. The text, of course, is evident, materially, as an object, in the concreteness of its paper, in the ink with which it is written. This may in some sense be what Montaigne means when he suggests substance, ephemeral thought taking on body in the actual words visible on the page. By writing he endows himself with a concrete history, with a past essential to any concept of self. We are dealing with a man who insists on the weakness of his memory, on the impotence of that which is by nature inert, housed in the "storehouse of the mind." But the weak memory is an important thematic element, for on his own, without his book, it deprives him of that very past on which his quest depends. Like the man suffering from amnesia who must determine where he has come from to establish who he is, Montaigne must begin to record present moments to accumulate a past, to be able to look back, at future moments, at the shape(s) emerging from this movement through time. The history of Montaigne's thought is in this sense the substantialization of the man.

At the same time the words on the page are not his thought itself any more than the book is the man himself. In both cases we are dealing with symbols, at least one remove from the source. If Montaigne can be said to experience a certain materializing effect as he articulates himself as the written word, the reader performs the operation in reverse and from the concrete symbol reconstructs the man. From this point of view, where Montaigne exists, in relation to the text, is in the mind of the reader, and notions of substantiality appear weakened. Moreover, as we have already suggested, the Montaigne the reader imagines never really is but endlessly becomes, so that what is perceived in the mind's eye is itself fleeting and partial.

We come back to the metaphor of portrait. If the nature of the man as subject, the literary medium, and the experience of that medium all appear rooted in temporal discontinuity and thus call into question notions of substantiality—that is, of being in space—then the portrait may function to insinuate that quality by association. The familiar distinction between the arts of time (poetry, music) and those of space (painting, sculpture) suggests that painting has a physical mode of existence that differentiates it from the terms we have been using to describe the *Essais*.[15] Painting, it can be argued, is a tangible medium that exists in space, static and immobile. In the contemporary "realistic" art that Montaigne imagines as he establishes his metaphor, the painter seeks to reproduce a physical entity in its visible properties—that is, to capture the spatiality of the subject, an activity rendered particularly meaningful in the Renaissance through the advances of three-dimensional perspective. In portraiture, in particular, the model remains stationary as the painter attempts to fix being, to immobilize it in space and thus in time. And the experience of the viewer is one of stability accompanied by a sense of the totality, of simultaneous existence.

The distinctions between literature founded in mobility and painting in fixity are by no means clear-cut. The picture of a bird in flight or of an event about to occur stirs imaginings of movement, of action, in the mind of the spectator which give the experience a temporal dimension, just as a word description may be said to conjure up objects in space. The period spent standing before a painting, perhaps seeing previously unperceived elements or interrelating them, suggests duration just as the physical book and the act of reading share in spatiality. Or the painting may provoke a range of reaction or interpretation so that as part of an esthetic experience it participates in change, in instability. At the same time, differences do exist which allow the notion of portrait to influence our appreciation of the written essays. However much the fleeting apprehension of literature may look like that of painting, in literature what is apprehended is itself always fleeting, incomplete, while the painting remains a stable, complete, and enduring entity. Not absolutely enduring, in Montaigne's world, for even constancy, as he says in *Du repentir,* is nothing but a more languid motion; and not complete but a succession of portraits representing the continual essaying of the ever-changing self. But portrait nonetheless, solid and immobile in its physical existence, fixed in the "realistic" representation of its subject, itself setting "still." And hand-made, crafted by the artist-artisan. The metaphor of portrait imparts the sense of substance, the setting of being and its materialization. It conveys by association the uniqueness of the subject as the portraitist captures that moment when the model looks most like himself. The portrait sets down the man as he "really is"; it depicts him as Montaigne suggests men should be judged, "par leur estat rassis, quand elles [les âmes] sont chez elles, si quelque fois elles y sont; ou aumoins quand elles sont plus voisines du repos et de leur naifve assiette" (III, 2, 810). The image of the self in a settled state, at home or at rest, comes close to describing the sitter in a characteristic pose, at a time when his exterior features and expressions are most revealing of interiority. This is precisely the kind of subject most appropriate to the solid, static mode of painting.

Thus what we have called the strategy, or fiction, of consubstantiality depends in part on the reader's acceptance of the essays as portrait(s). But the portrait as material, as stillness, as being never establishes dominance, never gains ascendancy. It stands rather as the reverse of the medal of becoming, in a position of constant tension with it. The *Essais* are representative of becoming, both thematically and stylistically, as every student of Montaigne knows, but it is important to add that to reach out toward the essayist's goal (if not to reach it) the *Essais* must also tend toward being, toward a sense of entity. As we suggested earlier, the presentation of discontinuity, of fleeting moments as both the point of departure and the conclusion of existence in time, leads only to the situation described in *De l'oisiveté*. Some movement has to be made in the direction of stability if the lost soul is to be located someplace, if the "amas et pieces de chair informes" (I, 8, 32) which is the idle self are to take shape. By introducing the portrait into literature, line into language, Montaigne expresses the paradoxical interplay of the reality of becoming and the necessity of being, of inevitable movement and essential rest, of fragmentation and a sense of wholeness. He introduces those very qualities that represent the *end* of the effort to know, to form, not as a goal to be achieved but as the final term to be sought. The *repos*, staying and settling in himself, the order that he could not establish in idleness, returns in the essays of the Third Book as the measure of the beautiful life.[16] The portrait in words cannot achieve stability or being, but it must pretend to them.

IV

"Realistic" and "representative," which have appeared a number of times in our discussion of both the portrait and Montaigne's portrayal, invite further reflection, for these are common terms, often used by critics to underscore the coincidence of the historical and literary man, or the author's sincerity. Auerbach, for example, speaks of Montaigne's "realistic introspection" and of his "exact and factual description of a constantly changing subject" as if the essayist employs a simple mimetic process to transfer his model, whole, onto the page or canvas.[17] The sixteenth century expressed the concept of art imitating nature—in watered-down Aristotelian terms derived mostly from Horace—as vivid representation designed to create the illusion that the hearer or reader was actually in the presence of the original model.[18] But our comments on physiognomy and portraiture imply transformation rather than transfer, a basic change from formlessness to form. If the portrait depicts more than was visible to the naked eye by penetrating to interiority to draw out what "really is," in what sense can we speak of imitation? And if the writer is both the subject and object, the problem of perspective—esthetic and psychological—as it affects objectivity intrudes on the consideration of faithful representation. Our aim is not to go back over the oft-discussed and elusive subject of *mimesis* but rather to attempt a better grasp of what takes place in the process of depiction that is self-portrayal in the *Essais.*

Montaigne himself raises the question of change or distinction in *De l'exercitation*: "Il n'est description pareille en difficulté à la description de soy-mesmes, ny certes en utilité. Encore se faut-il testoner, encore se faut-il ordonner et renger pour sortir en place. Or je me pare sans cesse, car je me descris sans cesse" (II, 6, 378). *Testoner*, as "to comb one's hair," and *parer*, as "adorn," "embellish," dress up Montaigne in a way that covers and masks his natural self. He acknowledges as a kind of general truth that one is never quite the same at home in private as in public, that before one goes out into the world one spruces up to appear more presentable, or acceptable to popular taste, or to impress. At the same time, this artificial making-up would seem antithetical to the avowed purpose of self-discovery and to the claim that he has presented himself in his simple and ordinary fashion without retouching his portrait. Perhaps this tension is inevitable and artifice must accompany a public dimension, so that some distance always exists between the man in the raw and the one his readers come to know. Yet the sense of artifice may be lessened somewhat if we read *parer* etymologically as "arrange," "prepare," "set out," meanings that would move it closer to *ordonner* and *renger* and diminish the negative undertone of false embellishment. The emphasis lies on a transformative act, on a change from a state where things are not arranged to one where they are, where concessions to taste or vanity are subsumed in the larger framework of the relation of disorder to order. In his juxtaposition of *parer* and *descrire* Montaigne sets his going out in public as the act of writing, so that he arranges himself *to* write ("pour sortir en place") and, most significantly, *through* writing.

We have encountered notions of ordering before, most notably in *De l'art de conferer*, where in the juxtaposition of writing and debating we spoke of Montaigne's emphasis on form and order, its fundamental relationship to the emergence of truth, to the accessibility of any mode of being or expression.[19] And at the same time, discussion as an art, indeed as a verbal artifact, self-consciously constructed, was clearly apparent. However much Montaigne might long to reenact the natural—and idealized—arguments of shopboys and shepherds, he approximates that model only through the attitudes and actions he sets forth as the "art de conferer." Although separate and distinct from nature, this art functions not as its antithesis but as a means of rapprochement. When Montaigne speaks of ordering himself to bring himself out, he clearly suggests a form assumed or imposed which was not there before.

As Montaigne practices that art, imposes that order—that is, writes—we follow a movement away from what he is "by nature" toward a shape acquired through artifice. And because the form is new, the essayist has created something that goes beyond reproduction. The self described, it would appear, is something more, at least something other, than the self observed. In *Du démentir* Montaigne underscores the notion of transformation: "Et quand personne ne me lira, ay-je perdu mon temps de m'estre entretenu tant d'heures oisifves à pensements si utiles et aggreables? Moulant sur moy cette figure, il m'a fallu si souvent dresser et composer pour m'extraire, que le patron s'en est fermy et aucunement formé soy-mesmes. Me peignant pour autruy, je me suis peint en moy de couleurs plus nettes que n'estoyent les miennes premieres" (II, 18, 665). Through the use of the verbs *peindre* and *extraire* (which echoes *protrahere*) Montaigne affirms the identity of writing as painting and his goal of "bringing himself out," of making the invisible visible. And in the process, as the lines from *De l'exercitation* indicated, a fashioning and composing takes place, an arrangement emerges (that is, is imposed) that is not a part of the preliterary self. The less-clear colors of his original, inward self, of his model, become more distinct when exteriorized in the portrait and then, because art influences life, the sitter models himself after his own painting.

Montaigne intends to show that his book has made him as much as he has made his book, that the two not only affect each other but are identical, consubstantial, as he says in the next line. But however much he stresses the similarity of that interaction, two different movements appear to be in play. Although it is possible to see development here as (a) the desire to portray, (b) the firming up of the model, (c) the painting (or copying) of the firm model, this view fundamentally diminishes the centrality of the book by reducing it to mere imitation, not unlike what occurs as the last step when the model imitates the painting. What our discussion suggests is that the painting and the firming are a single, indivisible act, linked to the essayist's very sense of being. Again I would substitute "through" for "to" so that we see Montaigne composing himself *through* the act of bringing out, *through* the writing, rather than *to* bring himself out, as if he imposed an order before writing and then simply noted it down. The book is not only the record of order; it represents the process of arrangement itself.

The notions of form and of substance come together in Montaigne's use of the verb *mouler*. In the editions published during his lifetime, after claiming that the only contact he had with the public in this book was to borrow its tools of printing, he added, "il m'a fallu jetter en moule cette image, pour m'exempter la peine d'en faire faire plusieurs extraits à la main" (p. 664n). *Jetter en moule* refers to the mold in printing, to casting his language-picture in type, but the word is richly suggestive as it anticipates "Moulant sur moy cette figure . . ." with which the essayist was to replace it. To the impression of fixing his own image or, we can say, his own self in the stable medium of print, by its etymology *moule* (from the Latin *modus*) adds the sense of "measure," "arrangement," now the familiar accompaniment of exteriorization in Montaignian terms. When Montaigne writes the passage in the C text and deletes the lines just quoted, he uses the present participle literally, describing his own activity as "modeling." At the same time *mouler* carries along with it the other meanings we have noted, so that as

Montaigne models the portrait figure on himself we see him arranging and providing measure, casting the self in the substantial medium of the book. By providing what we have called the real locus of the self, writing keeps the mind from wandering off, firms up and shapes its ideas and conceptions, sets them and makes them accessible: "Aux fins de renger ma fantasie à resver mesme par quelque ordre et projet, et la garder de se perdre et extravaguer au vent, il n'est que de donner corps et mettre en registre tant de menues pensées qui se presentent à elle" (II, 18, 665).

Interestingly, the process we have described resembles that of literary invention, the uncovering of things existent but heretofore unknown, and their formulation or arrangement in a new way, embodied in words. The essayist comes upon his sense of self, of being to which he gives expression, or substance in his text. Speaking of the nature of imitation in sixteenth-century French poetics, Castor considers this merging of invention and representation into a single act to be its most profound expression.[20] And in his penetration and articulation of the true nature of things (that is, of his own true nature), in this activity that renders the invisible visible, Montaigne discloses his authentic divinity as on his own he becomes the source, if not the creator, of his being in the world. Creator would be anachronistic, we remember, for the Renaissance did not conceive of creation out of nothingness except by God. But in the transformation Montaigne effects from chaos to a degree of order, from fragmentation to a measure of continuity, from erratic motion to a greater sense of rest or fixity, his activity dramatically parallels that of the archetypal maker.

Montaigne reacts to the missing image, carried off, lost at La Boétie's death. The feeling of loss of self reappears continually through the essays, expressed both as the inclination of the mind (as *fantasie, esprit, âme*) to *se perdre,* to *extravaguer,* and in the sense that he is nothing (*rien*), a void, vain or empty. The general notion of vanity as inherent in the human condition, of worthlessness and hollowness as part of man's nature, is a Christian theme that we have seen Montaigne incorporate meaningfully into the secular context of the *Essais*. And his admission of his own lack of value both affirms his humility and assigns him a place among the wise. But at the same time these statements appear to characterize Montaigne's personal situation, the sense of his own absence or nothingness so eloquently articulated in *De l'amitié*. When he modestly proclaims his ignorance in *De la phisionomie*, "et ne traicte à point nommé de rien que du rien, ny d'aucune science que de celle de l'inscience" (III, 12, 1057), the nothing that he treats is not only his lack of knowledge but most specifically himself. In the emphasis on recovering, or uncovering, his true nature, on embodying and substantiating interiority, on fixing the lost or errant self, we see the counterpoint to nothingness.

There is, of course, no final resolution or reconstitution, no absolute recovery of being. The nostalgia for the essential self represented as union with La Boétie is separate from the experience of manifold selves; in the world of flux and contingency, multiple images replace the image. As we pointed out earlier in our discussion of conversion, the return to the self is inevitably accompanied by the tendency to flight just as the sense of self is continually overwhelmed by that of loss. Repetition, renewal, reaffirmation in the successive instances of the present moment constitute that activity which for Montaigne provides contact with being. As he quests and writes, his mind moving as it seeks to know, the essayist casts himself in his text: "D'autant que nous avons cher, estre; et estre consiste en mouvement et action. Parquoy chascun est aucunement en son ouvrage" (II, 8, 386). The canvas fills with the portraits of the self.

V

Our comments on the portrait should be refined to weigh the implications of self-portraiture. Perhaps Dürer's self-portraits

provide an analogy with that concentration on the self characteristic of Montaigne and on the awareness of the problems it
raises. The portraitist's dilemma involved distortion in the image
reflected in the convex mirror (we recall also Parmigianino's "Self
Portrait in a Convex Mirror"). In an early series of paintings, the
mouth diminishes to one side and the eyes appear to be on two
different planes. When Dürer recorded the half-length figure,
the fact of reversal posed another intriguing problem, for the
reversed head could be joined to a normal body, or the body itself
could be reversed. In later paintings, where a flat mirror has evidently been used to allow for a truer depiction, the artist
continues to confront the difficulties inherent in self-representation.[21] The problem of projecting one's image to allow observation and description appears inevitably to involve distortion. The
complexities of penetrating to an "other," of reading his physiognomy, are intensified by the deforming process of self-projec-
tion. The distance opened between the self as subject and object
to create that perspective which makes the painting possible in
the first place also serves to alienate the painter from himself, to
bring the identity of that self "out there" into question because it
is an "other." The sixteenth century was well aware of the illu-
sionistic power implicit in perspective, as its interest in anamor-
phic pictures confirmed (anamorphoses are enigmatic pictures
contrived to make sense only when viewed from a particular
angle).[22] And the baroque style in art, with its delight in the play
of illusion and *trompe l'oeil*, develops from the understanding that
the characteristics of vision determine the apprehension of the
object represented.

Montaigne is particularly alert to this difficulty, as he remarks
in *De l'exercitation*, "il n'est description pareille en difficulté à la
description de soy-mesmes" (378). His comment reflects on the
problem of penetrating the dark recesses of the other (self's) mind
and that posed by the potential for distortion as he dresses
himself up to go out in public, both subjects under discussion.
He also understands the deforming effects of vainglory, which he
examines in *De la praesumption*: "C'est un'affection inconsiderée,

dequoy nous nous cherissons, qui nous represente à nous mesmes autres que nous ne sommes" (II, 17, 631). For the man who aims to uncover his true nature, to represent himself faithfully, presumption and pride are to be avoided at all costs, for they cast a false image. And so we see Montaigne choosing the perspective of humility and modesty (although he points out the equally false picture produced by selling oneself short) to speak about himself in this essay so often considered among the most sincerely self-revelatory. Yet it would appear that any act of self-reference, by the very nature of its internal reflexive focus, must remain tentative. A passage we examined earlier in our discussion of thought and action bears repeating in full:[23]

> Ceux que la fortune . . . a faict passer la vie en quelque eminent degré, ils peuvent par leurs actions publiques tesmoigner quels ils sont. Mais ceux qu'elle n'a employez qu'en foule, et de qui personne ne parlera, si eux mesmes n'en parlent, ils sont excusables s'ils prennent la hardiesse de parler d'eux mesmes . . ., à l'exemple de Lucilius:
>
> > Ille velut fidis arcana sodalibus olim
> > Credebat libris . . .
> > [He would confide, as unto trusted friends,
> > His secrets to his notebooks.]
>
> Celuy là commettoit à son papier ses actions et ses pensées, et s'y peignoit tel qu'il se sentoit estre. [632]

However subtle the difference may seem between the great figure acting in the world to reveal what he *is* and the private man, writing, who comes out as he *feels* he is, this distinction strikes at the heart of our concern. The essayist minimizes the potential for discrepancy between what a man is and how he might appear to the outside, and the possibility of deceit and dissimulation, to suggest that the public man can, if he wants, disclose his true self because there are others to see and acknowledge what he does. When Montaigne describes the man who will only be spoken of if he speaks of himself in writing, he does not say that *his* thoughts and actions reveal what he is, but rather, as if to take note of the margin of error involved in the self-referential perspective, places him at one remove from certainty. Without that exterior frame of reference provided by the true "other," the writer serves as his own public, as the one who both acts and acknowledges; the very operation in which he is engaged calls itself into question.

VI

The notion of portrait, then, functions in multiple ways in the *Essais*. It translates the effort at self-representation, as a faithful visual rendering and, more importantly, as the attempt to uncover the motions of the mind. As a "spatial" medium, it serves as the primary metaphor of substance, a fundamental element in that strategy which allows Montaigne's claim to articulate and to anchor interiority in the material world. And in the analogy between the portraitist and the ultimate maker (yet without transcendental help) lies a glimpse of man as the founder of his own sense of being. To suggest that he can penetrate to the true nature of things, that he can succeed in rendering the invisible visible, that he attains a measure of order, continuity, and stability is to exalt man on his own and legitimize that concentration on the self which harkens back to the pagan world of antiquity. Progressively, Montaigne seeks to recover his own lost image.

But there is another side to the coin. Fixing the gaze intently on one's reflection in the mirror, either in admiration or in the attempt to practice the art of physiognomy—both aspects of the Renaissance cult of personality and its affirmation of man's place in the universe—raises serious questions, to which the Christian Middle Ages, with its distrust of optics as a vain devotion to appearances, would have testified. The projection of the self required by the effort at portrayal makes it more or less remote from the observer. Its existence verifiable as an object, the self undermines its identity precisely because it is an "other." The discrepancy that appears to operate in the sixteenth century between inner and outer man, between outwardness and interior reality, comes into play to obstruct the discovery of the motions of the mind. And, in fact, the whole of contemporary painting—and portraiture—is itself based on the development of the illusion-producing power of perspective, on its ability to give two dimensions the look of three, to create a feeling of depth and mass where there is none.

The metaphor of self-portrait appears correlative to the multi-dimensional, often paradoxical nature of the *Essais*. It represents Montaigne's effort to affirm certain qualities and characteristics of his work at the same time that it raises questions about, and weakens, the very thrust of the enterprise itself.

9

Words of Flesh and Blood

"Le sens esclaire et produict les
parolles; non plus de vent, ains de
chair et d'os" (III, 5, 873)

Montaigne's insistence on the substantiality of making and
forming the self underlies his preoccupation with language and
the implications of his own writing, for ultimately the value of
his enterprise derives from the way he handles the medium.
What he finally looks like to himself and to others depends on
how he casts himself into the language, how it receives and
shapes his imprint at the same time. The articulation of thought
becomes the measure of that judgment Montaigne seeks to assay,
as we noted earlier: "Nos gens appellent jugement, langage; et
beaux mots, les plaines conceptions" (III, 5, 873). The inference
here, of course, is that the language and fine words contain and
express the quality of the mind unequivocally. But the essayist
also understands the antithetical corollary, and his awareness of
the likelihood that words will veil, distort, or even betray him
constantly accompanies his urge to exteriorize himself, his need
to locate himself as an ordered form of discourse.

Montaigne stands between the ideal coincidence of thought
and expression and the imperative that "les mots aillent où va la
pensée," (III, 8, 924), imperative because it points up that
tendency of thought and expression to diverge and man's inclination to exploit that divergence. If there is a space separating sign
and referent, the man as he "is" risks being lost there. This

explains in part Montaigne's emphasis on personal sincerity, on the one hand, and his general notion that any action reveals a man ("Tout mouvement nous descouvre" [I, 50, 302]), on the other, as if this latter offered another route to inwardness if words failed. Language and thought must be coincidental if the one is to be sought in the other, if the authenticity of the "portrait" is to be guaranteed. But equally as central to the writer's purpose is the conviction that the word not be considered as a merely transparent sign of a world of substance outside itself. Montaigne will insist on the word as substantive and on the fact that he literally resides in it. The language of the *Essais* aims at being an incarnating medium, one that points not beyond but back to itself as an essential entity. Like the ideal portrait, it seeks actually to participate in the nature, life, and properties of the man whose image it is.[1]

I

We have been dealing all along with this preoccupation with materiality; in Montaigne's preference for the verb *faire* rather than *escrire* to describe the act of writing, in the metaphor of the painter which similarly moves him closer to the workman or artisan and imparts objective properties to his writings, in the claim of consubstantiality. The multiple dimensions of this effort share a common purpose, one intended to persuade the reader that the essays are an entity in the world, one that embodies, sensuously perceptible, the mind and the soul, the moral and spiritual qualities of the man himself. To say that the man and the book are one affirms their coincidence and at the same time underscores their separateness (as Montaigne himself does when he notes that he and his essays have a mutual influence on each other). And in this play of identity and difference lies Montaigne's claim to shaping himself and our understanding of the work as the origin of his sense of being. To speak of entity and of language as an incarnating medium extends the implications of the book as interiority externalized, as the invisible made visible, and echoes another incarnation, one also expressed in the juxtaposition of word and substance. Whether the writer was conscious of the parallel is, perhaps, a moot question. The unuttered analogy stands out, the resemblance of vocabulary and of process which sustains the impression of a man of flesh and blood, the source of his own making.

The suggestive metaphor of words with literal body is Montaigne's own, articulated in *De l'institution des enfans* to describe the quality absent from mediocre prose ("j'avois trainé languissant apres des parolles Françoises, si exangues, si descharnées et si vuides de matiere et de sens" [I, 26, 147]) and in *Consideration sur Cicéron* (I, 40) where he criticizes Cicero's emphasis on style and eloquence. As counterpoint, the essayist holds up the prose of Epicurus and Seneca, which he carefully distinguishes from empty and fleshless letters: "ne sont ce pas lettres vuides et descharnées" (I, 40, 252). His deep interest in *choses* (in the mind and in the world) turns him against words that exist for their own sake although, ironically, in Cicero's case he is willing to admit the possibility that the extreme perfection of style might somehow transcend itself to produce substance. Once more, that substance is depicted as body: we might say that Cicero's style, "estant en si extreme perfection, se donne corps elle mesme" (I, 40, 252).

Again, in *Sur des vers de Virgiles* (III, 5), Montaigne articulates his discussion in terms of words of flesh and blood. In the verse of Virgil and Lucretius he finds language solid enough to ruminate on, striking enough to be "tout epigramme, non la queuë seulement, mais la teste, l'estomac et les pieds" (873). Commenting on the relationship between thought and expression in the same passage, he insists on the supremacy of the concept in the mind and characterizes the language of the poet capable of true invention as *plein* and *gros, solid(e), vif(ves)* to underline its substantial and material properties. In order truthfully to represent *choses*, the words themselves must have bodily qualities: "Plutarque dit qu'il veid le langage latin par les choses; icy de mesme: le sens esclaire et produict les parolles; non plus de vent, ains de chair et d'os" (873).

This concretizing process that we uncover in the case of language parallels one of the most consistent and original image patterns in the *Essais*, the presentation of the mind in terms appropriate to the body: "Montaigne compare son esprit instinctivement et d'une façon spontanée à son corps, et c'est à cette personnification constante de toute chose abstraite que nous devons une bonne partie de ses images."[2] The several examples we have pointed out do not represent a systematic or sustained presentation. Rather they are suggestive indices—tantalizingly brief and with implications undeveloped—of Montaigne's overall effort to incorporate himself into his prose. As he himself says of these materializing words, "elles signifient plus qu'elle ne disent" (873).

Earlier in *Sur des vers de Virgile* Montaigne takes a different perspective to contrast his writing with his own person, which he calls "des essays en cher et en os" (844). He made a similar distinction in *De la ressemblance des enfans aux peres*, where his comments to Mme. de Duras distinguish between his portrait ("cette peinture morte et muette") and his "estre naturel" (II, 37, 784). In both instances Montaigne seeks to validate what he considers proper action, in this latter case to insist on the superiority of *faire* over *escrire* and in the former to subordinate imagination to physical activity, art to natural pleasure. Yet in *De la ressemblance,* in the very same context, Montaigne will state that he is to be found in his writings, that he seeks to reproduce the very traits and faculties with which Mme. de Duras is familiar in the flesh. He lodges them, he adds, in *un corps solide*, a solid and enduring body that will outlast his aged and withering physical self.

It is as if Montaigne were constantly reminded (and so reminds his reader) of the literary nature of his enterprise. What we might call the metaphoric spell, that sustained suspension of disbelief that allows the reader unbroken participation in the literary world, is repeatedly interrupted to bring the focus back to the point of contact between literature and life, to fix attention directly on the nature of the literary act. When in *Sur des vers de Virgile* Montaigne uses the exact vocabulary of *cher* (*chair*) and *os* first to characterize himself as *opposed* to the essays and then to describe the very properties of certain words, the juxtaposition sets before the attentive reader the paradoxical character of the *Essais* themselves. Clearly, it does not suffice for the essayist simply to record his thought, to register the meanderings of his mind. He maintains explicitly that thought takes on real substance, that the corpus of writing is as his own *corps*, and he implies that language itself, in its relation to thought, can have body. But what we have called the strategy of consubstantiality is constantly brought under the essayist's own scrutiny, continuously set alongside its opposite number, compared with the possibility that the portrait *is* only words to express the dynamic tension inherent in the central notion that language is the repository of reality.

Although the passages we have been examining treat the language of poetry, they are directly relevant to Montaigne's prose. The essayist suggests this parallel by elaborating on his own stylistic concerns immediately after his comments on the verse of Virgil and Lucretius. And later, in *De la vanité*, when he seeks to explain his penchant for digression, his reference to the "alleure poetique, à sauts et à gambades" (III, 9, 994) that he appreciates in Plutarch's prose (and imputes to his own) leads him to a direct comparison: "Mille poëtes trainent et languissent à la prosaïque; mais la meilleure prose ancienne (et je la seme ceans indifferemment pour vers) reluit par tout de la vigueur et hardiesse poetique, et represente l'air de sa fureur" (995). As he blurs the distinctions between poetry and prose Montaigne lends to his writing the potential for substance and truth that made poetic expression, at its source, "l'originel langage des Dieux."

The theme of "body" appears then to function at different levels. It affirms the validity of articulated thought as the true expression of interiority and introduces the notion of incarnation, the idea that Montaigne comes most meaningfully into being in his book. We see a variation of the divine word made flesh as the man makes himself in words of flesh and bone. It acknowledges language as "real" and sustains Montaigne's effort to recover himself through it. On his own he uses the power of the verb to move from chaos, loss, and dispersion to a sense of order and form that permits self-knowledge. He comes back to himself, as we suggested earlier in our remarks on conversion, in search of his true image. And like the quest that is its own end, the book is its own end. It does not refer to something preexistent; it pretends only to *be* Montaigne.

Through the network of associations that turn around the notion of body, Montaigne claims his real, physical presence in the work, both by *saying* he is there and by giving the reader the *sense* that he is there; the thematic thread has stylistic consequences. Whether or not he casts the abstract into concrete terms instinctively and spontaneously as Gray suggests (following St. Beuve's lead: "pensée, image, chez lui, c'est tout un"), that tendency clearly dominates the essays and invites further inquiry.[3] A number of excellent studies have analyzed the poetic and compositional processes that create the sense of plasticity. Let us examine the implications of some of their conclusions, and some of our observations, in the context of consubstantiality and incarnation.[4]

II

To speak of the concreteness of Montaigne's prose, particularly evident in his choice of vocabulary and in his imagery, is to restate a commonplace. The emphasis on experience and physical sensation as opposed to abstract reasoning, on the union of body and mind, on the subordination of words to things all nourish the essayist's attempt to lend his thought, and his prose, a quality the reader perceives as substantial, tangible, or sensually apprehensible. Sayce underlines the characteristic solidity and plenitude of Montaigne's style and the world it creates, "a world densely packed with concrete objects which have their own substantial existence quite apart from their functions as illustrations, examples, metaphors and so on."[5] The two passages Montaigne chooses to illustrate poetry's power to animate its subject, to provide its reader with an experience more realistic than actuality itself, both depict lovemaking among the gods, which Montaigne contrasts with the sterile abstraction of the Renaissance treatise: "Les sciences traictent les choses trop finement, d'une mode trop artificielle et differente à la commune et naturelle" (III, 5, 874). If he were of the trade, he adds, he would naturalize art as much as these others artify nature. The vocabulary singled out for special mention in Virgil and Lucretius—the concrete nouns, the active, vividly descriptive verbs, the adjectives chosen for visual or tactile effect—is the language he himself employs, one he endows with material properties that allow it to be bent, turned, and stretched to give weight and depth to its meaning and use.

Words of stuff (*estoffe*) that can be fashioned, metaphors savory to the reader with a good nose, both participate in and represent that Montaignian world of substance with which we are familiar, where love is thirst (III, 5, 877), where pleasures like health are meaty and marrowy (II, 37, 785), ideas are digested (I, 26, 151), discussants fence (III, 8), and judgment is enthroned (III, 13, 1074). The abstract philosopher straddles the epicycle of *Mercure* (II, 17, 634), those with transcendental humors try to walk on stilts while the wise man judges all by the measure of his rump (III, 13, 1115). We encounter Montaigne ruminating, relishing pleasure to study it, to know it just as he listens to come to know his own self, his *forme maistresse* (III, 2, 811). "Je ne me juge que par vray sentiment, non par discours" (III, 13, 1095), he maintains at the end of the *Essais,* as if reasoning and its abstract language are replaced by listening to and watching himself, by feeling. This is dramatically evident in *De l'experience,* where his personal intimacy with his illness and his advancing age becomes the source of knowledge, of both himself and the world. The loss of a tooth, for example, offers Montaigne a microcosmic experience of the natural passage of time and of his own inevitable death more directly and more profoundly than any of the philosophers he excludes from his world.

Early in our study of the *Essais* we watched Montaigne move away from the historical time and space he occupied before the writing, withdraw from that outside world incapable of serving as the wellspring of any sense of being. We saw him dismantle that structure, attack and weaken its underpinnings, its confidence in man and the extent of his intellectual reach, its reliance on the power of discursive reason. He pictured that world as the disparity between its arrogant appearance and the reality of its hollowness. But that vision has its counterpoint in the *Essais* as well. Against pride Montaigne has raised humility, against pretense sincerity, against false knowledge learned ignorance. Ephemeral language has gained substance just as the unnatural world of abstraction has ceded to a universe of concrete things, of material existence. And in this context Montaigne seeks contact with his essential self, to which he refers variously as *patron* and *forme,* by articulating thought—that is, by lending voice to interiority. In the book that is the record of that articulation, the man claims a reality which shares the substantiality of the other objects that people its world. Here his *moy,* his *essence,* are as real, as accessible, as the words that embody them. Montaigne's object in writing, it would appear, is to acquire that sense of entity, of object-ness with which things are endowed. To suggest his own incarnation in the book, in words of flesh and blood, is to fashion for himself a sense of being in the world; it is to be his own source and end.

Barthes' comments on *écrire* as an intransitive verb can be extended from Proust's narrator, whom he chooses as exemplary to describe this aspect of Montaigne's *Essais.* "In the middle verb to write the distance between writer and language diminishes asymptotically. In subjective writings . . . which are active, the agent is not *interior* but *anterior* to the process of writing. . . . In the modern verb of middle voice to write, however, the subject is immediately contemporary with the writing, being effected and affected by it."[6] In the coincidence of "I speaking" and "I spoken of" the writer stands inside the writing as the agent of the action—that is, he affects himself in acting. "The field of the writer is writing itself not as the pure form of art for art's sake but as the only area (*espace*) for the one who writes."[7]

Before he begins to write, we can speak of Montaigne as absence, absence from the world from which he has purposely withdrawn, and, more intimately, absence from himself experienced as the loss of his true image, his sense of dispersion and fragmentation. It is through the writing that he seeks to gain presence, inside the writing where he can be said to exist. As we have stressed, the movement described is not creation from nothing but rather, on the one hand, the recovery of a sense of what has been lost and, on the other, through the imposition of a measure of form and order, the fashioning of a self that is intelligible. In Barthes' terms, Montaigne both causes the writing and is caused by it; in a real sense it is his only true locus. Both his history and his memory reside wholly within the book: "A faute de memoire naturelle j'en forge de papier" (III, 13, 1092). As we suggested in our discussion of imitation and the portrait, the literary form does not express an interiority constituted previous to and outside of language. The writing itself is incarnation, the writer his own maker. Yet we must emphasize as well the many elements that undermine, postpone, and make presence problematic. Rather than being fully realized, it is continually deferred; through the *Essais*, presence is conceived as process.

III

Incarnation, consubstantiality, statements that he and his book are one underlie Montaigne's concern that in this case inside and outside coincide, that thought and expression correspond. They sustain his claim to sincerity and affirm his difference from the world and his refusal of what seems the inevitable disparity of appearance and reality. The ordinary use of language, its equivocal relationship to what it signifies, and thus its imperfect use as an instrument of knowledge find their counterpoint in the book when word and thing are one. In his own case, Montaigne seeks a reintegration of sign and referent, the establishment of an absolute, primal discourse where, as he himself says, "les mots aillent où va la pensée." At this level the word exceeds mere clarity of meaning, becomes more than a direct reference. In fact, language can be said to have transcended its referential function to participate once again in the world of things.

At least this is what Montaigne implies, although he and his reader know that any such moments of convergence are tentative, constantly threatened with dissolution, and that each essay must be a microcosmic reexperience of the entire dialectic. The endlessly renewed effort at self-portrayal, taking place in the change and flux of human time, reveals a multiplicity of faces as subject and object change, as perspective varies; but contradiction and disparity do not affect overall truth: "Tant y a que je me contredits bien à l'adventure, mais la verité, comme disoit Demades, je ne la contredy point" (III, 2, 805). To claim, as Montaigne does, that he and his work are one or to speak, as we have, of his real presence in a discourse that pretends to primacy neither denies the richness and complexity of the portrait nor seeks to minimize the difficulty of painting it with words. Rather it sets the outer limits of the ideal, the bounds of that utopian dream conceived as the perfect friendship that Montaigne strives to recover. A goal he does not, and cannot, reach: "Si mon ame pouvoit prendre pied, je ne m'essaierois pas, je me resoudrois." So that while Montaigne is never entirely there in the book, what is there is entirely Montaigne.

This correspondence underlies the style we have come to appreciate as peculiarly Montaignian, so personal a mode of expression that it seems to have flowed automatically, spontaneously, from his pen. The essayist equates himself with it to affirm its truthfulness, implying that he and his style are one, that to know the one is to make contact with the other: "Mon stile et mon esprit vont vagabondant de mesmes" (III, 9, 994). The mobility and flux that characterize human existence and the nature of the thought process itself inform all aspects of composition: overall structure, phrasing, tempo, vocabulary, imagery. Montaigne looks to the informality and freedom of the conversational style, its vigor and naturalness, as the authentic means to articulate interiority. To the artificially ordered and stylized forms of rhetoric which falsify the real nature of things, Montaigne prefers the oral mode: "Le parler que j'ayme, c'est un parler simple et naif, tel sur le papier qu'à la bouche; un parler succulent et nerveux, court et serré, non tant delicat et peigné comme vehement et brusque: . . . plustost difficile qu'ennuieux, esloingné d'affectation, desreglé, descousu et hardy" (I, 26, 171). In the opening lines of Book Three he explicitly characterizes it as his own: "Je parle au papier comme je parle au premier que je rencontre" (III, 1, 790). His ability to involve his reader as interlocutor, his own dialogue of question and answer, of comment and judgment with himself, function together with the flowing, uneven movement of his phrases and sentences, the suppression of connectives, and the concreteness of his vocabulary to give the prose an improvised, conversational feel.[8] Self-consciously, he has sought to express the movement of his *fantasies*: "mon dessein est de representer en parlant une profonde nonchalance et des mouvemens fortuites et impremeditez, comme naissans des occasions presentes" (III, 9, 963). *Dessein, representer, comme naissans* indicate that he works at achieving a stylistic effect that comes off as unstudied and unpremeditated. This is precisely what Montaigne admires in Plutarch: "que ces gaillardes escapades, que cette variation a de beauté, et plus lors que plus elle retire au nonchalant et fortuite" (994). That is, all the more so when it looks as if it is nonchalant and fortuitous. Plato's *Phaedrus* strikes him by its change and diversity, elements that the ancients did not fear: "et ont une merveilleuse grace à se laisser ainsi rouler au vent, ou à le sembler." Montaigne points up the variety and movement of his own work although he insists on an interior order or composition; it is the inattentive reader who loses his subject, not he, for there is always a word, an image, that picks up the thematic thread. He loves poetry's leaps and gambols, and is willing to accept Platonic implications of fiction and untruth as he juxtaposes this style with his own to highlight its freedom and spontaneity. And the best ancient prose, we recall, shines with the same vigor and boldness.

Montaigne's conversational style is an art, like the art of conversation itself. Freed from the usual pejorative connotations of artificial and dissimulative, it relates to the natural as the essayist's practice of the *art de conferer* to the discussions of the shopboys. Here it denotes a skill to be learned and practiced as a means to truth, an act self-consciously performed to replicate the structure and sense of the ideal posed as natural. Conversation, Montaigne holds, is the most fruitful and natural exercise of the mind, for its dialectical exchange provides that order which is the medium of truth. And his comments on its art broaden most meaningfully to include the book itself, as if the nature and mode of discussion were an epitome of the act of essaying.[9] The *Essais,* considered as an extended dialogue with the self, would then require an appropriately oral style. Although the composition of *De l'art de conferer* (Villey places it at 1586-1587) postdates the beginnings of what can be called the stylistics of conversation, it coincides with a notable flowering of that style in the Third Book and the later additions to the first two books.[10] Our intention is not to identify the essay as the source but rather as the confirmation of the link among the arts of essaying, conversing, and style.

All this appears to fall within the general Western tradition, which, from the time of the ancients, has considered speech to be a more faithful—because more proximate—expression of the soul than the written word. In the *Phaedrus,* Socrates distinguishes between the living word of knowledge, communicated orally and graven in the soul (the true way of writing), and the written word that is no more than an image of it, a memorandum for those who already know (275a-278h). Aristotle conceives of the sounds emitted by the voice as symbols of affections or impressions of the soul and written words as symbols of words spoken (*De Interpretatione,* 16a,3). In the immediacy of its expressions, as a natural effect of the correspondence of voice and soul or of voice and being, the spoken word serves as the genuine medium of interiority. Traditionally, writing stands outside, at the second remove from things thought in the mind, as Derrida points out:

> la voix est au plus proche du signifié, qu'on le détermine rigour-
> eusement comme sens (pensé ou vécu) ou plus lâchement comme
> chose. Au regard de ce qui unirait indissolublement la voix à l'âme
> ou à la pensée du sens signifié, voire à la chose même (qu'on le
> fasse selon le geste aristotélicien . . . ou selon le geste de la théo-
> logie médiévale déterminant la *res* comme chose créée à partir de
> son *eidos*, de son sens pensé dans le logos ou l'entendement infini
> de Dieu), tout signifiant, et d'abord le signifiant écrit, serait dé-
> rivé. Il serait toujours technique et représentatif.[11]

Derrida attributes the perpetuation of this logo- and phono-centered tradition (which he marks as a point of origin of the distinction between *signifié* and *signifiant*) and the corresponding devaluation of *écriture* through the Middle Ages to Christian metaphysics, to the "créationnisme et . . . l'infinitisme chrétiens lorsqu'ils s'approprient les ressources de la conceptualité grecque."[12]

At the same time, as we saw earlier, the Christian Middle Ages sustains a view affirming the primacy of the book.[13] Derrida acknowledges this seeming paradox but insists that the metaphorical nature of the archetypal books of scripture, of nature, of memory, eternal and universal, the ideal union of logos-referent-sign, always calls up the imperfect, physical, textual writing of man and thus diminishes it.[14] Montaigne's own reservations express this sense of imperfection, and yet at the same time he commits himself to a book. In his case the metaphor functions as well to enhance the value of physical books and confirm the potential of the written word as a source of truth.

To pursue this further will take us too far afield. Let us simply note the development of these two different emphases, both of which nourish the composition of the *Essais*. We have already looked at the properties acquired by Montaigne's conversational mode: the tradition that considers speech the more genuine medium of the soul clearly lends an element of authenticity, of truthfulness, which would be lacking in unidimensional written style. At the same time, our earlier comments on language, and Montaigne's notion of the airy medium of words, appropriately characterize the ephemeral quality of speech. Even if he accepts the primacy of oral expression, as his own preference indicates, the nature of his enterprise seems to demand that it take the form of a book. Unlike the revered Socrates, Montaigne's quest for wisdom and self-knowledge must unfold as the written text. If his language is to contain or embody interiority, if its order is to determine his sense of self, if it is to provide his past, be his history, it must assume a form that is accessible—that is, which itself has being in space and endures: "ceux qui se repassent par fantasie seulement et par langue quelque heure, ne s'examinent pas si primement, ny ne se penetrent, comme celuy qui en faict son estude, son ouvrage et son mestier, qui s'engage à un registre de durée . . ." (II, 18, 665). Thus we come back once again to the primacy of the book to find in the tension between the conversational mode and the written medium, between the movement of thought and the fixity of prose, between the immediacy of the voice and the mediacy of the pen, the heart of the dialectic that is Montaigne's quest for the self.

The difference between oral and written modes reflects the opposition for the speaker between natural and artificial. His claims of an inability to organize his material, to sustain a prolonged development, his insistence that chance rather than art underlies the movement of his thought ("les fantasies de la musique sont conduictes par art, les miennes par sort"), distinguish the *Essais* from the early-sixteenth-century preference for the organized and elaborate style and structure of Ciceronian prose to allow it the freedom and spontaneity associated with conversation. His preference for Seneca's flowing, open style (to which he refers as *parler*) seems another way of emphasizing the oral over the written quality of the work: "Comme à faire, à dire aussi je suy tout simplement ma forme naturelle: d'où c'est à l'adventure que je puis plus à parler qu'à escrire" (II, 17, 638). Not that the spoken word is at all times the genuine item, for it too can be contaminated by artificiality and contrivance, as Montaigne points out in his critique of rhetoric ("cette science de gueule") in *De la vanité des paroles* (I, 51). But his strongest accent seeks to convey the impression that his reader is a listener, that if the way he writes has a style it must be recognized as that of speech: "si je dois nommer stile un parler informe et sans regle, un jargon populaire et un proceder sans definition, sans partition, sans conclusion, trouble" (II, 17, 637). Even as he attributes a "style comique et privé" (I, 40, 252) to his writing, he stresses how this is naturally his manner, how it characterizes his language as well. Auerbach's suggestion that this is an unmistakable allusion to the realistic style of antique comedy, the *sermo pedester* or *humilis*, confirms the emphasis Montaigne desires to place on the genuineness of his presentation.[15]

For the reasons we have indicated, Montaigne prefers to disavow the literariness of the *Essais*, to conceal and dissimulate his art, his concern with the very aspects of prose style which produce the unstudied effect he achieves.[16] An unrehearsed presentation is what he is after, one that expresses the natural disjointed and disconnected, the changing and fragmented self. At the same time, order, form, and continuity—as expressions of that end toward which he strives—appear to depend on the nature of his activity as writing, and on the art it involves. Montaigne seeks to escape the implications of art as artifice and avoid imposing a form from without, forcing a structure on his work and his thought. He maintains that the shape emerges from the inside, faithful to the movement, variety, and diversity of human life. And so he sets his thought down on the page, ostensibly as he thinks it and, he would have us believe, as he says it. This written record provides the enduring account without which there can be no sense of self—that is, perceptible order or continuity. In this regard the essayist appears to fulfill the conditions necessary for keeping the soul from losing itself (*De l'oisiveté*), for examining and penetrating to the essentials of the self, and for training the mind to operate with some measure of order (*Du démentir*).

The same tension between movement and stability underlies Montaigne's attitude toward French and Latin. The sixteenth-century efforts to return Latin to its purer classical form by purging it of those elements acquired in its duration as a living language reflect Renaissance nostalgia for the revered ancient world (and disdain for its medieval heirs) and reveal a longing for stability, for a written language existing as if immobile, outside of time. Contemporary preoccupation with literary style, with building up French by analogy with classical Latin (and Greek as well), was clearly meant to set modes of written expression, to render the vernacular worthy of dealing with the loftier subjects of intellection, free from the contingencies of present moments. But if the general trend through the century appears as the effort to reduce the gap separating the two languages, for his own reasons Montaigne chooses to stress their differences. He strikes a modest pose, deprecating his work, to explain why he does not write in Latin; if his had been durable matter, if he had expected (or intended) it to survive, he would have written in a stable language. The real issue, of course, is not that of modesty but of appropriateness, for French as he describes it corresponds to the nature of his subject. Montaigne emphasizes the variation of the language in full evolution, and says of it, as he might of himself, "il escoule tous les jours de nos mains" (III, 9, 982). He is not looking to convey impressions of stability or fixity through his choice of language, but rather of movement and changing form. The medium he chooses, like the man he portrays, is meant to express becoming.

The choice, of course, imposes itself, but it is interesting to note that although French is, indeed, in the process of dynamic development, the tendency through the latter part of the century progresses toward more restricted form, less overall freedom. In

terms of syntactical order, this trend had begun in the fifteenth
century and was to culminate in the establishment of the seven-
teenth-century classical style. The appearance of the first linguistic studies of French and the efforts to construct grammars
acknowledged the rapid change the language was undergoing
(and, like Montaigne, recognized that writers were quickly out-
dated) and sought to slow it down by setting forms and usage.[17]
Generally speaking, though, Montaigne's emphasis on the
changing character of French in the sixteenth century is correct.
And the freedom it allowed him in syntactical structure, in
vocabulary, phrasing, and the use of connectives lies at the very
center of that interplay between written and oral style.

III

The desire for consubstantiality, the longing to possess spatial
entity, depends on the written word for fulfillment. And a sense
of constancy and duration derive from it as well. The ancients
attributed a stability, even a kind of permanence, to writing,
which they distinguished from the fluid, fleeting world of
speech, as the Roman proverb warned: *verba volant, scripta manent.*
As if spatial form conferred a measure of materiality and, because
space and time intersect, of fixity. The Western tradition has
long expressed abstract intellectual activity in spatial terms. One
thinks of the logical *topoi* or rhetorical invention from the Greeks
and Latins through the Middle Ages. Medieval rhetoricians used
schematically diagrammed layouts and visual images in manu-
scripts to teach the art of memory.[18] But it remained for the
Renaissance to exploit the visual constructs and models and
extend the spatial implications of the written word. In the main,
the development of printing served as stimulus. The process itself
dramatized the concept of the "fixed" word; it offered new possibilities for the physical disposition of language; and, practically
speaking, it facilitated the reproduction of visual schemata. If we
situate Petrus Ramus' emphasis on charts and geometrical pat-

tern in this framework (as representative of a general contemporary fad of diagrammatic logic), his enterprise becomes an effort to simplify scholastic logic through the greater use of visual modes of conceptualization, to endow the evanescent world of discourse with spatial dimension, to give words the substance and manipulability of things.[19] Where Ramist dialectic converged with contemporary poetic practice, poets sought to embody concepts in words whose physical arrangement conveyed meaning. And Renaissance rhetoricians like Scaliger stressed the disposition and placement of figures as a central element of composition and style.[20]

The sixteenth century's general conception of writing as a spatial art, one that lends materiality and stability to the fleeting world of speech, to the abstract world of intellection, brings us back to Montaigne and his words of flesh and blood, and to what he appears to share with Ramus. The essayist's notion of consubstantiality and his efforts to effect a spatial entity through language by reducing the disparity between words and things, indeed his conception of words *as* things, parallel the logician's spatializing efforts. Montaigne's emphasis on a nonrhetorical form, on simplicity of expression and natural style, finds its counterpart in the Ramist plain-style, described by an English advocate as "a close, naked, natural way of speaking." In both cases we find a reaction to the verbal excess of rhetorical eloquence and scholastic jargon, of words prized for their own sake, which keep meaning from getting through.

If the comparison of Ramus and Montaigne reveals certain points of convergence, the differences it raises are more telling and help to put aspects of the *Essais* into greater relief. To sharpen the juxtaposition let us examine what can be considered the deepest implications of Ramist rhetoric (which emerge most clearly in the hands of its later practitioners):

> By its very nature, Ramist rhetoric asserts . . . that there is no way to discovery or to understanding through voice, and ultimately seems to deny that the processes of person to person communication play any necessary role in intellectual life.

> [Speech] is resented . . . as an accretion to thought, hereupon
> imagined as ranging noiseless concepts or "ideas" in the silent
> field of mental space.[21]

Clearly the voiceless, depersonalized world described here is not
Montaigne's. Although sharing Ramus' concern with the spatiality of language and thought, he does not make his choice
absolute or exclusive. While fleeting discourse challenges the
urge for stability and duration, Montaigne does not attempt to
suppress it or to replace it wholly by the written word. In the
world of the *Essais,* the personal, individualized voice speaks loud
and clear, to be written down, as the only means to discovery or
understanding. Montaigne appears to situate his work at that
point where the spoken becomes the written word, as if to seize
simultaneously the spontaneous genuineness of the voice and the
spatial fixity of the printed page.

Montaigne requires voice—although he must attempt to
neutralize certain of its properties—just as he must write, and
overcome its drawbacks, as if each medium compensated for the
problems of the other. If the written word is solid, frozen in
print, then in its immobility it threatens to betray the real nature
of "things" as Montaigne sees it. How distorted the world of
change must appear locked in written syntax. And if oral
discourse represents essential instability, flight, and evanescence,
by itself it leads nowhere, or everywhere, which as Montaigne
said is the same thing. Discourse, to be meaningful, must
acquire a measure of form, of order, which the writing provides;
and the corollary is also true, that writing to be meaningful
must be authentic discourse, as the juxtaposition of discussion
and essaying suggests in *De l'art de conferer*. The acquisition of
knowledge, and, most fundamentally, knowledge of the self,
depends on speaking through writing: "Je parle au papier."
Socratic dialogue may serve as a model but here, for lack of a true
interlocutor, it must take place with the self, within the realm of
writing.

"Method" occupies the center of Ramist dialectic and by its etymology (following after, way through) reveals its source as a spatial concept designating the pursuit of knowledge or the mode of inquiry. This interest in orderly procedure, in system or structure, which was to reach an apogee of sorts in the seventeenth century with Bacon and Descartes, permeated a wide field of Renaissance activity, and we find works on method in disciplines as diverse as letter writing, rhetoric, dialectic, and theology. In this sense the Ramist approach merely exaggerated the contemporary search for intellectual order, the urge to define the internal structures of knowledge and to develop procedures for teaching the various disciplines, which motivated humanists, pedagogues as well as poets (particularly in the area of what is called scientific poetry). Hence the dialectician's emphasis on rules, on the arrangement of axioms, on the use of syllogism, which become the means for the demonstration as well as the building up of knowledge. Spatial conceptions based on a visualist metaphor of the act of cognition impart a maximum sense of order and control.

In our discussion of the *Essais* we have tended to speak of a number of different "spaces." In chapter 2 we explored the notion of an outside, physical space from which Montaigne withdraws to fix his attention and activity on the locale of interiority. In determining the reality of the life of the mind, we have considered the dynamics of writing as the effort to overcome the metaphorical space separating words and things required for the faithful rendering of that life (chapter 5). And finally, in the last two chapters, we have used the notion of spatiality to explore the implications of consubstantiality and the function of essaying oneself in writing. All of this comes together as a single, overall dialectic by which Montaigne moves from the physical world and himself in it to an interior space from which he re-emerges physically as the book. It is to that middle term or space that the consideration of Ramus' method and its visual path brings us.

Method is anathema to Montaigne. Taking the syllogism as

representative, he uses vigorous invective and the force of satire to disarm and destroy its pretensions. Distinguishing true philosophy from dialectical method, he states, "C'est 'Barroco' et 'Baralipton' qui rendent leurs supposts ainsi crotez et enfumés, ce n'est pas elle: ils ne la connoissent que par ouïr dire" (I, 26, 161). Montaigne ridicules syllogistic reasoning through parody: "Voire mais, que fera-il si on le presse de la subtilité sophistique de quelque syllogisme: le jambon fait boire, le boire desaltere, parquoy le jambon desaltere? Qu'il s'en mocque. Il est plus subtil de s'en mocquer que d'y respondre" (171). These dialectical tricks ("finesses dialectiques") subordinate matter to form to create a disequilibrium that obscures reality. Like the eloquent words that cloak the nature of things, they are distorting shapes imposed from without. In the tension between matter and form so often expressed as the relation of inside to outside, words depend on things and in the instance of ideal expression become one with them. Perverse dialectics manipulates empty words freely (since they are only insubstantial outsides) and forms them into configurations it pretends are real.

Method implies a fixed system with clear, precise organization and an orderly movement through that structure to a set goal, to conclusive results—knowledge, truth in science, medicine, logic, letter writing, grammar. Montaigne's world is opposed to method at all points: its fixity, systematization, orderliness, its confident assurance of success. In *De la vanité* where he valorizes ignorance and what man does not know, the essayist uses the metaphor of the voyage as life as essays to describe the only motion appropriate to man:

> Je ne l'entreprens [the voyage] ny pour en revenir, ny pour le parfaire; j'entreprens seulement de me branler, pendant que le branle me plaist. [III, 9, 977]

> S'il faict laid à droicte, je prens à gauche; si je me trouve mal propre à monter à cheval, je m'arreste. . . . Je ne trace aucune ligne certaine, ny droicte ny courbe. [985]

The progression of his life through time is "un mouvement d'yvroigne titubant, vertigineux, informe, ou des joncs que l'air manie casuellement selon soy" (964). And when Montaigne describes the quest for the self, his effort to follow the workings of his mind, he again speaks of movement, this time in interior space: "C'est une espineuse entreprinse, et plus qu'il ne semble, de suyvre une alleure si vagabonde que celle de nostre esprit; de penetrer les profondeurs opaques de ses replis internes; de choisir et arrester tant de menus airs de ses agitations" (II, 6, 378). His style follows the errant progress of his thought: "Mon style et mon esprit vont vagabondant de mesmes" (III, 9, 994).

Movement is a commonplace in Montaigne, change the single-most characteristic element of the world he describes.[22] Physical reality (from the continents to the pyramids to the human body), political states, ideas, opinions, fashions, himself from moment to moment, all exist as becoming in time: "il n'y a aucune constante existence, ny de nostre estre, ny de celuy des objects. Et nous, et nostre jugement, et toutes choses mortelles, vont coulant et roulant sans cesse" (II, 12, 601). Human activity, whether reading ("J'avois trainé languissant . . . : au bout d'un long et ennuyeux chemin . . ." [I, 26, 147]), the study of true philosophy ("mais si peut on y arriver . . . par des routtes ombrageuses" [161]), or the effort to attain the natural ("Nature est un doux guide. . . . Je queste partout sa piste" [III, 13, 1113]) appears as progression along a path or road. But however sequential or chronological it appears, whether the progressive aging of the body, the successive portraits of the self, or what is described above as the easy, pleasant road to virtue, movement tends to be discontinuous and tentative, without formal order. The way is often difficult to maintain, as Montaigne will point out in *De la cruauté* as he looks from another angle at the road to virtue: "cette aisée, douce et panchante voie, par où se conduisent les pas reglez d'une bonne inclination de nature, n'est pas celle de la vraye vertu. Elle demande un chemin aspre et espineux" (II, 11, 423). The traveler so often has trouble finding his way and, as his vagabond mind and style denote, his movement is one of "here and there," a wandering aimless and endless. When Montaigne speaks of *s'essayer*, the starts and stops, the uneven and irregular gait, the multidirectional thrusts dominate. The familiar passage from *De Democritus et Heraclitus* bears repeating in full:

> Le jugement est un util à tous subjects, et se mesle par tout. A cette cause, aux essais que j'en fay ici, j'y employe toute sorte d'occasion. Si c'est un subject que je n'entende point, à cela mesme je l'essaye, sondant le gué de bien loing; et puis, le trouvant trop profond pour ma taille, je me tiens à la rive: et cette reconnoissance de ne pouvoir passer outre, c'est un traict de son effect, voire de ceux dequoy il se vante le plus. Tantost, à un subject vain et de neant, j'essaye voir s'il trouvera dequoy lui donner corps. . . . Tantost je le promene à un subject noble et tracassé, auquel il n'a rien à trouver de soy, le chemin en estant si frayé qu'il ne peut marcher que sur la piste d'autruy. Là il fait son jeu à eslire la route quy luy semble la meilleure, et, de mille sentiers, il dict que cettuy-cy, ou celuy là, a esté le mieux choisi. . . . Tout mouvement nous descouvre. [I, 50, 301-302]

The process conforms to the nature of things, the procedure is without method, a systemless system for moving about, for allowing the motion to describe its own order and form. Fortune, chance, random movement each plays its role; spontaneity, diversity, variety dominate.

We should, perhaps, open a short parenthesis here to remind ourselves that when the narrative voice speaks the claims he makes are his own—that is, valid only within his book. He wants the reader to believe, for example, that he converses with the paper as with anyone he meets, that what we read is unmediated thought, spreading out naturally on the page. On the other hand, his own comments on style cited above and the skillful stylistic art that recent studies have revealed show the writer crafting his work to give it the look, or, more appropriately, the feel, of spontaneity. While the procedure is not fixed or systematic, it is calculated and controlled. If "spontaneous" style or form exists anywhere, it is only *inside* the literary world of the book. We will come back to discuss questions of verisimilitude, of the relation of art and nature, in the *Essais* at greater length in the next chapter.

The Renaissance accent on configurations in space, stable or in motion, logical or astronomical, Ramist or Copernican, broadens a traditional tendency to describe intellectual cognition by visualist analogies.[23] The coincidence of knowing and perceiving was present in Greek, suggesting perhaps that of the senses it was considered the most informative, the most reliable. Montaigne's involvement in space builds up a world of concrete, visible entities whose accessibility or impenetrability is expressed in terms of lusters and faces which sometimes dazzle and deceive, sometimes open up to study and contact. As we noted earlier, man's imperfect eyesight also becomes an obstacle to truth. Montaigne's quest for self-knowledge demands that he look at himself: "Regardez dans vous" (III, 9, 1001). And he does: "Moy qui m'espie de plus prez, qui ay les yeux incessamment tendus sur moy, comme celuy qui n'ay pas fort à-faire ailleurs," although his own troubled vision ("ma veuë . . . desreglée" [II, 12, 565]) sees a multiplicity of conflicting faces whose meaning is difficult to sort out. As he says in *De l'art de conferer*, he tries to see himself as something apart, as a tree or a neighbor—that is, to exploit spatiality by providing perspective. Montaigne juxtaposes *voir* and *estudier* to justify his frank and open manner as the basis of moral rectitude and of self-amendment: "Il faut voir son vice et l'estudier pour le redire. Ceux qui le celent à autruy, le celent ordinairement à eux-mesmes. Et ne le tiennent pas pour assés couvert, s'ils le voyent; ils le soustrayent et desguisent à leur propre conscience" (III, 5, 845). Whether man hides from himself or things hide from him, to pierce the veil of appearance, to penetrate the disparity between inside and outside, to know in Montaignian terms is to see.

While Montaigne's use of the metaphor of vision underlines that side of cognition related to discursive reason, to explanation traditionally posed in these terms, he does not circumscribe knowing in this way. The visualist analogy—with the stability

and materiality it implies—is particularly appropriate to the
essayist's quest for spatial entity. At the same time, he extends
the means to knowledge by opening himself up to the potential
of the other senses. In the passage quoted above from *De Democritus et Heraclitus,* essaying his judgment on various subjects
becomes stabbing, pinching, licking as well as seeing. Montaigne listens (*escouter*) to his ideas since he has to write them
down, just as he describes contact with essential form as a
function of listening: "il n'est personne, s'il s'escoute, qui ne
descouvre en soy une forme sienne, une forme maistresse . . ."
(III, 2, 811). To appreciate the vigorous poetry of Virgil and
Lucretius he ruminates their words to draw out their true flavor.
Through *De l'experience* he describes what he has learned from the
"feel" of experience: "il se sent par experience que . . ." (1067).
Montaigne lets himself be guided by the general law of the
world, which he locates by feel: "Je la sçauray assez quand je la
sentiray" (1073). And when he distinguishes his attitude toward
life from those who merely "pass the time," he juxtaposes *estudier*
with *savourer* et *ruminer* to suggest that he understands and
possesses life by analogy with the sense of taste (1112).

Montaigne's last essay (III, 13) explores the ground we have
been covering, posing reason and experience as the two means to
knowledge. With characteristic irony, he acknowledges the
traditional superiority accorded to reason and the rather second-
rate position held by experience ("moyen plus foible et moins
digne"), and in the name of truth—"chose si grande, que nous ne
devons desdaigner aucune entremise qui nous y conduise"—sets
out to reverse the roles. Intellection is played against apprehension in an immediate and lively way to affirm experience as man's
most useful source of information about himself and the world.
The subjects of health, eating, sleeping—the natural preoccupations of a speaker concerned with illness and advancing age—
form a thematic framework where what is learned from books (or
from doctors) pales before one's own bodily sensations, where
abstract speculation or concern with the future deprive the self-
consciously old man of the "feel" of his fleeting last days. This

emphasis on physical living translates into an impressive pattern of sensory analogies to knowing by experience, which are woven through the fabric of the essay. Wisdom, happiness, and the recognition of one's own condition do not derive from examples drawn from Caesar's life but from listening to the voices of one's own: "Escoutons y seulement: nous nous disons tout ce de quoy nous avons principalement besoing" (1074). That accent on feeling we noted above receives unequivocal statement when Montaigne rejects discursive reasoning and the language in which it operates: "Je ne me juge que par vray sentiment, non par discours" (1095). Whether speaking of his effort to seize each day ("je le retaste, je m'y tiens" [1111]) or the difference between the scholarly classifications and categories and his own general and groping presentation ("à tastons" [1076]), the senses of touch, taste, and hearing serve as physical correlatives to knowing. It is interesting to note that these senses function analogously in the extrarational experience of mystics.

The move away from reason to nonintellectual ways of knowing (expressed as the most concrete senses) signals the desire for equilibrium. Montaigne deflates overblown reason to redress the imbalance caused by the subordination of experiential knowledge. By enhancing nonverbal means of apprehension he also limits the range of language, with its inherent ambiguities and obscurities. But however much Montaigne denigrates man's rational side and his tendency to lofty pursuits, his purpose is control rather than suppression, redirection rather than negation. Reason occupies a center in this many-centered, most intellectual discussion of the nonintellectual side of knowing and living.[24] In fact, the *Essais* themselves can be considered the intellect's own look into the nature of its activity. The visual metaphor thus continues to play its dual role as an interpreter of spatial reality and the correlate of reason and explanation. Even as he is listening and feeling, Montaigne has his eye on himself: "Si chacun espioit de pres les effects et circonstances des passions qui le regentent, comme j'ay faict de celle à qui j'estois tombé en partage, il les verroit venir, et ralantiroit un peu leur impetuosité et leur course" (1074). He savors and ruminates a pleasurable moment and brings reason into the process: "Je consulte d'un contentement avec moy . . . ; je le sonde et plie ma raison à le recueillir" (1112). Montaigne sets his soul to admire herself (*se mirer*) in this prosperous state. And while there are few instances of light as clarity in the *Essais*, since imperfect reason takes for truth what is most often false brilliance or superficial luster ("je ne sçay quelle apparence de clarté et verité imaginaire" [1068]), vision and reason are inevitably and, one senses, necessarily associated with the concrete senses. Montaigne feels himself, as perhaps the most physical way to affirm his existence in space, but he still has a need to see himself—that is, to think about himself, to intellectualize.

Our earlier discussion of the reality of the mind, of life lived most meaningfully through the intellect, posited the relationship between feeling and thinking as the distinction between actual experience and reflection.[25] There we spoke of vicarious experience, of physical life distanced in time and in space and relived in the mind as its most significant expression. Here Montaigne's juxtaposition of actual and intellectual experience, of knowing as feeling and watching—in effect his insistence on the physical expressed through the written—appear to restate the same dynamic. Its multiple dimensions elevate the realm of the particular and temporal by posing it as subject worthy of study, indeed as the only subject so worthy, and lower the intellect from the abstract heights toward which it yearns to fix it on the individual man in time. The physical and the mental converge as Montaigne affirms the union of mind and body, as he collapses physics and metaphysics to make the whole self the single valid object of concern. This is the point where life and literature merge, where essays become consubstantial to the self. It is the point where art becomes the means to truth, where being becomes the end of art.

PART IV
LIFE AND ART

10
Life and Art

"J'ay un dictionnaire tout
à part moy" (III, 13, 1111)

I

The discussion of art in the *Essais* has to wend its way carefully
through the implications both pejorative and positive of Montaigne's varied use of the word. Generally speaking, the subject
arises as the negative term in the couple *nature-art*, a favorite
antithesis that spreads out to inform a wide range of familiar
Montaignian oppositions that we have touched upon in the
course of our study: ignorance-knowledge; the primitive-the
cultured; philosophy-the way of nature; conscience-law; conversational style-rhetoric and oratory.[1] When Montaigne speaks of
art, he implies an obscuring veil that the working of speculative
reason, pride, the desire to know or to impress casts over a kind
of essential form or way of being inherent in things. Human
constructs and artifacts also becloud "true nature," seen in
temporal and spatial terms as a remove closer to the "real" point
of man's origin (in this lies the basis of Montaigne's primitivism).
They disguise and distort the face of nature considered the vivi-
fying force of the universe and the supreme good. In each case
what is inherent has been subordinated to what is external, what
is real to what is artificial, manmade. Something original, something essential, something at the very heart of being human
appears to get lost, whether it is expressed as "nostre mere

nature" (I, 26, 157), to which the ideal pupil is referred, or "nostre grande et puissante mere nature" (I, 31, 206), which regulates primitive societies, whether as the faculty of judgment common to all or the laws of nature ("les loix de nature" [III, 10, 1009]), whether as something akin to *natura naturans* or to *natura naturata*. And it gets lost to art.

Art meets with poor treatment since it represents contrivance that smothers the source of virtue, truth, knowledge, pleasure: "Ce n'est pas raison que l'art gaigne le point d'honneur sur nostre grande et puissante mere nature. Nous avons tant rechargé la beauté et richesse de ses ouvrages par nos inventions, que nous l'avons du tout estouffée" (I, 31, 205). The effort to escape the misery of his condition through art only plunges man deeper into it: "A peine est-il en son pouvoir, par sa condition naturelle, de gouter un seul plaisir entier et pur, encore se met-il en peine de le retrancher par discours: il n'est pas assez chetif, si par art et par estude il n'augmente sa misere" (I, 30, 200). In the *Apologie* Montaigne attacks the false premise used to distinguish man from the animals by imagining all creatures in the hands of beneficent nature. Human art is not the outgrowth of freedom or the sign of dignity; it signals man's alienation from his rightful and proper place in the universal scheme of things. Nature as *maratre* is a perverse myth engendered by human pride to valorize the achievement of its art.

In that continuing movement of the *Essais* which is recovery as well as discovery, Montaigne seeks to reestablish what he senses as lost: his grasp of the self enjoyed in the perfect friendship, his image held by La Boétie before his death—that stability and wholeness represented by their union. The preference for nature, the desire to penetrate the false way she has been painted (III, 13, 1073), to seek out her true path beneath the artificial tracks that cover her (1113)—whether what is meant by nature is the animating force of the universe or the way things "are"—manifest the same effort at recuperation. In the essays the quest for self-knowledge and the pursuit of nature and the natural are merely differing faces of the same dialectic. The *forme sienne* and *forme maistresse* of each man seem to stand at their juncture.

To suggest that the natural equals the good in every circumstance, and that art is always bad, however, is to oversimplify their relationship.[2] In *De l'affection des peres aux enfans* (II, 8) Montaigne takes a view of reason different from that dictated by the framework of the *Apologie* to see in it man's distinct, and privileged, faculty:

> Puisqu'il a pleu à Dieu nous doüer de quelque capacité de discours, affin que, comme les bestes, nous ne fussions pas servilement assujectis aux loix communes, ains que nous nous y appliquassions par jugement et liberté volontaire, nous devons bien prester un peu à la simple authorité de nature, mais non pas nous laisser tyranniquement emporter à elle; la seule raison doit avoir la conduite de nos inclinations. [387]

The tendency to subordinate nature to reason and judgment, or perhaps to bring them together to attain a higher form of human behavior, increases through the *Essais*.[3] Montaigne appears willing to treat nature more equivocally, to allow, as in this case, that man not slavishly submit to it but rather use his reason either to override it or enhance its impulse by adding the consent of judgment, freely practiced. In *De la cruauté* (II, 11) he suggests that virtue achieved by reason overcoming temptation stands higher than natural goodness or innocence even though he has to place God and Socrates beyond all consideration. When Montaigne reaffirms the imperative "know thyself" at the end of *De la vanité*, he recognizes the demand that man overcome his natural inclination to preoccupation elsewhere: "Pour ne nous desconforter, nature a rejetté bien à propos l'action de nostre veuë au dehors" (III, 9, 1000). Benevolent nature, it appears, protecting man from the disconcerting view of his own inadequacy, must be overcome if man is to seek himself as he is. The visualist metaphors that dominate the close of the essay underscore the place of reason and judgment in the quest for self-knowledge.

Montaigne allows himself the same latitude as he deals with art, for although it remains firmly anchored in opposition to nature, there are occasions when, like things intellectual, it functions positively. Art can be military skill and science, compatible with valor when applied for the public good (II, 27, 698); it can even be the practice of medicine, which when properly used becomes a field for forming one's judgment, a source of wisdom (III, 9, 931). Montaigne's effective diversionary tactics, which draw the grieving widow from her mourning, apply to himself as well when faced with the loss of his friend: "Ayant besoing d'une vehemente diversion pour m'en distraire, je me fis, par art, amoureux, et par estude, à quoy l'aage m'aidoit" (III, 4, 835). While the essayist inverts his subject through *De la diversion* to make man's propensity to distraction a sign of the weakness of mind and soul, diversion remains an art that has its season. And when it comes to thoughts of his own death, he claims in *De la vanité* to try to burrow and hide from it by design: "Je cherche à coniller et à me desrober de ce passage, non par crainte, mais par art" (III, 9, 978).

In his tribute to Epaminondas Montaigne praises the paradoxical union of violence and virtue in what he calls the rich composition of his soul. Juxtaposing nature and art, he allows each as the possible cause of moral strength: "Ce courage si gros, enflé et obstiné contre la douleur, la mort, la pauvreté, estoit ce nature ou art qui l'eust attendry jusques au poinct d'une si extreme douceur et debonnaireté de complexion?" (III, 1, 801). The essayist draws the same parallel in *De la vanité*, this time in a pejorative context, when he confirms man's excessive preoccupation with the opinions of others: "Qui que ce soit, ou art ou nature, qui nous imprime cette condition de vivre par la relation à autruy, nous faict beaucoup plus de mal que de bien" (III, 9, 955). Here again the suggestion that both art and nature can lead to both good and bad blurs the distinctions between them and makes their coupling as antithesis weaker. Art may produce virtue and courage just as nature may lead man away from himself.

The potential of art to play a meaningful positive role in

human life looms distinctly in the *Essais,* particularly in the last book, as if to suggest that the obscurities, disguises, and distortions it produces derive from perverse practice and excess. Nowhere is the notion of proper employ more evident than in *De l'art de conferer,* whose centrality in the work we have already noted. Here *art* is a skill acquired, attitudes and postures assumed in order to reach a higher level of human conduct. The way of discussion becomes a means to the way of living, both because usage and custom form part of the man and because discussion, essays, and life blend in a common activity. Montaigne pinpoints the tension between the proper and improper use of this art, as aware of the danger of verbal encounter as of its promise. He argues against the "moyen scholastique et artiste" of treating a subject in favor of a "moyen naturel, d'un sain entendement" (III, 8, 926) and against the "excellence artificielle" of the Master of Arts (927) at the same time that he affirms the value of discussion as *art.* The theme of ineptitude implies that the problem is less art than its use. As in the case of reason and learning, misuse by the weak-minded and the clumsy outweighs the inherent drawbacks of *science* or *discours*: "C'est chose de grand poix que la science; ils fondent dessoubs: pour estaller et distribuer cette noble et puissante matiere, pour l'employer et s'en ayder, leur engin n'a ny assez de vigueur, ny assez de maniement: elle ne peut qu'en une forte nature; or elles sont bien rares" (931-32).

The essay on managing one's will makes a parallel statement about the tension between inclination and design. The natural tendency of the will to give too much of itself, to mortgage itself to things exterior or be carried off by them, must be tempered by what can only be called an art of self-control, of counterpoint, which recognizes one's own nature (custom and fortune are here absorbed in nature) and seeks to keep its activities within bounds: "La carriere de nos desirs doit estre circonscripte et restraincte à un court limite des commoditez les plus proches et contigues; et doit en outre leur course se manier, non en ligne droite qui face bout ailleurs, mais en rond, duquel les deux

pointes se tiennent et terminent en nous par un brief contour"
(III, 10, 1011). The gaze fixed on the self in the effort to know
also functions to direct; reason and judgment trying themselves
out have a managing role to play as well. In the *Apologie* Montaigne suggests that art limit the range of man's reach: "On a
raison de donner à l'esprit humain les barrieres les plus con-
traintes qu'on peut. En l'estude, comme au reste, il luy faut
compter et regler ses marches, il luy faut tailler par art les limites
de sa chasse" (II, 12, 559). While the context obviously differs as
the essayist seeks to humble reason and its questing, the idea of
art imposing limitations, governing and administering, has a
familiar ring.

Montaigne's characteristic attitudes on life are generally
lumped together in what is often called his "art of living."
Drawn for the most part from the Third Book and based on the
interplay of nature, custom, reason, judgment, and the watchful
eye, this "art" represents his efforts to come to grips with pain
and discomfort (both bodily and spiritual) and to heighten the
enjoyment of pleasure and the physical experience of life. The
quotation from Manilius which opens *De l'experience* indeed
suggests that experience can lead to an art of living if one heeds
its examples:

> Per varios usus artem experientia fecit:
> Exemplo monstrante viam (1065).
> [Experience, by example led
> By varied trials art has bred.]

In a general way, our discussion bears on this rather broad sense
of *art*. At the same time, we must take into account the varied
and precise dimensions of *art* in the *Essais*, for, as we have seen,
the concept is not unequivocal. For all of its made-up and
managed qualities, art is indivisibly related to nature and truth.
Or perhaps we should say because of those qualities, for it is art as
literature that becomes the means to life. When we began our
study of the *Essais* we attempted to focus on the work on its own
terms, to understand the fiction—that is, the art of what looks so

much like life. Now we want to turn the problem the other way to inquire how what is art can open out on life. Rather than deny or subordinate the notion that the *Essais* are *art*, or literature, we begin to understand that only in that role do they bear a meaningful relation to life. Art and life, the made-up and the real, are bound together as one.

II

Montaigne's familiar leit-motif of the world as a theater functions at multiple levels to express his views on existence and human behavior. In characteristic baroque metaphor, he imagines life lived as roles played on a stage, but here the role and reality are confused, indeed the two as indistinguishable give rise to deep feelings of instability, of fragmentation, of the illusory nature of life. While this perspective finds expression in countless works of the late-sixteenth and seventeenth centuries—one thinks of Shakespeare, Cervantes, Corneille—these common baroque elements are the basis of Montaigne's personal vision. They are precisely the qualities associated with the death of La Boétie, which we have watched the essayist engage and encounter through the *Essais*.

But the world as a stage is more than the backdrop for the partial, disoriented self, for Montaigne links the idea of roles to the problem of authenticity. In the constant tension between inside and outside, between private self and public persona, man seeks continuously to suggest that he is as he appears. Position, status, eloquence in speech and elegance in manner disguise what lies beneath, always threatening to stick to the skin, as in the case of the orator whose counterfeit melancholy became real (III, 4). Montaigne aims at the discrepancy between the parts played and the real, essential dimension of being.[4] He strives to peel back the mask, to uncover the sham of illusion, to break through artifice and superficies to disclose substance. The borrowed form of the actor (*forme empruntée*, [838]) obscures and endangers that

personal ruling pattern (*forme sienne, forme maistresse,* [III, 2, 811])
which is the very heart of individuality: "La plus part de nos
vacations sont farcesques. 'Mundus universus exercet histrioni-
am.' Il faut jouer deuement nostre rolle, mais comme rolle d'un
personnage emprunté. Du masque et de l'apparence il n'en faut
pas faire une essence réelle, ny de l'estranger le propre" (III, 10,
1011).

Social man assumes postures and puts on airs in the public
arena, but Montaigne implies that life as a stage is not exclusively a function of the outside world. However much the mask is
to be regarded with suspicion, the playing of roles itself remains
an inextricable part of human existence. In the early essays on
death the "real" moment at man's inevitable end concludes life's
play and illusion, but it too is a role, albeit an authentic one. As
the title of the essay indicates, he maintains in *Qu'il ne faut juger
de nostre heur, qu'après la mort* (I, 19) that a happy fate cannot be
attributed to a man "qu'on ne luy aye veu joüer le dernier acte de
sa comedie. . . . En tout le reste il y peut avoir du masque. . . .
Mais à ce dernier rolle de la mort et de nous, il n'y a plus que
faindre, il faut parler François" (79-80). It is not that the play
ends so that life (or death, in this case) can take over; rather, the
play that is pretense—*masque,* as Montaigne says—gives way to
the real play. Lucretius would separate life as play from reality:

> Nam verae voces tum demum pectore ab imo
> Ejiciuntur, et eripitur persona, manet res.
> [At last true words surge up from deep within our breast,
> The mask is snatched away, reality is left.]

Montaigne uses the vocabulary of drama to describe that reality.
Death is still the last act of the comedy, its final confrontation
the last scene. The play has become authentic, real, we said
earlier in an apparent paradox, but if life is a play, one's own role
can be counterfeited or faced up to. Masks may be worn in that
play within the play of life, roles changed at will until death
forces man to play himself.

Life is theater and the self a role at the point where illusion and reality converge and intermingle: "quelque personnage que l'homme entrepraigne, il joue tousjours le sien parmy" (I, 20, 81). As he affirms the familiar analogy between human development and the cycle of the seasons to underscore the certainty of death, Montaigne situates them as dramatic action unfolding through time: "la distribution et varieté de tous les actes de ma comedie se parfournit en un an" (93). The emphasis is less on masks, worn consciously or unconsciously, and rather on the broader implications of the metaphor of the play, on the idea that man even plays at being himself. Here as elsewhere in the *Essais* Montaigne refers to his own life as comedy, a function of his modest role, consistent with his tendency to deprecate his activities and achievements, and to articulate the low style he finds appropriate to his subject.

Comedy, theater, laughter imply audience as Montaigne looks out from his physical and psychological remove at the spectacle of life about him. Whether at home in his tower or away on a voyage, the essayist is always the outsider—that is, he stands as a spectator apart from the world. His purpose is study, and what he hopes to gain is wisdom and virtue. Montaigne articulates this lesson in *De l'institution des enfans* (I, 26), although he is content to leave literal theater as mere diversion for the people. On the ideal level at which the essay is written, and with the analogy of essaying constantly in the background, the outside world serves as a book where the student learns how to do (152), as a school where he learns of others (154), but most importantly as a mirror where the individual learns about himself: "Ce grand monde . . . c'est le miroüer où il nous faut regarder pour nous connoistre de bon biais" (157). Detachment, the immobility or passivity of the onlooker, is required as one benefits personally from watching. Montaigne paraphrases Pythagoras' analogy of life as the Olympic Games to legitimize the function of the observer: "Les uns s'y exercent le corps pour en acquerir la gloire des jeux; d'autres y portent des marchandises à vendre pour le gain. Il en est, et qui ne sont pas les pires, lesquels ne cerchent autre fruict que de regarder comment et pourquoy chaque chose se faict, et estre spectateurs de la vie des autres hommes, pour en juger et regler la leur" (158).

Later, in *De la phisionomie*, Montaigne returns to the confusion of life and theater and to himself as spectator. Here, as opposed to the comedy of individual life he poses the tragedy of national calamity:

> Comme je ne ly guere és histoires ces confusions des autres estats que je n'aye regret de ne les avoir peu mieux considerer présent, ainsi faict ma curiosité que je m'aggrée aucunement de veoir de mes yeux ce notable spectacle de nostre mort publique, ses symptomes et sa forme. Et puis que je ne la puis retarder, suis content d'estre destiné à y assister et m'en instruire.
>
> Si cherchons nous avidement de recognoistre en ombre mesme et en la fable des Theatres la montre des jeux tragiques de l'humaine fortune. [III, 12, 1046]

Not diversion but instruction, which is, after all, one of the cornerstones of Montaigne's activity in the *Essais*. The outside world is again considered and absorbed into the individual, interior domain. The passive onlooker—in this case justified by his helplessness—turns this public spectacle to personal advantage; his active role begins in the process of *s'instruire* and *amender*.

The observer of the world is most profoundly the observer of the self; the metaphor of theater and its roles touches all aspects of human life, as we have seen. Montaigne plays the parts both of actor and spectator to his own action and, as in the case of public spectacle, he seeks to learn, to know about himself, and to acquire wisdom and virtue. In the world of the *Essais* those who err do so because they deny the necessity, or the validity, or the practice of this play of the self. The failure to look, or to see, results in arrogance, in the tendency to take oneself too seriously as absolute term, to assume that one's role is always authentic. Without separation, without distance, the self cannot locate and know itself, cannot distinguish borrowed roles from real. However paradoxical it may appear, the dichotomy of the self, its fragmentation, is a condition necessary to wholeness and authenticity. Truth resides in the interaction of spectator and actor.

III

The discussion of art, theater, and roles leads back to its source in the *Essais* as literature and in the relation of literature to life. We have seen Montaigne purposely blur the distinctions in his juxtapositions of art and nature and in the metaphor of life as a play. In *De la vanité* he judges ideas in the same mode Horace used to describe the poet's aim: "Je ne me soucie pas tant de les avoir vigoreuses et doctes, comme je me soucie de les avoir aisées et commodes à la vie: elles sont assez vrayes et saines si elles sont utiles et aggreables" (III, 9, 951). As he does throughout the essays (and particularly in the Third Book), Montaigne reduces the general to the particular, substituting criteria relevant to the individual (useful and pleasing) for universal considerations (truth and soundness). The Horatian *utile* and *dulce* apply to elements of life as if it were a work of art. Again, in *De mesnager sa volonté*, the true friendship for oneself is presented in these same terms: "une amitié salutaire et reiglée, également utile et plaisante" (III, 10, 1006). And as if to affirm the literary overtones, Montaigne says of the man who attains this level, "il est vrayement du cabinet des muses."[5] Truth derives from a view of life that can only be called artistic.

Literary criteria also apply to the *Essais* themselves, as Montaigne justifies his inclusion of fabulous testimonies:

> en l'estude que je traitte de noz moeurs et mouvemens, les tesmoignages fabuleux, pourveu qu'ils soient possibles, y servent comme les vrais. Advenu ou non advenu . . . c'est tousjours un tour de l'humaine capacité, duquel je suis utilement advisé par ce recit. Je le voy et en fay mon profit egalement en umbre qu'en corps. . . . Il y a des autheurs, desquels la fin c'est dire les evenements. La mienne, si j'y sçavoye advenir, seroit dire sur ce qui peut advenir. [I, 20, 105]

Claiming to be absolutely faithful to the original accounts of his stories, the essayist introduces the notion of verisimilitude, of things possible. In terms reminiscent of Aristotle, Montaigne suggests that in the area of human behavior and motives, the potential, that which might have happened, is more useful, more informative and, one senses, more true than that which has happened. At this point, he digresses to wonder out loud how historians can pretend to describe what "really" was, given the unreliability of witnesses, the difficulty of discerning intentions. Against the conjecture of history masquerading as reality Montaigne sets the possibility of literature as a way to truth.

The implications of this view that art provides the means to truth, and, in a deeper sense, to life, are multiple. The dialectic of the quest for self-knowledge rests on the premise that seeing oneself involves projecting an image, in Montaigne's case a construct, a counterpart in words whose motion can be charted, whose ideas and activities considered and judged.[6] The dominant vision is artistic, one might even say poetic, as the *Essais* penetrate the superficies of historical reality to consider most profoundly human experience and the essayist's own. The military bearing of the imagined self, his ideal union with La Boétie, his lack of memory and of science and his situation in the Third Book as an old man good only for musing about himself, are aspects of the personal presentation whose textual significance transcends biographical import. The utopianism of friendship, death proceeding from life in the cycle of nature, the voyage that is life, the ideal of the past, Montaigne's primitivism, these are all elements of the world in which that projected self seeks meaning that would be called literary. The purpose is not to build up an imaginary structure for its own sake, nor to make a fiction that expressly distorts and misleads. The *Essais* are a construct from beginning to end, but they aim at all points to contact life.

The roles Montaigne plays in the *Essais*, the various postures and perspectives he assumes in the diverse contexts of different essays, function at this convergence. We no longer have to confine ourselves to an evolutionary reading of the work in biographical terms, considering the change from Stoic through the crisis of skepticism to a kind of Epicurean humanism as a personal journey, for positions taken and argued have a deeper significance. Any subject matter, and the view taken of it, sets the mind in motion to reveal the quality of its judgment. A point of view is not inevitably a matter of conviction but of trial (or tryout) and exercise. Montaigne can slip into the skin of the Stoic, skeptic, or Epicurean as he can argue both sides of a question or be the devil's advocate to point up paradox (as in *De la phisionomie*). Whether he plays the confident teacher in *De l'institution des enfans* (in spite of his initial protestation to the contrary) or assumes the humble posture of *De la praesumption*, the exteriorization provides the opportunity for stocktaking. His area of concern is always himself: "Le monde regarde tousjours vis à vis; moy, je replie ma veue au dedans, je la plante, je l'amuse là. Chacun regarde devant soy; moy, je regarde dedans moy: je n'ay affaire qu'à moy, je me considere sans cesse, je me contrerolle, je me gouste" (II, 17, 657). *Contrerolle* demands remove, as the vocabulary of vision suggests, a perspective provided by the distance between the projected self acting its part and the self as onlooker watching and judging. The capacity to sift out the truth from his attitudes and actions—*trier le vray* (658), he says in the same context—depends on parts played and moved away from. If he were not conscious of his many roles—that is, if he were not watching and taking stock, apart from the self acting—he would lose his freedom and his potential for knowledge.

Attitudes assumed and positions held may also derive from a strategy that allows Montaigne to regulate and control his inclinations and desires, to walk, as he says in *De mesnager sa volonté*, "tousjours la bride à la main" (1008). The man who gives himself up wholly to his role, who cannot see it as such, forfeits his independence. Distance and *dédoublement* permit him to locate the self and, if it is leaning too far in one direction, bring it back in the other. From one posture Montaigne will move to another, exaggerated, to strike an ultimate balance: "Pour dresser un bois courbe on le recourbe au rebours" (1006). A role played, dictated

not by sincerity or depth of belief but by the demands of freedom:
"Comme, estant jeune, je m'opposois au progrez de l'amour que
je sentoy trop avancer sur moy, et estudiois qu'il ne me fut si
aggreable qu'il vint à me forcer en fin et captiver du tout à sa
mercy, j'en use de mesme à toutes autres occasions où ma volonté
se prend avec trop d'appetit: je me panche à l'opposite de son
inclination" (1014).

The validity and efficacy of the effort at self-knowledge, at
self-control, which Montaigne expresses as *s'instruire* and *amender*,
depend in the final analysis on art, on the dialectic of *s'essayer*, on
these discussions by and with the self. The projected image of the
self and the construct that is the essayist's vision of the world
most meaningfully represent Montaigne's "art" of living. In this
endless movement back and forth between life and literature, the
distinctions are blurred: indeed, as we have seen, the two are one,
for in Montaigne's case writing is living.

Two sides of a single act. The writer as artist, as *facteur*, comes
into the truth of things by conferring shape, arrangement. This is
not the false uniformity of the *artistes* who attempt to "renger en
bandes cette infinie diversité de visages, et arrester nostre incon-
stance et la mettre par ordre" (III, 13, 1076), but an order
consistent with the nature of things, for matter determines form
and form renders the substance accessible—that is, meaningful.
The rejection of that world which cannot provide a sense of
being, the progressive delineation of the self, the reaffirmation of
the "outside" as a function of the self are elements of that form
which emerge through the act of writing. By "making" the
book, Montaigne "invents" the man.

If we look at the other side of the act, the living, we find coincidental movement. In *Du repentir* Montaigne disclaims any
intention of instructing the world or of trying to form Man, or
even of remaking himself since he is already fashioned. And yet
his whole activity involves instructing, amending, and reforming
himself; not refashioning from scratch, but taking on a shape
consistent with his nature and the larger scheme of things. We
watch Montaigne continually attempting to introduce this kind

of unity between his personal substance and its form: "Composer nos meurs est nostre office . . . et gaigner . . . l'ordre et tranquillité à nostre conduite" (III, 13, 1108). He seeks to be guided by conscience and to recognize and accept the personal characteristics given him by nature and habit and the limitations they imply (*De l'experience* treats nature and habit almost identically as formative and restrictive forces). And to the notion that virtue is its own reward Montaigne adds the pleasure that accompanies moral action: "Il y a certes je ne sçay quelle congratulation de bien faire qui nous resjouit en nous mesmes. . . . Ces tesmoignages de la conscience plaisent; et nous est grand benefice que cette esjouyssance naturelle" (III, 2, 807).[7] By conceiving of the virtuous life, and the good life as naturally pleasing, and by associating reason (*l'ame*) with pleasure both to temper (and thus add seasoning) and to extend it, Montaigne gives pleasure a moral dimension and justifies its centrality (III, 13, 1110-12). He imparts form to his life and thus determines its quality, value, and meaning.

The accent on pleasure accompanies Montaigne's sense of *usage* in *De l'experience* as custom, habit, as experience and as use. *Usage* is that which helps make man what he is; it is that from which he draws his lessons and, equally as important, it is what he makes of things and of his life. Human history and individual experience both provide examples of conduct moral and physical from which a man can learn about himself and the world. The practice of essaying is that of education: "Je m'estudie plus qu'autre subject" (III, 13, 1072). And its purpose is to allow man to use his own conditions properly ("l'usage des nostres" [1115]), to enjoy his being rightfully ("de sçavoyr jouyr loiallement de son estre").

The dialectic of learning, using, and enjoying has distant Horatian echoes, but we have seen life treated as art before. It suggests that, like the writer or poet, man makes and shapes his own life consistent with the raw materials of (his) nature and that in this case, as reader and audience as well, he does so for his own pleasure and utility. The movement between the two roles is

circular and constant as the essayist turns to live life and the man
to essay it. In a pertinent analogy between life and the music of
the spheres, where he describes the interrelation of pleasure and
pain as counterpoint and harmony, Montaigne again collapses
the distinction between what is natural and what is art: "Nostre
vie est composée, comme l'armonie du monde, de choses contraires, aussi de divers tons, douz et aspres, aigus et plats, mols et
graves. Le musicien qui n'en aymeroit que les uns, que voudroit
il dire? Il faut qu'il s'en sçache servir en commun et les mesler. Et
nous aussi les biens et les maux" (III, 13, 1089). Like the
musician, the man composes and arranges parts of his own life for
himself. In a peculiarly Montaignian tautology, the writer, the
subject, the "artifact" and the reader are one.

IV

Thematically and formally, the mode is circular and self-enclosed.
The tendency to view the *Essais* as linear and open-ended remains
valid as the reader uncovers traces of evolution—Stoic to skeptic
to Epicurean humanism; the effort to recover the lost utopia—
and acknowledges the unending quest for self-knowledge. But we
recognize as well that the work opens out to close back upon
itself. The writer is his own reader, as Montaigne suggests in *De
la praesumption* by his rhetorical question on the worth of his
effort: "Et puis, pour qui escrivez vous?" (657). And in parallel
postures, both the self as its own best friend and the book as
another self stand face to face; the man makes the book as the
book makes the man (II, 18, 665). As if the *Essais* were enclosed
in sets of mirrors, self-reflecting images express the essential
circularity of the Montaignian dialectic: the internal focus of the
"self-seeker," the movement out from and back to the self
describing the secular conversion and the play of infinite regress,
the writer observing himself observing, and so on.

Montaigne's point of departure is the fragmentation, the multiplicity of the "self" and its experience that distances man (in

modern terms, alienates him) from direct and immediate apprehension of himself and the world. The Second Book begins with
echoes of the opening essay of the First Book, stressing inconstancy and diversity as a function of the disparate soul:

> Cette variation et contradiction qui se void en nous, si souple, a
> faict qu'aucuns nous songent deux ames, d'autres deux puissances
> qui nous accompaignent et agitent, chacune à sa mode, vers le bien
> l'une, l'autre vers le mal, une si brusque diversité ne se pouvant
> bien assortir à un subjet simple. [II, 1, 335]

> Nous sommes tous de lopins, et d'une contexture si informe et
> diverse, que chaque piece, chaque momant, faict son jeu. Et se
> trouve autant de difference de nous à nous mesmes, que de nous
> à autruy. [337][8]

The space between man and himself as subject and object,
between the mind and things external, derives from the situation
of man in time, from a view of the world as discontinuous. And
language, ambiguous and opaque, is at once a source and sign of
this fragmentation depicted as a falling away from a primitive
state when name and thing coincided, when the grasp of experience was direct.

Montaigne turns to writing not to accomplish unadulterated
mimetic transfer of experience, for to do so would reproduce the
conditions of his point of departure. While he seeks to remain
true to the nature of things as they are, the *Essais* demand transformation to allow form, accessibility, meaning. They work
toward Montaigne's goals—self-portraiture, self-knowledge—
precisely because they are other than, or more than, the raw
material of experience. We see this in what we have called the
artistic or literary vision—that series of myths or metaphors
which structure the work—and we see it most meaningfully in
Montaigne's claim that he and the essays are consubstantial. This
notion expresses the heart of his attempt to cover the ground
between himself as subject and object and correspondingly to
make language function more perfectly as the union of word and
thing. By making the artifact and claiming for it substance as a

self-sufficient entity, the origin and end of its meaning, Montaigne brings about a kind of incarnation.[9] And because the body created is his own, he stands by analogy with God as his own maker. Not a creator *ex nihilo,* which is the exclusive province of Divinity but as one who, like the writer-inventer, fashions preexistent matter to come into the true nature of things. Montaigne never doubts the existence of that self he seeks to know; he is, after all, a Christian. At the same time he alone is the source of its discovery, of its uncovering through that process of exteriorization which is the writing of the *Essais.*

The materialization of the immaterial and the consequent sense of being in and through the book are concepts inextricably bound to Montaigne's language, for they imply the necessity of breaking through its referential role, of overcoming the disparity of word and thing, of endowing with substance the sign floating free in the airy medium. We have seen Montaigne use these very terms in *Sur des vers de Virgile* (III, 5) to express how poetic language becomes one with the world, how words from *vent* become *chair* and *os* (873). And we recognize as well the implications for man depicted as wind: "nous sommes par tout vent" (III, 13, 1107). Able writers, he says in this regard, do not create new languages. They take a given vocabulary, often overworked, trite, and weak, and infuse it with new vigor and life: "Ils n'y aportent point des mots, mais ils enrichissent les leurs, appesantissent et enfoncent leur signification et leur usage." Through the creation of metaphor, the talented mind calls up new associations and relationships, evokes new realities. Weight, depth, body, and texture in the language allow Montaigne to naturalize his art and to respond to his basic concern as he speaks of his writing: "Me represente-je pas vivement?" (875). The medium allows a faithful portrayal and, we gather as well from his suggestive use of *vivement,* one that is living, alive.

In his choice of French over Latin Montaigne singles out the unstable, evolving quality of the vernacular. What good and useful writings do, he says, is to set the language, to pin it down in time: "C'est aux bons et utiles escrits de le clouer à eux" (III,

9, 982). The essayist exploits its shifting, changing character to express the nature of things in movement and the uncertainties and ambiguities to which its use gives rise. And while he maintains in *De l'experience* that man should accept his basic airiness and not desire stability and solidity (III, 13, 1107), we note all along how he tangles with language to give it substance, how his play with its diversity emerges as the other side of the effort to control and to order. Montaigne claims a vocabulary all his own when he describes his personal sense of *passer le temps*: "J'ay un dictionnaire tout à part moy" (1111). We see him working with an ordinary, hackneyed idiom, taking it out of the realm of the casual, rather empty, and expressionless everyday usage to infuse it with particular and precise meaning, to make it value-charged. Montaigne pins down *passer le temps* and *passe-temps* as *couler et eschapper* from life, "la passer, gauchir . . . ignorer et fuir," to set them against the seizing and savoring, the possession of life.

Montaigne's personal vocabulary goes beyond a single expression to inform his vision of reality built up through the *Essais.* The process of redefining words and concepts, of attaching particular words to specific contexts, and of giving them qualitative value endows his language with meanings and implications expressive of his attitudes. This does not mean that language overcomes all ambiguities, that it is rendered wholly one-dimensional, that absolute correspondence is achieved with things. Neither the real world nor Montaigne's vision of it allows this monism. Rather, we see the essayist attempting as far as possible to make language his own; we see the tension between his effort and its resistance; and, we should add, we see him reveling at times in the richness, the suggestiveness, the variety that language allows. He strives to make his language intersect with himself—that is, representative of his own singularity and diversity. In this case, what Montaigne *says* and what he *is* coincide.[10]

The most striking examples of this personal vocabulary occur in the Third Book where Montaigne gives his individual stamp to *repentir, vanité, experience,* concepts that appear to include by themselves almost all that is essential to our understanding of the

Essais. In the process he takes related notions out of their familiar contexts to refashion them: true *science* becomes "sçavoir vivre cette vie" (III, 13, 1110); man's worst *maladie*, "mespriser nostre estre"; nobility and *grandeur de l'ame,* "sçavoir se ranger et circonscrire." In *Du repentir* he takes over *la constance* as "un branle . . . languissant" (III, 2, 805). True *doctrine* passes from the accepted view of *science* to Montaigne's *ignorance*, from something acquired from without to something found naturally within (III, 12, 1039).

In the first two books *la philosophie* is given a new look, combined with virtue and pleasure (I, 26, 161); *l'amitié* receives Montaigne's personal stamp (I, 28); *l'institution* is recast (I, 26). *Des cannibales* (I, 31) redefines *sauvage* and *barbare* and *De la gloire* (II, 16) moves the sense of true glory from "une approbation que le monde fait des actions que nous mettons en evidence" (619) to what derives from living one's life tranquilly, according to oneself (622). And, of course, Montaigne's most personal and permanent vocabulary contribution is the *essai* (I, 26, 146; I, 50, 301; II, 10, 407; III, 2, 805; III, 13, 1079).

This list is not meant to be complete; it serves rather to highlight the implications of a new vocabulary. Not neologisms sustaining an imaginary vision but clearly a world built on pilings different from those supporting that outside reality which is Montaigne's point of reference. Or perhaps it is closer to say different from the world the *Essais* "replace." We come back again to the concept of self-sufficiency, to the *Essais* as a construct governed by particular laws or forces, sustaining specific values or attitudes. Because variety, change, instability are major thematic threads, the work does not dissolve into indescribable multiplicity, nor does it move so much or so fast as to become wholly tentative. These very themes form part of a larger fabric that imposes its norms on the reader. The *Essais* cannot be narrowly considered or defined, but it does not follow that they thus mean everything, and nothing. The dominant strains of movement and diversity operate in the context of a self to be known, of an individual ruling pattern to be discovered, of a nature (whose path has been confounded with artificial tracks) to be uncovered and followed. If absolute certainty exceeds his reach and skeptical detachment characterizes Montaigne's outlook, he never doubts the weight of conscience and the force of virtue. The essays are at the same time negation and affirmation and at this point of convergence the figure of Montaigne emerges, what he rejects as important as what he accepts, what he is not as central as what he is. The reader must constantly bear in mind that Montaigne owes his reality to the text, and that the text functions as source precisely because it is self-contained.

What we describe in these terms is art, but art as imaginative literature conflicts with our common understanding of the *Essais* as a faithful self-portrait. The point we have been underlining in this section, however, and which Montaigne himself illuminates, is that art and life are not antithetical, that in fact they commingle, that, by extension, art may be true even if it is not real. The *Essais* are not a fiction, although it is clear that aspects of the world presented derive from what we have called an artistic vision of reality. We acknowledge the centrality of this vision because it ultimately differentiates the work from the formless, chaotic forces of life, endows it with the degree of self-sufficiency or enclosure that allows it existence as an object. Here, apart, through what itself has entity, the essayist strives to bring himself out, to exteriorize and materialize interiority. And, we understand, here alone is where this dialectic can operate. Without Montaigne's art there is no life. Art alone allows him form, accessibility, meaning, and a sense of being.

V

Montaigne's *Essais* are Janus-like. One face looks out toward the rich composition of experiential life, of existential or historical reality in its contradiction and paradox, its opaque, impenetrable forces, its tensions unsettling and unresolvable. The other side faces inward toward form and order, in the disposition of inter-related norms that impose themselves on the reader; in the constitution of entity, enclosed; in the expression of the aspira-tion for unity and reconciliation. The same might be said of literature in general, of traditional drama, for example, which embodies reality's stresses and its inclination toward chaos at the same time as it transcends them in aesthetic resolution, as it offers a vision characterized by order and design. But the equilib-rium is tentative, the tension between these opposing impulses extreme, for even as order is affirmed it is undermined as art's illusion. The *Essais* make the dialectic of tension their central, explicit concern. Rather than dramatizing the symbolic interplay of forces, the work affirms its historicity as the exposition of the conflict unfolding. The man as writer brings to reality as insta-bility, movement, and multiplicity the longing for form, whole-ness, and direction, which are the province of art. The *Essais* focus on the very point of contact between nature and art, on what is the archetypal moment of creation: of the world God shapes from chaos and darkness, of the human body sculpted from the mass of stone, of Montaigne himself emerging through the book as if from the "amas et pieces de chair informes" he describes in *De l'oisiveté* (I, 8, 32). What distinguishes the work is the recognition of limitation, of restriction that reality places on the formal or esthetic impulse—that is, on the urge to bring himself about through the work. The outside world intrudes upon the artistic just as Montaigne's desire for form, for meaning, imposes itself on history.

Montaigne's effort to give body to his writing, to constitute it as a substance and by this process delineate or invent himself, is constantly threatened by the forces of dispersion and fragmenta-tion. The antagonism is played out both inside the man as the conflicting sides of his own nature and between the man and the outside world as social, political, intellectual pressures. Most importantly, Montaigne must come to grips with language if he is to release it from its purely referential function to identify the work as body with his own. Not individual names that are suddenly united with things but the corpus of language standing as a totality, participating in the very life and properties of the man. We return once again to the *Essais* as a portrait, drawn in a language expressive rather than literal or communicative, or perhaps more properly called iconic, to stress its mutuality with Montaigne.[11] And this language continually threatens to fly off on its own, to impose meaning beyond the essayist's intent, to lose itself in obscurity and ambiguity. Language and portrait must constantly be renewed, as the quest for self-knowledge pursued endlessly in accordance with man's temporality, with his recognition and acceptance of becoming.

The balance in that tension between life and literature favors the life forces. The problem is how to meet them on their own ground, to recognize them without distorting them and at the same time to achieve that measure of form which allows meaning. Permanence and fixity are delusions of being in the world of the *Essais*; the man, his life, and the art through which he comes out must coincide with the real nature of things: "Nostre vie n'est que mouvement" (III, 13, 1095). But if movement tends toward multiplicity and disintegration, it is also the root of the sense of being, perhaps of being itself: "nous avons cher estre: et estre consiste en mouvement et action" (II, 8, 386). Not the unchanging being ascribed to God, but being that is human, which, by its very nature, is movement and action, and which expresses that nature *through* movement and action. The genius of Montaigne is to have found an art that remains faithful to the reality of being—and thus renders its delineation valid— while at the same time allowing for form which makes that reality accessible and meaningful, and thus remains true to itself as art. And language, with the same qualities as life, with the same elements as being, is the very source of substantiality, the very medium that allows for the authentic materialization of the immaterial, as Montaigne affirms in Homer: "Ses parolles, selon Aristote, sont les seules parolles qui ayent mouvement et action; ce sont les seuls mots substantiels" (II, 36, 753).

Notes

1. Friendship and Literature

1. Quotations are from *Les Essais de Michel de Montaigne,* ed. Pierre Villey (Paris, 1965), published under the direction of V. L. Saulnier by the Presses Universitaires de France. References are given by book, essay, and page number.

2. See F. Gray, "Montaigne's Friends," *French Studies* 15 (1961): 203-217; also C. Brush, "The Essayist Is Learned: Montaigne's *Journal de voyage* and the *Essais,*" *Romanic Review* 42 (1971): 16-27.

3. See A. Wilden, "Par divers moyens on arrive à pareille fin: A Reading of Montaigne," *MLN* 83 (1968): 577-597; also D. Frame, *Montaigne's Essais: A Study* (Englewood Cliffs, N.J., 1969), p. 10; M. Butor, *Essais sur les Essais* (Paris, 1964); A. Thibaudet, *Montaigne,* ed. Floyd Gray (Paris, 1963), p. 143ff. Wilden describes the privileged unity of friendship (p. 581) and examines the essays' function as surrogate "other" in terms of the model of "psychoanalytic intersubjectivity" (p. 582). My own concerns are textual and literary, although our views on the symbolic value of the friendship, and of its absence, coincide.

4. Gray, "Montaigne's Friends," p. 211.

5. G. Castor, *Pléiade Poetics* (Cambridge, 1964), pp. 103-113.

6. Aristotle, *Nicomachean Ethics,* IX, 9, 10, 1170B; Cicero, *On Friendship.*

7. It is important to note that Montaigne himself did not use paragraphs. The early editions of the *Essais* were faithful to this presentation of the text.

8. The translations of Montaigne are those of D. Frame, *The Complete Essays of Montaigne* (Stanford, Calif., 1948). These lines of Catullus are on p. 144.

9. Butor observes that the *Servitude volontaire* would have occupied the physical center of the book (since the essay presently numbered 29 would not have been included), *Essais sur les Essais,* pp. 72-79.

10. The line, which is found in the 1588 edition, was deleted, Saulnier suggests, out of consideration for Mlle. de Gournay.

11. J. E. Sullivan, *The Image of God* (Dubuque, Iowa, 1963), p. 138. The parallel I have been drawing seems to suggest that Montaigne knew Augustine's *Confessions.* Villey assumes that the *De civitate Dei* alone was included in Montaigne's library and that he might have read the *De ordine* (see E. Limbrick,

"Montaigne et S. Augustin," *BHR* 34 [1972]: 49-64). From a Christian point of view, Montaigne's conception of friendship (as mystical union outside of grace), his depiction of his fall from the *vol hautain et superbe* of that union to the mutability and weightiness of life (reminiscent of *pondus amorus*), where he seeks to renew the image on his own, might be described as the hagiography of the sinner, one that seems to parallel the *Confessions* in counterpoint. Further study of these and other echoes of the *Confessions* ("L'homme ne peut estre que ce qu'il est" [II, 12, 520], for example, which repeats Augustine's "Et quis homo est quilibet homo cum sit homo" [IV, 1]), might prove valuable to Montaigne scholarship.

12. My comments on *epistrophe* draw heavily from P. Aubain, *Le Problème de la conversion* (Paris, 1963), pp. 19-66.

13. Ibid., p. 58.

14. Epictetus, *Le Manuel d'Epictète,* translated by Du Vair (1641), p. 291.

15. In his seminal *Montaigne* Thibaudet speaks briefly of "la conversion vers le dedans" and of "cette conversion qu'implique la religion du moi," p. 456. While his context differs from mine, he does suggest a coincidence between religious and what I have called secular conversion.

2. The Space Occupied and the Time Lived

1. See Donald Frame, *Montaigne: A Biography* (London, 1965). F. Brown, *Religious and Political Conservatism in the Essais of Montaigne* (Geneva, 1963); J-P Boon, *Montaigne: Gentilhomme et essayiste* (Paris, 1971); M. Dréano, *La Religion de Montaigne,* rev. ed. (Paris, 1969); J. Plattard, *Montaigne et son temps* (Paris, 1933); J. Prévost, *La Vie de Montaigne* (Paris, 1926); F. Strowski, *Montaigne* (Paris, 1931); and P. Villey, *Les Sources et évolution des Essais de Montaigne* (Paris, 1933) are among the critics who are interested in biographical reconstitution.

2. Villey, 2: 51-55; D. Frame, *Montaigne's Discovery of Man* (New York, 1955), pp. 36-37.

3. H. Hedy-Erlich, *Montaigne: la critique et le langage* (Paris, 1972), p. 46.

4. *Ame* is variously translated as "soul" and "mind" to suggest the richness of Montaigne's usage.

5. R. Sayce, *The Essays of Montaigne: A Critical Exploration* (London, 1972), p. 193. See also G. Atkinson, *Les Nouveaux horizons de la Renaissance française* (Paris, 1935).

6. Sayce, *The Essays of Montaigne,* pp. 88-90.

3. The Rhetoric of Humility

1. See F. Gray, "The 'nouveaux docteurs' and the Problem of Montaigne's

Consistency in the 'Apologie de Raymond Sebond,'" *Symposium* 18 (1964): 22-34.

2. Frame submits that the notion of an apology of Sebond's book was suggested to Montaigne by M. de Valois after he had written the sections on man's inferiority to the animals, the failure of knowledge to lead to happiness and virtue, and the virtues of Pyrrhonism, and that he used it as a pretext to put everything together (*Montaigne's Essais: A Study*, pp. 27-28).

3. In the editions published during Montaigne's lifetime the end of this line read, "soubslever par la grace divine, mais non autrement."

4. See Sayce, *The Essays of Montaigne*, p. 223.

5. Pascal, M. *de Saci* in *Oeuvres complètes* (Paris, 1954), p. 569.

6. Montaigne's use of *abêtir*, and its meaning for Pascal, are debated by B. F. Bart, "Abêtir in Pascal and Montaigne," *RPh* 9 (1955-56): 1-6; B. Foster, "Pascal's Use of *abêtir*," *FS* 17 (1963): 1-13; S. Haig, "A Further Note on Pascal's *abêtir*," *FS* 18 (1964); 29-32; E. Moles, "Pascal's Use of *abêtir*," *FS* 19 (1965): 379-384. Mole suggests that for Montaigne *abêtir* implies both the prudent recognition of the limitations of abstract reasoning and the notion of *docta ignorantia*.

7. Sayce, *The Essays of Montaigne*, p. 176.

8. Thibaudet, *Montaigne*, pp. 181-182.

4. The Primacy of the Book

1. E. R. Curtius, *European Literature and the Latin Middle Ages*, trans. W. Trask (1953; reprint, New York, 1963), pp. 302-347.

2. H. de Lubac, *Histoire et esprit: L'intelligence de l'Ecriture d'après Origen* (Paris, 1950), pp. 336-373.

3. Jean Leclerq, "Aspects spirituels de la symbolique du livre au XIIe siècle," *L'Homme devant Dieu* 2 (1963): 67.

4. R. Sebond, *La Théologie naturelle*, trans. M. de Montaigne in the *Oeuvres complètes de Michel de Montaigne*, ed. A. Armaingaud (Paris, 1932), 9: ix-x.

5. See M. Foucault, *Les Mots et les choses* (Paris, 1966), pp. 32-59, for a discussion of the notion of correspondences in the Middle Ages.

6. For an analysis of these changes in the text, see D. Frame, "Did Montaigne Betray Sebond?," *RR* 38 (1947): 297-329.

7. In *Pléiade Poetics* G. Castor suggests that Renaissance neo-Platonism effectuates a rehabilitation of the fine arts by making them a step on the ladder that leads from the world of appearances to that of Being. In the context of the *Apologie*, Montaigne's aim is clearly to disparage man's effort to elevate himself.

8. E. Huguet, *Dictionnaire de la langue française du seizième siècle*, (Paris, 1925), 4: 96.

9. Foucault, *Les Mots et les choses,* chap. 2, pp. 32-59.

10. Castor describes this phenomenon fully, *Pléiade Poetics,* pp. 190-191.

11. See H. Weber, *La Création poétique au XVIᵉ siècle en France* (Paris, 1956), pp. 463-557, and A-M. Schmidt, *La Poésie scientifique en France au XVIᵉ siècle* (Paris, 1938).

12. Curtius, *European Literature and the Latin Middle Ages,* p. 326, and P. O. Kristeller, *Renaissance Thought* (1955; reprint, New York, 1961), pp. 3-23, underline the bookish nature of late medieval and Renaissance humanist activity.

13. F. Gray, "Montaigne's Friends," *FS* 15 (1961): 203-217.

14. R. La Charité, "Montaigne's Early Personal Essays," *RR* 42 (1971): 5-15.

15. Montaigne consistently describes books as food, and studying or learning in terms of eating; see *Des livres* (II, 10, 414, 417). Both R. Sayce, *The Essays of Montaigne,* p. 294, and Carol Clark, "Montaigne and the Imagery of Political Discourse," *FS* 24 (1970): 337-355, discuss this metaphor.

16. Montaigne implies that one builds on the *inclination naturelle* (I, 26, 149) of the student, that one looks to develop "les propensions naturelles" (149), "selon la portée de l'ame qu'il a en main" (150). The confidence that one can so clearly identify and isolate what is "natural" to the student is one term of the paradox of the self that is both present and absent at the same time. The act of essaying provides the link between that self or nature dimly glimpsed (experienced as absence) and the self as it delineates and expresses itself, exteriorized in the text. This process will be our concern in the following chapters.

17. Du Bellay, *La Deffence et illustration de la langue françoyse,* ed. H. Chamard (Paris, 1948), p. 42.

18. Ronsard, *Oeuvres complètes,* ed. Gustave Cohen (Paris, 1966), p. 390.

19. See M. A. Screech, "An Aspect of Montaigne's Aesthetics: Entre les livres simplement plaisants . . . (II, 10: *Des livres*)," *BHR* 24 (1962): 576-582.

20. The paradoxical relationship between Montaigne's own book and those of others is described by A. Glauser, *Montaigne paradoxal* (Paris, 1972), pp. 61-77.

5. The Range of Words

1. The image of texts spawning texts might also be used to characterize what happens in Montaigne's case. As chapter 4 indicated, he draws on the books of others, and his own, as interpolated notes and comments generate additions and even new chapters in the *Essais.* Paradoxically, Montaigne includes himself in

the class of useless scribblers and at the same time attempts to set his book apart, as we will see in chapter 6.

2. R. Sebond, *La Théologie naturelle,* chap. 193, p. 348.

3. See H. Friedrich, *Montaigne,* trans. R. Rovini (Paris, 1968), pp. 169-172; Thibaudet, *Montaigne,* p. 127, p. 507, for discussion of internal-external.

4. See also *Des noms* (I, 46, 279).

5. See Ronsard in the "Abrégé de l'art poétique," *Oeuvres complètes,* ed. P. Laumonier (Paris, 1914-1953), 14: 13.

6. See chap. 4.

7. See G. Castor, *Pléiade Poetics,* chap. 2 and R. Griffin, *The Coronation of the Poet,* Part I.

8. T. Sebillet, *Art poétique françoys,* ed. F. Gaiffe (Paris, 1932), I: 3.

9. See Griffin, *The Coronation of the Poet,* p. 8; for a contemporary view, J. C. Scaliger, *Poetices libri septem* (Lyon, 1581), chap. 28.

10. See W. Ong, *Ramus: Method and the Decay of Dialogue* (Cambridge, Mass., 1958), p. 129. In Ramist logic, the root opposition set up in generating the notion of "things" is not between the mental and the extramental. Things are constituted in opposition not to the mind, but to the word.

6. Singularity and Substance

1. For an analysis of Montaigne's use of *marqueterie,* see B. Bowen, "What Does Montaigne Mean by *marqueterie?*" *SP* 67 (1970): 147-155. Here, once again, in the notion of thefts, Montaigne embodies a central paradox of the *Essais:* the search for the self as something that exists (endowed with a *forme maîtresse*) and the sense of the self as absent, or lost, as something to be composed of borrowings.

2. The complexity and diversity of Montaigne studies is evident in the juxtaposition of this view, which claims an evolution from the aim of personal self-portraiture to more universal concerns, to the view quoted earlier, which sees a development from the impersonal early essays to the more individualized later additions.

3. V. L. Saulnier, introductory notes to *Du démentir,* p. 663.

4. See M. McGowan, *Montaigne's Deceits: The Art of Persuasion in the Essais* (London, 1974), chap. 1.

5. See R. Colie, *Paradoxia Epidemica* (Princeton, 1966), esp. pp. 374-395. A. Glauser examines the form and function of paradox in *Montaigne paradoxal.* Cf. also Barbara Bowen, *The Age of Bluff* (Urbana, Ill., 1972).

6. In a richly suggestive observation Thibaudet speaks of Rembrandt's efforts at self-portraiture in terms applicable to Montaigne: "Il n'a pas voulu se raconter, mais *produire* chez lui quelque chose de permanent," *Montaigne,*

p. 499. His varied references to Rembrandt (pp. 74, 444) underscore the value of comparing painting and writing, as I do in chap. 8.

7. The Life of the Mind

1. E. M. Padelford, "Select Translations from Scaliger's 'Poetics,'" *Yale Studies in English* 26 (1905): 456.

2. Thibaudet notes the function of the book as another self, as surrogate friend and offspring in *Montaigne*, pp. 72-73, 132-133.

3. I. D. McFarlane, "Montaigne and the Concept of the Imagination," in *The French Renaissance and its Heritage* (London, 1968), pp. 117-137, and G. Castor, *Pléiade Poetics*, have already performed this valuable task.

4. The dominant present tense in the *Essais* might be said to affirm Montaigne's emphasis on the here and now, although it is also frequently the "eternal" present. On Montaigne's treatment of time, cf. Georges Poulet, *Etudes sur le temps humain* (Paris, 1950), pp. 1-15.

5. E. B. McGilvary, *Toward a Perspective Realism*, quoted in C. Guillen, *Literature as System* (Princeton, 1971), pp. 368-369.

6. See Sayce, *The Essays of Montaigne*, p. 297.

8. On the Face of Things

1. See J. Pope-Hennessy, *The Portrait in the Renaissance* (New York, 1966).

2. Sayce, *The Essays of Montaigne*, p. 53.

3. R. Sayce, "Baroque elements in Montaigne," *FS* 8 (1954): 1-15; I. Buffum, *Studies in the Baroque from Montaigne to Rotrou* (New Haven, 1957).

4. Albert Châtelet and Jacques Thuillier, *French Painting: From Fouquet to Poussin*, trans. Stuart Gilbert (Geneva, 1963), pp. 124-126.

5. Pope-Hennessy, *The Portrait in the Renaissance*, p. 101.

6. C. Guillen, "Toward a Definition of the Picaresque" in *Literature as System*, pp. 89-93.

7. Guillen (p. 90) quoting from Butcher's *Aristotle's Theory of Poetry and Fine Art* (London, 1911), pp. 133-134.

8. Guillen, p. 91 (Spitzer, *Romania* LXVIII [1944-1945], p. 474).

9. R. W. Lee, "Ut Pictura Poesis: The Humanistic Theory of Painting," *The Art Bulletin*, XXII, 4 (1940): 197-269.

10. Périgord was Protestant country and Montaigne thus appeared a supporter of Henry of Navarre.

11. In the '88 text Montaigne had written "en ces deux visages . . ." instead of "deux sortes."

12. Even biblical exegesis, which has a clear historical basis, takes on new and varied forms and methods. One has only to look at Pico's biblical

interpretation and his interest in Cabala. Protestants like Melanchthon, on the other hand, rejected the belief in textual ambiguity and obscurity. See E. Lowinsky, *Secret Chromatic Art in the Netherlands Motet* (New York, 1946), chap. 9.

13. Guillen characterizes Shakespeare's challenge in the same terms, his problem being to portray *homo interior* by means of perceptible action on the stage.

14. E. Gilson, *Painting and Reality* (New York, 1959), pp. 27-50. My observations in this section are suggested by Gilson's remarks on the physical and aesthetic existence of art.

15. See Lessing's *Laocoön*.

16. III, 2, 810; III, 3, 827; III, 10, 1020; III, 13, 1116.

17. Auerbach, "L'humaine condition" in *Mimesis,* trans. W. Trask (New York, 1957), pp. 249-273.

18. G. Castor, *Pléiade Poetics,* pp. 51-62. In the *Abrégé* and the 1587 preface to the *Françiade* Ronsard comes closer to the Aristotelian concept of imitation than any of his contemporaries. His view of verisimilitude appears to capture some of the spirit of Aristotle's notion that art represents particulars so as to make the universals embodied in them accessible.

19. See chap. 5.

20. G. Castor, *Pléiade Poetics,* pp. 179-180.

21. Pope-Hennessy, *The Portrait in the Renaissance,* pp. 127-129.

22. Guillen, "Metaphor of Perspective" in *Language as System,* pp. 296-297.

23. See chap. 6.

9. Words of Flesh and Blood

1. Murray Krieger, *A Window to Criticism* (Princeton, 1964).

2. Floyd Gray, *Le Style de Montaigne* (Paris, 1958), p. 164. Thibaudet stresses the physicality of the *Essais* as Montaigne's words "de chair et d'os," *Montaigne,* p. 492.

3. St. Beuve, *Port Royal,* ed. Doyon and Marchesne, III: 54.

4. On style, cf. Gray, *Le Style de Montaigne*; A. Thibaudet, *Montaigne*; R. Sayce, *The Essays of Montaigne*; Z. Samaras, *The Comic Element of Montaigne's Style* (Paris, 1970).

5. Sayce, *The Essays of Montaigne,* p. 291.

6. R. Barthes, "To Write: Intransitive Verb?" in *The Language of Criticism and the Science of Man,* eds. R. Macksey and E. Donato (Baltimore, 1970), p. 143.

7. Ibid., p. 144.

8. See Auerbach, *Mimesis,* pp. 249-273.

9. This analogy is developed in chap. 5.

10. Gray in his *Style de Montaigne* characterizes stylistic differences between the first two books and the third in his chapters on exterior and interior order, pp. 185-256.

11. J. Derrida, *De la grammatologie* (Paris, 1967), pp. 22-23.

12. Ibid., p. 24. Of course, Derrida's objective is to undermine the tradition that devalues the written for the sake of the spoken because, for him, *écriture* is primary, not derived. Caught up in the tradition, Montaigne reflects its paradoxical weakness.

13. See chap. 4.

14. Derrida, *De la grammatologie*, pp. 26-31.

15. Auerbach (p. 272) denies that *comique* implies "humorous," although other critics (Frame, Sayce, Bowman, Samaras) speak of Montaigne's comic element.

16. See particularly M. McGowan, *Montaigne's Deceits: The Art of Persuasion in the Essais* for an examination of stylistic techniques by which Montaigne dissimulates his art.

17. W. v. Wartburg, *Evolution et structure de la langue française* (Berne, 1965), pp. 143-166.

18. See F. Yates, *The Art of Memory* (Chicago, 1966).

19. See W. Ong, *Ramus: Method and the Decay of Dialogue* (Cambridge, Mass., 1958), pp. 296-318. I am indebted to Ong for my views on the spatial dimension of writing and on Ramus in general.

20. See R. Griffin, *The Coronation of the Poet* (Berkeley and Los Angeles, 1969), pp. 22-24.

21. Ong, *Ramus: Method and the Decay of Dialogue*, pp. 290-291. Ramus labors at divorcing dialectic and rhetoric, but the two converge in their assumption of a world where vision subordinates voice.

22. Movement in Montaigne is the central concern of Yves Delègue, "Du paradoxe chez Montaigne," *CAIEF* 14 (1962): 241-253, and Jean Starobinski, "Montaigne en mouvement," *NRF* (January-February 1960): 16-22, 254-266. See also Thibaudet, *Montaigne,* esp. pp. 531-553.

23. Ong, *Ramus: Method and the Decay of Dialogue,* pp. 107-110.

24. W. G. Moore makes this point in his essay, "Montaigne's Notion of Experience," *The French Mind* (Oxford, 1952).

25. See chap. 6.

10. Life and Art

1. For a more extended list of antitheses deriving from the couple *nature-art,* see A. Micha, "Art et nature dans les Essais," *BSAM* II, 19 (1956): 50-55.

2. See M. McGowan, *Montaigne's Deceits,* p. 144.

3. Frame points to this tendency in *Montaigne's Essais: A Study* (Englewood Cliffs, N.J., 1969), pp. 39-41.

4. Examples appear in I, 42, 261; II, 10, 415; II, 36, 753.

5. The military life is extolled as *plaisante* and of great *utilité* in *De l'experience* (III, 13, 1096).

6. See chap. 1.

7. The ease and pleasure of virtue is articulated in *De l'institution des enfans* (I, 26, 161). In *De la cruauté* (II, 11, 423) virtue's difficult road is stressed.

8. See also III, 9, 964.

9. M. Krieger, *A Window to Criticism*, pp. 3-28, 165-219, discusses the poem as effigy and the miraculism that accompanies its incarnation.

10. Montaigne's notion of the faithful and representative portrait expresses the degree to which he seeks to make the signs imprinted in the book resemble him. His effort to remain faithful to himself as depicted there is the other side of that desire for coincidence. The essayist is recognizable in the book and through the book; the reality he achieves he owes to language.

11. See Philip Hallie, *The Scar of Montaigne* (Middletown, Conn., 1966), pp. 94-117.

Bibliography

Aristotle. *Nichomachean Ethics.* Translated by Martin Ostwald. New York, 1962.

————. *On Interpretation.* Translated by H. P. Cook. Cambridge, Mass., 1962.

Atkinson, Geoffroy. *Les Nouveaux horizons de la Renaissance française.* Paris, 1935.

Aubigné, Agrippa d'. *Oeuvres.* Edited by Henri Weber. Paris, 1969.

Aubain, P. *Le Problème de la conversion.* Paris, 1963.

Auerbach, Erich. *Mimesis.* Translated by W. Trask. Berne, 1946; reprint, New York, 1957.

Augustine. *Confessions of St. Augustine.* Edited by John Ryan. New York, 1960.

Baraz, Michel. *L'Etre et la connaissance selon Montaigne.* Paris, 1968.

Barthes, Roland. "To Write: Intransitive Verb?" *The Language of Criticism and the Science of Man.* Edited by R. Macksey and E. Donato. Baltimore, 1970.

Bates, B. W. *Literary Portraiture in the Historical Narrative of the French Renaissance.* New York, 1945.

Boas, George. *The Happy Beast in French Thought of the Seventeenth Century.* Baltimore, 1933.

Boon, Jean-Pierre. *Montaigne: gentilhomme et essayiste.* Paris, 1971.

Bowen, Barbara. What Does Montaigne Mean by *marqueterie?" SP* 67 (1970): 147-155.

————. *The Age of Bluff: Paradox and Ambiguity in Rabelais and Montaigne.* Urbana, Illinois, 1972.

Bowman, Frank. *Montaigne: Essays.* London, 1965.

Brown, Frieda. *Religious and Political Conservatism in the Essais of Montaigne.* Geneva, 1963.

Brunschvigg, Léon. *Descartes et Pascal, lecteurs de Montaigne.* Paris, 1944.

Brush, Craig. "The Essayist Is Learned: Montaigne's *Journal de Voyage* and the *Essais*." *RR* 42 (1971): 16-27.

Buffum, Imbrie. *Studies in the Baroque from Montaigne to Rotrou.* New Haven, 1957.

Butor, Michel. *Essais sur "les Essais."* Paris, 1968.

Castor, Graham. *Pléiade Poetics.* Cambridge, 1964.

Châtelet, Albert, and Thuillier, Jacques. *French Painting: From Fouquet to Poussin.* Translated by S. Gilbert. Geneva, 1963.

Cicero. *Laelius.* Translated by L. Laurand. Paris, 1928; reprint 1968.

————. *On Old Age and On Friendship.* Translated by F. O. Copley. Ann Arbor, Mich., 1967.

Clark, Carol. "Montaigne and the Imagery of Political Discourse." *FS* 24 (1970):337-355.

Colie, Rosalie. *Paradoxia Epidemica: The Renaissance Tradition of Paradox.* Princeton, 1966.

————. *The Resources of Kind.* Berkeley, Los Angeles, London, 1973.

Curtius, E. R. *European Literature and the Latin Middle Ages.* Translated by W. Trask. New York, 1953; reprint 1963.

Delègue, Yves. "Du Paradoxe chez Montaigne." *CAIEF* 14 (1962): 241-253.

Derrida, Jacques. *De la grammatologie.* Paris, 1967.

Dréano, Mathurin. *La Religion de Montaigne.* Revised edition. Paris, 1969.

Du Bellay, Joachim. *La Deffence et illustration de la langue françoyse.* Edited by H. Chamard. Paris, 1948.

Du Vair, Guillaume. *La Philosophie morale des stoïques.* Paris, 1641.

Epictetus. *Entretiens.* Translated by J. Souilhé. 4 vols. Paris, 1949; reprint 1969.

————. *Manuel* in *Les Stoïciens.* Edited by P. M. Schuhl. Paris, 1962.

Foucault, Michel. *Les Mots et les choses.* Paris, 1966.

Frame, Donald. "Did Montaigne Betray Sebond?" *RR* 38 (1947):297-329.

————. *Montaigne: A Biography.* London, 1965.

————. *Montaigne's Discovery of Man.* New York, 1955.

————. *Montaigne's Essais: A Study.* Englewood Cliffs, N.J., 1969.

Friedländer, Max. *Landscape, Portrait, Still-Life.* New York, 1950.

Friedrich, Hugo. *Montaigne.* Translated by R. Rovini. Paris, 1968.

Gilson, Etienne. *Painting and Reality.* New York, 1959.

Glacken, Clarence. *Traces on the Rhodian Shore.* Berkeley and Los Angeles, 1967.

Glauser, Alfred. *Montaigne paradoxal.* Paris, 1972.

Gray, Floyd. *Le Style de Montaigne.* Paris, 1958.

———. "Montaigne's Friends." *FS* 15 (1961):203-217.

———. "The 'nouveaux docteurs' and the Problem of Montaigne's Consistency in the 'Apologie de Raymond Sebond.'" *Symposium* 18 (1964):22-34.

———. "The Unity of Montaigne in the Essais." *MLQ* 22 (1961): 79-86.

Griffin, Robert. *Coronation of the Poet: Joachim Du Bellay's Debt to the Trivium.* Berkeley and Los Angeles, 1969.

Guillen, Claudio. *Literature as System.* Princeton, 1971.

Hallie, Philip. *The Scar of Montaigne.* Middletown, Conn., 1966.

Hedy-Ehrlich, Hélène. *Montaigne: la critique et le langage.* Paris, 1972.

Holyoake, S. J. "The Idea of 'jugement' in Montaigne." *MLR* 63 (1968):340-351.

Huguet, Edmond. *Dictionnaire de la langue française du seizième siècle.* 7 vols. Paris, 1925-1967.

Jamieson, I. W. A. "Augustine's *Confessions:* The Structure of Humility." *Augustiniana* 24 (1974): 234-246.

Jeanson, Francis. *Montaigne par lui-meme.* Paris, 1951.

Krieger, Murray. *A Window to Criticism: Shakespeare's Sonnets and Modern Poetics.* Princeton, 1964.

Kristeller, Paul Oskar. *Renaissance Thought: The Classic, Scholastic, and Humanist Strains.* New York, 1961.

La Charité, Raymond. "Montaigne's Early Personal Essays." *RR* 42 (1971):5-15.

———. *The Concept of Judgment in Montaigne.* The Hague, 1968.

Leclercq, Jean. "Aspects spirituels de la symbolique du livre au XIIe siècle" in *L'Homme devant Dieu.* Paris, 1963-1964. 2:63-72.

Lee, R. W. "Ut Pictura Poesis: The Humanistic Theory of Painting." *The Art Bulletin* 22 (1940):197-269.

Limbrick, Elaine. "Montaigne et S. Augustin" *BHR* 34 (1972):49-64.

Lowinski, Edward. *Secret Chromatic Art in the Netherlands Motet.* New York, 1946.

de Lubac, Henri. *Histoire et esprit: l'intelligence de l'Ecriture d'après Origen.* Paris, 1950.

McFarlane, I. D. "Montaigne and the Concept of the Imagination" in *The French Renaissance and its Heritage*. London, 1968.

McGowan, Margaret. *Montaigne's Deceits: The Art of Persuasion in the Essais*. London, 1974.

McLuhan, Marshall. *The Gutenberg Galaxy*. Toronto, 1962.

Micha, Alexandre. "Art et nature dans les *Essais*" *BSAM* II, 19 (1956): 50-55.

Miller, Perry. *The New England Mind: The Seventeenth Century*. Cambridge, Mass., 1954.

Montaigne, Michel de. *Les Essais de Michel de Montaigne*. Edited by Strowski, Gebelin, and Villey. (Edition Municipale) 4 vols. Bordeaux, 1906-1920.

——. *Les Essais de Michel de Montaigne*. Edited by Pierre Villey. Reprinted under the direction of V. L. Saulnier. Paris, 1965.

——. *Oeuvres complètes*. Edited by Thibaudet and Rat. Paris, 1962; reprint 1965.

——. *The Complete Essays of Montaigne*. Translated by Donald Frame. Stanford, Calif., 1948; reprint 1957, 1958.

Moore, W. G. "Montaigne's Notion of Experience" in *The French Mind, Studies in Honour of Gustave Rudler*. Oxford, 1952.

Munro, Thomas. *The Arts and Their Interrelations*. Cleveland, 1967.

Ong, Walter J. *Ramus: Method and the Decay of Dialogue*. Cambridge, Mass., 1958.

——. *The Presence of the Word*. New Haven, 1967.

Padelford, E. M. "Select Translations from Scaliger's Poetics." *Yale Studies in English* 26 (1905).

Panofsky, Erwin. *Early Netherlandish Painting*. 2 vols. Cambridge, Mass., 1953; reprint 1958.

Pascal. *Oeuvres complètes*. Edited by J. Chevalier. Paris, 1954.

Plattard, Jean. *Montaigne et son temps*. Paris, 1933.

Pope-Hennessy, J. *The Portrait in the Renaissance*. New York, 1966.

Pouilloux, Jean-Yves. *Lire les "Essais" de Montaigne*. Paris, 1969.

Poulet, Georges. *Etudes sur le temps humain*. Paris, 1950.

Prévost, Jean. *La Vie de Montaigne*. Paris, 1926.

Rider, Frederick. *The Dialectic of Selfhood in Montaigne*. Stanford, Calif., 1973.

Rigolot, François. *Poétique et onomastique*. Paris, 1976.

Ronsard, Pierre de. *Oeuvres complètes*. Edited by G. Cohen. 2 vols. Paris, 1966.

St. Beuve, C. A. *Port-Royal.* Edited by Doyon and Marchesne. 10 vols. Paris, 1926-1932.

Samaras, Zoé. *The Comic Element of Montaigne's Style.* Paris, 1970.

Sayce, Richard. "Baroque Elements in Montaigne." *FS* 8 (1954):1-15.

―――. "Montaigne et la peinture du passage." *Saggi e ricerche di letteratura francese* 4 (1963):9-59.

―――. *The Essays of Montaigne.* London, 1972.

Scaliger, Jules César. *Poetices libri septem.* Lyon, 1581.

Schmidt, Albert-Marie. *La Poésie scientifique en France au XVIe siècle.* Paris, 1938.

Screech, M. A. "An Aspect of Montaigne's Aesthetics: 'Entre les livres simplement plaisants . . .' (II, 10: Des livres)." *BHR* 24 (1962): 576-582.

Sebillet, Thomas. *Art poétique françoys.* Edited by F. Gaiffe. Paris, 1932.

Sebond, Raymond. *La Théologie naturelle.* Translated by Michel de Montaigne in *Oeuvres complètes de Michel de Montaigne.* Edited by A. Armaingaud. 12 vols. Paris, 1932.

Seneca. *Ad Lucilium Epistulae Morales.* Translated by R. M. Gummere. Cambridge, Mass., 1917; reprint 1961.

Smalley, Beryl. *The Study of the Bible in the Middle Ages.* South Bend, Ind., 1964.

Starobinski, Jean. "Montaigne en mouvement." *Nouvelle revue française* (January-February, 1960):16-22, 254-266.

Strowski, Fortunat. *Montaigne.* Paris, 1931.

Sullivan, J. E. *The Image of God.* Dubuque, Iowa, 1963.

Tetel, Marcel. *Montaigne.* New York, 1974.

Thibaudet, A. *Montaigne.* Edited by F. Gray. Paris, 1963.

Tigerstedt, E. N. "The Poet as Creator: Origin of a Metaphor." *Comparative Literature Studies* 5 (December 1968):455-488.

Villey, Pierre. *Les Sources et l'évolution des Essais de Montaigne.* 2 vols. Paris, 1933.

von Wartburg, W. *Evolution et structure de la langue française.* Berne, 1946; reprint 1965.

Weber, Henri. *La Création poétique au XVIe siècle en France.* Paris, 1956.

Wilden, Anthony. "Par divers moyens on arrive à pareille fin: A Reading of Montaigne." *MLN* 83 (1968):577-597.

Xenakis, Iason. *Epictetus.* The Hague, 1969.

Yates, Francis. *The Art of Memory.* Chicago, 1966.

Index

Index of Essays